Visual QuickStart Guide

Excel X

For Mac OS X

Maria Langer

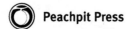 Peachpit Press

Visual QuickStart Guide
Excel X for Mac OS X
Maria Langer

Peachpit Press
1249 Eighth Street
Berkeley, CA 94710
510-524-2178 • 800-283-9444
510-524-2221 (fax)

Find us on the World Wide Web at: www.peachpit.com
To report errors, please send a note to errata@peachpit.com
Peachpit Press is a division of Pearson Education

Editor: Nancy Davis
Indexer: Emily Glossbrenner
Cover Design: The Visual Group
Production: Maria Langer, Connie Jeung-Mills

Colophon

This book was produced with Adobe PageMaker 6.5 on a Power Macintosh G3/300. The fonts used were Kepler Multiple Master, Meta Plus, and PIXymbols Command. Screenshots were created using Snapz Pro X on a Strawberry iMac.

Notice of Rights

Notice of Liability

Trademarks

ISBN 0-201-75842-3

9 8 7 6 5 4 3 2 1

Printed and bound in the United States of America.

Dedication

To my grandmother,
Maria Soricelli,
for her 90th birthday

Thanks!

To Nancy Davis, for keeping up with my feverish pace on this project. Nancy never ceases to amaze me with her ability to catch all kinds of boo-boos in my manuscripts, tiny and not-so-tiny. We make a great team—what other author/editor pair can get books out so quickly?

To Connie Jeung-Mills, for her sharp eyes and gentle layout editing.

To Emily Glossbrenner, for indexing yet another one of my books in record time.

To Nancy Ruenzel, Marjorie Baer, and the other powers-that-be at Peachpit Press, for allowing me to update my Excel VQS for Excel X. And to the rest of the folks at Peachpit Press for doing what they do so well.

To Erik Ryan and Irving Kwong at Microsoft and Danica Smith at Waggener Edstrom for helping me get the software I needed to complete this book. To Bart Chellis at Microsoft for providing some clarifications I needed for Chapter 10. And to Microsoft Corporation for supporting Mac OS X and continuing to improve the best spreadsheet program on earth.

And to Mike, for the usual reasons.

www.marialanger.com

TABLE OF

CONTENTS

TABLE OF CONTENTS

TABLE OF CONTENTS

INTRODUCTION TO EXCEL X

Figure 1 Excel X is built for Mac OS X and has all the interface elements of Aqua.

Introduction

Microsoft Excel X, a component of Microsoft Office v.X, is the latest version of Microsoft's spreadsheet application for Macintosh users. Now built for Mac OS X (**Figure 1**) and more powerful than ever, Excel enables you to create picture-perfect worksheets, charts, and lists based on just about any data.

This Visual QuickStart Guide will help you take control of Excel by providing step-by-step instructions, plenty of illustrations, and a generous helping of tips. On these pages, you'll find everything you need to know to get up and running quickly with Excel X—and more!

This book was designed for page flipping. Use the thumb tabs, index, or table of contents to find the topics for which you need help. If you're brand new to Excel or spreadsheets, however, I recommend that you begin by reading at least the first two chapters. **Chapter 1** provides basic information about Excel's interface. **Chapter 2** introduces spreadsheet concepts and explains exactly how they work in Excel.

If you've used other versions of Excel and are interested in information about new Excel X features, be sure to browse through this **Introduction**. It'll give you a good idea of the new things Excel has in store for you.

One last word of advice before you start: don't let Excel intimidate you! Sure, it's big, and yes, it has lots of commands. But as you work with Excel, you'll quickly learn the techniques you need to get your work done. That's when you'll be on your way to harnessing the power of Excel.

New & Improved Features in Excel X

Excel X includes several brand new features, as well as improvements to some existing features. Here's a list.

Built for Mac OS X

Excel X is built for Mac OS X and takes full advantage of the features of this new operating system. It also utilizes the Mac OS X Aqua interface throughout its interface elements (**Figure 1**).

AutoRecover

Excel automatically saves information about your workbook files in the background while you work. If Excel unexpectedly quits because of a computer or power problem, the document —with all of your changes up to the last automatic save—is automatically opened when you restart Excel.

Customizable keyboard shortcuts

Excel now enables you to set your own keyboard shortcuts for menu commands. You can assign keyboard shortcuts with the new Customize Keyboard dialog (**Figure 2**).

Transparent charts

The Quartz technology that's part of Mac OS X makes it possible to create transparent charts (**Figure 3**). (This feature is not available in the Windows version of Excel.)

Compatibility

Excel X is compatible with Excel 2001 and Excel 98 for Macintosh, as well as Excel 2002 (XP), Excel 2000, and Excel 97 for Windows.

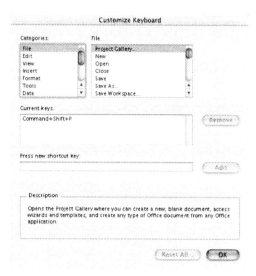

Figure 2 You can use the New Customize Keyboard dialog to set your own keyboard shortcuts.

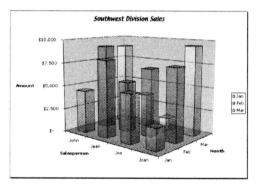

Figure 3 Excel X enables you to make chart elements transparent.

THE EXCEL WORKPLACE

Meet Microsoft Excel

Microsoft Excel is a full-featured spreadsheet application that you can use to create worksheets, charts, lists, and even Web pages.

Excel's interface combines common Mac OS X screen elements with buttons, commands, and controls that are specific to Excel. To use Excel effectively, you must have at least a basic understanding of these elements.

This chapter introduces the Excel workplace by illustrating and describing the following elements:

◆ The Excel screen, including window elements

◆ Menus, shortcut keys, toolbars, and dialogs

◆ Document scrolling techniques

◆ Excel's Help feature, including the Office Assistant

✔ Tips

■ If you're brand new to Mac OS X, don't skip this chapter. Many of the interface elements discussed in this chapter apply to all Mac OS programs, not just Excel.

■ If you've used previous versions of Excel or Mac OS, browse through this chapter to learn about some of the interface elements that are new to this version of Excel.

The Excel Screen

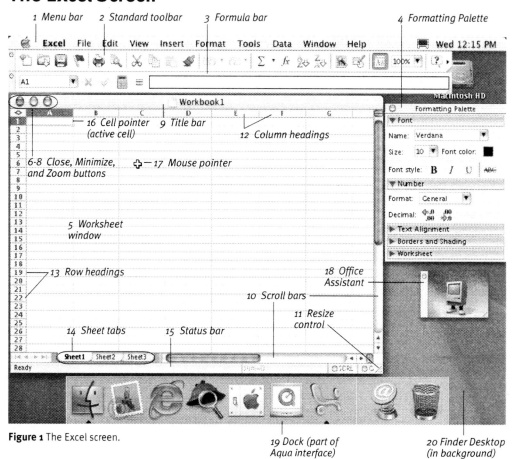

1 Menu bar   2 Standard toolbar   3 Formula bar   4 Formatting Palette

Figure 1 The Excel screen.

19 Dock (part of Aqua interface)

20 Finder Desktop (in background)

Key to the Excel screen

1 Menu bar

The menu bar appears at the top of the screen and offers access to Excel's commands.

2 Standard toolbar

The Standard toolbar offers buttons for many basic Excel commands. This toolbar is similar in other Microsoft Office X applications.

3 Formula bar

The formula bar displays the contents of the active cell and that cell's address or reference.

4 Formatting Palette

The Formatting Palette offers buttons and menus for formatting document contents.

THE EXCEL SCREEN

5 Worksheet window

The worksheet window is where you'll do most of your work with Excel. This window has columns and rows which intersect at cells. You enter data and formulas in the cells to build your spreadsheet.

6 Close button

The close button offers one way to close the window.

7 Minimize button

The minimize button enables you to collapse the window into the Dock. To display the window again, click its icon in the Dock.

8 Zoom button

The zoom button enables you to toggle the window's size from full size to a custom size that you create with the resize control.

9 Title bar

The title bar displays the document's title. You can drag the title bar to move the window. (You can also move a window by dragging any of its edges.)

10 Scroll bars

Scroll bars enable you to shift the window's contents to view different parts of the document.

11 Resize control

The resize control enables you to resize the window to a custom size.

12 Column headings

Column headings are the alphabetical labels that appear at the top of each column.

13 Row headings

Row headings are the numbered labels that appear on the left side of each row.

14 Sheet tabs

Each Excel document has one or more sheets combined together in a workbook. The sheet tabs enable you to switch from one sheet to another within the workbook.

15 Status bar

The status bar displays information about the document.

16 Cell pointer (active cell)

The cell pointer is a heavy or colored border surrounding the active cell. The active cell is the cell in which text and numbers appear when you type.

17 Mouse pointer

When positioned within the worksheet window, the mouse pointer appears as a hollow plus sign. You can use the mouse pointer to select cells, enter data, choose menu commands, and click buttons.

18 Office Assistant

The Office Assistant provides help and tips as you work.

19 Dock

The Dock, which is part of Mac OS X's Aqua interface, offers quick access to commonly used programs and minimized windows.

20 Finder Desktop

The Finder Desktop appears in the background as you work with Excel. Clicking the Desktop switches you to the Finder.

The Mouse

As with most Mac OS programs, you use the mouse to select text, activate buttons, and choose menu commands.

Mouse pointer appearance

The appearance of the mouse pointer varies depending on its location and the item to which it is pointing. Here are some examples:

◆ In the worksheet window, the mouse pointer usually looks like a hollow plus sign (**Figure 1**).

◆ On a menu name (**Figure 2**) or command, the mouse pointer appears as an arrow pointing up and to the left.

◆ In the formula bar (**Figure 3**) or when positioned over a cell being edited (**Figure 4**), the mouse pointer appears as an I-beam pointer.

◆ On a selection border, the mouse pointer looks like a hand (**Figure 5**).

To use the mouse

There are four basic mouse techniques:

◆ *Pointing* means to position the mouse pointer so that its tip is on the item to which you are pointing (**Figure 2**).

◆ *Clicking* means to press the mouse button once and release it. You click to make a cell active, position the insertion point, or choose a toolbar button.

◆ *Double-clicking* means to press the mouse button twice in rapid succession. You double-click to open an item or to select a word for editing.

◆ *Dragging* means to press the mouse button down and hold it while moving the mouse. You drag to resize or reposition a window, select multiple cells, or choose menu commands.

Figure 2 The mouse pointer looks like an arrow when pointing to a menu name or command.

Figure 3 The mouse pointer looks like an I-beam pointer when positioned over the formula bar...

Figure 4 ...or the contents of a cell being edited.

Figure 5 The mouse pointer looks like a hand when positioned over a selection border.

Figure 6
The Edit menu.

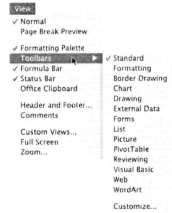

Figure 7 The Toolbars menu under the View menu.

Menus

All of Excel's commands are accessible through its menus. Excel has two types of menus:

◆ Standard menus appear on the menu bar at the top of the screen. **Figures 6** and **7** show examples of standard Excel menus.

◆ Shortcut menus appear at the mouse pointer. **Figure 10** on the next page shows an example of a shortcut menu.

Here are some rules to keep in mind when working with menus:

◆ A menu command that appears in gray (**Figure 6**) cannot be selected.

◆ A menu command followed by an ellipsis (...) (**Figures 6** and **7**) displays a dialog.

◆ A menu command followed by a triangle has a submenu (**Figure 7**). The submenu displays additional commands when the main command is highlighted.

◆ A menu command followed by the Command key symbol or Shift and Command key symbols and a letter or number (**Figure 6**) can be chosen with a shortcut key.

◆ A menu command preceded by a check mark (**Figure 7**) has been "turned on." To toggle the command from on to off or off to on, choose it from the menu.

✔ Tips

■ The above menu rules apply to the menus of most Mac OS applications, not just Excel.

■ I discuss dialogs and shortcut keys later in this chapter.

MENUS

To choose a menu command

1. Point to the menu from which you want to choose the command.

2. Click on the menu name to display the menu (**Figure 6**).

3. Click the command you want (**Figure 8**).

   or

   If the command is on a submenu, click on the name of the submenu to display it (**Figure 7**) and then click on the command you want (**Figure 9**).

   The command may blink before the menu disappears, confirming that it has been successfully selected.

✔ Tip

- Throughout this book, I use the following shorthand to refer to menu choices: *Menu Name > Command Name* or *Menu Name > Submenu Name > Command Name*. For example, to instruct you to choose the Copy command from the Edit menu, I'll write "Choose Edit > Copy."

To use a shortcut menu

1. Point to the item on which you want to use the shortcut menu.

2. Hold down Control and press the mouse button. The shortcut menu appears (**Figure 10**).

3. Click to choose the command you want.

✔ Tips

- The shortcut menu only displays the commands that can be applied to the item to which you are pointing.

- Shortcut menus are often referred to as *contextual menus*.

Figure 8
Choosing the Paste command from the Edit menu.

Figure 9 Choosing the Drawing command from the Toolbars submenu under the View menu.

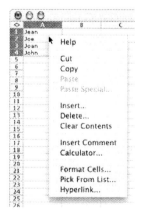

Figure 10
A shortcut menu for selected cells.

USING MENUS

Shortcut Keys

Shortcut keys are combinations of keyboard keys that, when pressed, choose a menu command without displaying the menu. For example, the shortcut key for the Paste command on the Edit menu (**Figure 8**) is ⌥ ⌘ V. Pressing this key combination chooses the command.

✔ Tips

■ All shortcut keys use at least one of the following modifier keys:

Key Name	Keyboard Key
Command	⌥ ⌘
Shift	Shift
Option	Option
Control	Control

■ A menu command's shortcut key is displayed to its right on the menu (**Figure 8**).

■ Many shortcut keys are standardized from one application to another. The Save, Print, and Quit commands are three good examples; they're usually ⌥ ⌘ S, ⌥ ⌘ P, and ⌥ ⌘ Q.

■ **Appendix A** includes a list of shortcut keys.

■ You can customize Excel X to modify or add shortcut keys. Although instructions for customizing the keyboard are beyond the scope of this book, you can explore this feature for yourself by choosing Tools > Customize and clicking the Keyboard button in the Customize dialog that appears.

To use a shortcut key

1. Hold down the modifier key for the shortcut (normally ⌥ ⌘).

2. Press the letter or number key for the shortcut.

For example, to choose the Paste command, hold down the Command key and press the V key.

Toolbars & Palettes

Excel includes a number of toolbars and palettes for various purposes. Each one has buttons or menus that activate menu commands or set options.

Figure 11 The Standard toolbar.

By default, Excel automatically displays a toolbar and a palette when you launch it:

◆ The **Standard toolbar** (**Figure 11**) offers buttons for a wide range of commonly used commands.

◆ The **Formatting Palette** (**Figure 12**) offers buttons and menus for formatting selected items.

Figure 12
The Formatting Palette.

✔ Tips

■ The options that appear in the Formatting Palette (**Figure 12**) vary depending on what is selected.

■ You can expand the Formatting Palette by clicking a triangle beside a tool category heading (**Figure 13**).

■ Other toolbars may appear automatically depending on the task you are performing with Excel.

■ Buttons with faint icon images cannot be selected.

■ A button that appears in a light gray box with rounded edges is "turned on."

■ You can identify a button by its ScreenTip (**Figure 14**).

■ A toolbar can be docked or floating. A docked toolbar is positioned against any edge of the screen. A floating toolbar can be moved anywhere within the screen.

Click here to display tools in this category.

Figure 13
Clicking a triangle beside each tool category heading expands the Formatting Palette to display more options. Here's the Formatting Palette with all categories of tools displayed.

Figure 14
A ScreenTip appears when you point to a button.

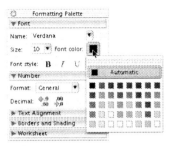

Figure 15 The Font Color menu appears when you click the Font Color button.

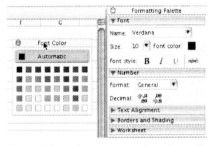

Figure 16 Drag the menu away from the toolbar.

Figure 17
The menu appears as a floating menu or palette.

Figure 18
Click the triangle beside the menu to display the menu.

Figure 19 Enter a new value and press [Return].

To view ScreenTips

Point to a toolbar or palette button. A tiny yellow box containing the name of the button appears (**Figure 14**).

✔ Tip

■ This feature was known as *ToolTips* in previous versions of Excel.

To use a toolbar or palette button

1. Click once on the button for the command or option that you want to activate to select it (**Figure 14**).

2. If the button displays a menu (**Figure 15**), click once on a menu option to select it.

✔ Tip

■ Button menus that display a dotted move handle along the top edge (**Figure 15**) can be "torn off" and used as floating menus or palettes. Simply display the menu and drag it away from the toolbar. When the palette appears (**Figure 16**), release the mouse button. The menu is displayed as a floating menu with a title bar that displays its name (**Figure 17**).

To use a toolbar or palette menu

1. Click on the triangle beside the menu to display the menu and its commands (**Figure 18**).

2. Click a command or option to select it.

✔ Tip

■ Menus that display text boxes (**Figure 18**) can be changed by typing a new value into the text box. Just click the contents of the text box to select it, then type in the new value and press [Return] (**Figure 19**).

WORKING WITH TOOLBARS & PALETTES

To display or hide a toolbar

Choose the name of the toolbar that you want to display or hide from the Toolbars submenu under the View menu (**Figure 7**).

If the toolbar name has a check mark to its left, it is currently displayed and will be hidden.

or

If the toolbar name does not have a check mark to its left, it is currently hidden and will be displayed.

✔ Tip

■ You can also hide a toolbar by clicking its close button.

To display or hide the Formatting Palette

Choose View > Formatting Palette (**Figure 20**).

If the Formatting Palette has a check mark to its left (**Figure 20**), it is currently displayed and will be hidden.

or

If the Formatting Palette does not have a check mark to its left, it is currently hidden and will be displayed.

✔ Tip

■ You can also hide the Formatting Palette by clicking its close button.

To move a toolbar or palette

Drag the move handle (**Figure 21**) or title bar for the toolbar or palette to reposition it on screen.

To resize a toolbar

Drag the resize control in the lower-right corner of the toolbar (**Figure 22**). When you release the mouse button, the toolbar's size and shape change (**Figure 23**).

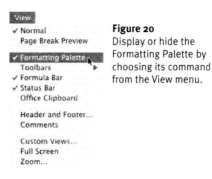

Figure 20
Display or hide the Formatting Palette by choosing its command from the View menu.

Move handle

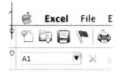

Figure 21
The move handle for a toolbar is like a tiny vertical title bar without a title.

Figure 22 Drag the lower-right corner of a toolbar...

Figure 23 ...to resize it.

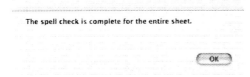

The spell check is complete for the entire sheet.

OK

Figure 24 The dialog that appears at the end of a spelling check just displays information.

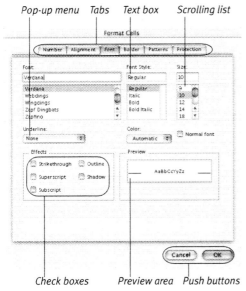

Pop-up menu Tabs Text box Scrolling list

Check boxes   Preview area   Push buttons

Figure 25 The Font tab of the Format Cells dialog.

Dialogs

Like most other Mac OS applications, Excel uses dialogs to communicate with you.

Excel can display many different dialogs, each with its own purpose. There are two basic types of dialogs:

◆ Dialogs that simply provide information (**Figure 24**).

◆ Dialogs that offer options to select (**Figure 25**) before Excel completes the execution of a command.

✔ Tip

■ Often, when a dialog appears, you must dismiss it by clicking OK or Cancel before you can continue working with Excel.

Anatomy of an Excel dialog

Here are the components of many Excel dialogs, along with information about how they work.

◆ **Tabs** (**Figure 25**), which appear at the top of some dialogs, let you move from one group of dialog options to another. To switch to another group of options, click the appropriate tab.

◆ **Text boxes** (**Figure 25**) let you enter information from the keyboard. You can press Tab to move from one text box to the next or click in a text box to position the insertion point within it. Then enter a new value.

◆ **Scrolling lists** (**Figure 25**) offer a number of options to choose from. Use the scroll bar to view options that don't fit in the list window. Click an option to select it; it becomes highlighted and appears in the text box.

Continued on next page...

Continued from previous page.

◆ **Check boxes (Figure 25)** let you turn options on or off. Click in a check box to toggle it. When a check mark or X appears in the check box, its option is turned on.

◆ **Radio buttons (Figure 26)** let you select only one option from a group. Click on an option to select it; the option that was selected before you clicked is deselected.

◆ **Pop-up menus (Figure 25)** also let you select one option from a group. Display a pop-up menu as you would any other menu (**Figure 27**), then choose the option that you want.

◆ **Preview areas (Figure 25)**, when available, illustrate the effects of your changes before you finalize them by clicking the OK button.

◆ **Push buttons (Figures 24, 25, and 26)** let you access other dialogs, accept the changes and close the dialog (OK), or close the dialog without making changes (Cancel). To choose a button, click it once.

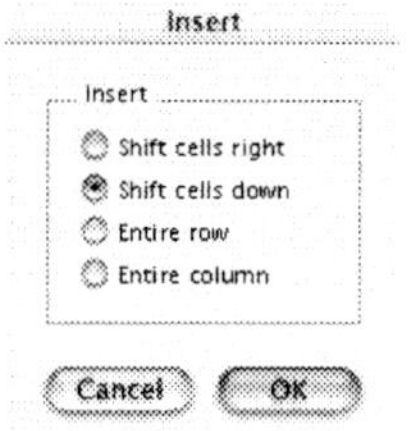

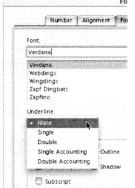

Figure 26
The Insert dialog uses radio buttons to get your selection.

Figure 27
Displaying a pop-up menu.

✔ Tips

■ When the contents of a text box are selected, whatever you type will replace the selection.

■ Excel often uses text boxes and scrolling lists together (**Figure 25**). You can use either one to make a selection.

■ If a pair of tiny triangles appears to the right of a text box, you can click a triangle to increase or decrease the value in the text box.

■ In some scrolling lists, double-clicking an option selects it and dismisses the dialog.

■ You can turn on any number of check boxes in a group, but you can select only one radio button in a group.

■ The Excel Help system sometimes refers to pop-up menus as drop-down lists.

■ A push button with an extra border around it is the default button; you can "click" it by pressing [Enter].

■ You can usually "click" the Cancel button by pressing [Esc] or [⌘ .].

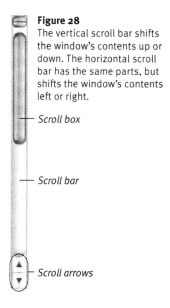

Figure 28
The vertical scroll bar shifts the window's contents up or down. The horizontal scroll bar has the same parts, but shifts the window's contents left or right.

Scroll box

Scroll bar

Scroll arrows

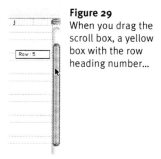

Figure 29
When you drag the scroll box, a yellow box with the row heading number...

Figure 30 ...or the column heading letter appears.

Scrolling Window Contents

You can use Excel's scroll bars to shift the contents of a document window so you can see items that don't fit in the window.

✔ Tip

- I tell you more about working with document windows in **Chapter 4**.

To scroll window contents

Click the scroll arrow (**Figure 28**) for the direction that you want to view. For example, to scroll down to view the end of a document, click the down arrow.

or

Drag the scroll box (**Figure 28**) in the direction that you want to view. As you drag, a yellow box with a row or column heading appears on screen. It indicates the topmost row (**Figure 29**) or leftmost column (**Figure 30**) that will appear on screen when you release the mouse button. Release the mouse button to view the indicated part of the document.

or

Click in the scroll bar above or below the scroll box (**Figure 28**). This shifts the window contents one screenful at a time.

✔ Tips

- Having trouble remembering which scroll arrow to click? Just remember this: click up to see up, click down to see down, click left to see left, and click right to see right.

- Although some keyboard keys change the portion of the document being viewed, they also move the cell pointer. I tell you about these keys in **Chapter 2**.

- You can use the Mac OS X General preferences pane to change the way scroll arrows appear on the scroll bars. **Figure 28** illustrates the default configuration.

The Office Assistant

The Office Assistant displays an animated character (**Figure 31**) that can provide tips and assistance while you work. While enabled, the Office Assistant is the main interface for working with Excel's onscreen Help feature.

To enable or disable the Office Assistant

Choose Help > Use the Office Assistant (**Figure 32**). The Office Assistant will disappear.

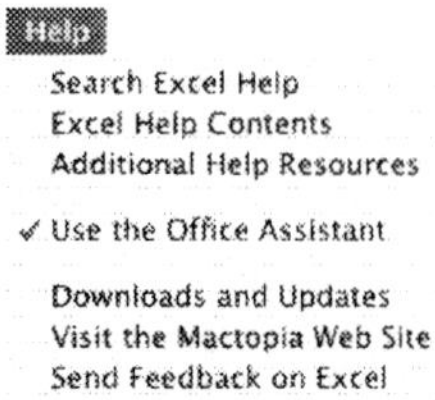

If a check mark appears to the left of the command (**Figure 32**), the Office Assistant is enabled and choosing the command will disable it.

or

If a check mark does not appear to the left of the command, the Office Assistant is not enabled and choosing the command will enable (and display) it.

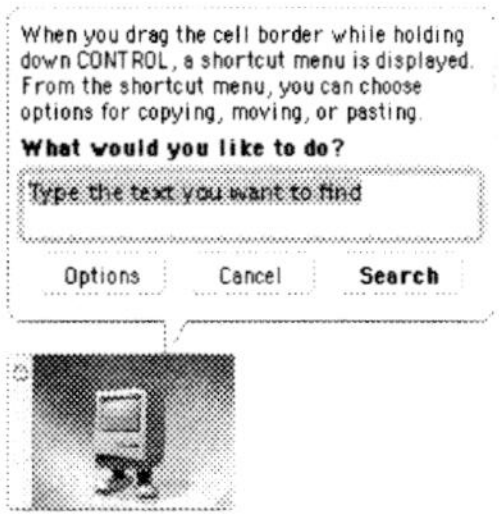

To display the Office Assistant

Click the Office Assistant button 🔍 on the Standard toolbar. The Office Assistant appears.

To close the Office Assistant

Click the close button in the Office Assistant window (**Figure 31**). The Office Assistant will wave goodbye before disappearing.

To move the Office Assistant

Drag the Office Assistant's move handle to reposition it on screen.

To get tips

1. Click the lightbulb that appears in the Office Assistant window (**Figure 31**) when the Office Assistant has a tip for you. The tip appears, along with a prompt to get more information (**Figure 33**).

2. Click Cancel to close the tip.

Figure 31
The Office Assistant.

Help
Search Excel Help
Excel Help Contents
Additional Help Resources

✓ Use the Office Assistant

Downloads and Updates
Visit the Mactopia Web Site
Send Feedback on Excel

Figure 32
Excel's Help menu.

When you drag the cell border while holding down CONTROL, a shortcut menu is displayed. From the shortcut menu, you can choose options for copying, moving, or pasting.
What would you like to do?

Type the text you want to find

Options   Cancel   **Search**

Figure 33
An Office Assistant tip.

USING THE OFFICE ASSISTANT

Figure 34
Get the Office
Assistant's attention...

Figure 35
...and then enter
a description of
what you want
to do.

Figure 36 A list of possible topics appears
in a balloon beside the Office Assistant.

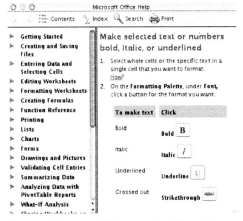

Figure 37 When you click a topic, the Microsoft
Office Help window appears with information about
that topic.

To get context-sensitive help

1. Click the Office Assistant to get its attention. A balloon with instructions appears
   (**Figures 33** and **34**).

2. Type a brief description of what you want to
   do into the text box (**Figure 35**) and click
   the Search button. A list of possible topics
   appears in another balloon (**Figure 36**).

3. Click a topic that interests you. A Microsoft
   Office Help window like the one in **Figure
   37** appears. Information about the topic
   appears in the right side of the window.

4. When you are finished reading help information, click the Microsoft Office Help
   window's close button.

USING THE OFFICE ASSISTANT

Excel Help

Excel has an extensive onscreen Help feature that provides information about using Excel to complete specific tasks. You access Excel Help via the Office Assistant (as discussed on the previous page) or commands under the Help menu (**Figure 32**).

To browse Help

1. Choose Help > Excel Help Contents (**Figure 32**). The Microsoft Office Help contents window appears (**Figure 38**).

2. Navigate through topics and information as follows:

    ▲ To expand a topic in the left side of the window, click the triangle beside it. Subtopics appear beneath it.

    ▲ Click underlined links to display information and subtopics in the right side of the window.

Figure 39 shows an example of expanded help topics with subtopic links, along with step-by-step instructions for completing a task.

✔ Tips

■ You can click the left arrow button in the Help window to browse topics you browsed earlier in the help session.

■ You can also display help contents (**Figure 38**) by clicking the Contents button in any Microsoft Office Help window.

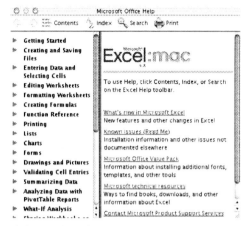

Figure 38 Choosing Excel Help Contents from the Help menu with the Office Assistant turned off displays Help contents.

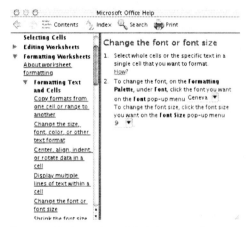

Figure 39 Navigate through help by expanding topic outlines and clicking underlined links.

Figure 40 Clicking the Index button in the Microsoft Office Help window displays a link for each letter of the alphabet.

Figure 41 Click a letter to display topics beginning with that letter.

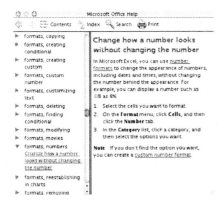

Figure 42 Continue clicking topics and links until the information you want appears on the right side of the window.

To use the Help Index

1. Choose Help > Excel Help Contents (**Figure 32**). The Microsoft Office Help contents window appears (**Figure 38**).

2. Click the Index button. A link for each letter of the alphabet appears on the left side of the screen (**Figure 40**).

3. Click the letter for the topic that interests you. A list of main topics beginning with that letter appears beneath the letter links (**Figure 41**).

4. Navigate through topics and information as follows:

   ▲ To expand a topic in the left side of the window, click it. Subtopics appear beneath it.

   ▲ Click underlined links to display information and subtopics in the right side of the window.

Figure 42 shows an example of subtopic links, along with step-by-step instructions for completing a task.

WORKSHEET BASICS

Numeric values

Text values   *Formula: =B1-B2*

◇	A	B
1	Sales —	— $1,000.00
2	Cost —	— 400.00
3	Profit —	$600.00

Figure 1 This very simple worksheet illustrates how a spreadsheet program like Excel works with values and formulas.

◇	A	B
1	Sales	$1,150.00
2	Cost	400.00
3	Profit	$750.00

Figure 2 When the value for Sales changes from $1,000 to $1,150, the Profit result changes automatically.

How Worksheets Work

Microsoft Excel is most commonly used to create *worksheets*. A worksheet is a collection of information laid out in columns and rows. As illustrated in **Figure 1**, each worksheet cell can contain one of two kinds of input:

◆ A *value* is a piece of information that does not change. Values can be text, numbers, dates, or times. A cell containing a value usually displays the value.

◆ A *formula* is a collection of values, cell references, operators, and predefined functions that, when evaluated by Excel, produces a result. A cell containing a formula usually displays the results of the formula.

Although any information can be presented in a worksheet, spreadsheet programs like Excel are usually used to organize and calculate numerical or financial information. Why? Well, when properly prepared, a worksheet acts like a super calculator. You enter values and formulas and it calculates and displays the results. If you change one of the values, no problem. Excel recalculates the results almost instantaneously without any additional effort on your part (**Figure 2**).

How does this work? By using cell *references* rather than actual numbers in formulas, Excel knows that it should use the contents of those cells in its calculations. Thus, changing one or more values affects the results of calculations that include references to the changed cells. As you can imagine, this makes worksheets powerful business planning and analysis tools!

Launching Excel

To use Excel, you must open the Excel application. This loads Excel into RAM (random access memory), so your computer can work with it.

To launch Excel by opening its application icon

1. In the Finder, locate the Microsoft Excel application icon (**Figure 3**). It should be in the Microsoft Office or Microsoft Excel folder on your hard disk.

2. Click the icon once to select it, then choose File > Open or press ⌘ O.

   or

   Double-click the icon.

   The Excel splash screen appears briefly (**Figure 4**), then the Project Gallery window appears (**Figure 5**).

✔ Tip

■ You can disable the display of the Project Gallery window at startup by turning off the check box at the bottom of its window (**Figure 5**). When disabled, a blank document window appears instead. I tell you about the Project Gallery later in this chapter.

To launch Excel by opening an Excel document icon

1. In the Finder, locate the icon for the document that you want to open (**Figure 6**).

2. Click the icon once to select it, then choose File > Open or press ⌘ O.

   or

   Double-click the icon.

   The Excel splash screen appears briefly (**Figure 4**), then a document window containing the document that you opened appears (**Figure 7**).

Figure 3
The Microsoft Excel application icon.

Microsoft Excel

Figure 4 The Excel X splash screen.

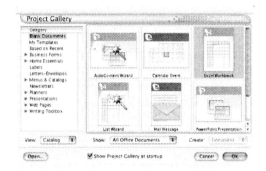

Figure 5 When you launch Excel by opening the Excel application icon, it displays the Project Gallery window.

Figure 6
An Excel document icon.

SW Division Sales.xls

Figure 7 When you launch Excel by opening an Excel document icon, it displays the document you opened.

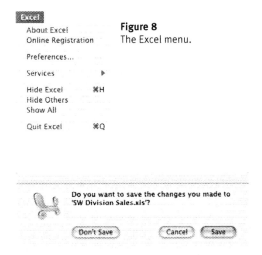

Figure 8
The Excel menu.

Do you want to save the changes you made to 'SW Division Sales.xls'?

Don't Save   Cancel   Save

Figure 9 A dialog like this appears when a document with unsaved changes is open when you quit Excel.

Quitting Excel

When you're finished using Excel, you should use the Quit Excel command to close the application. This completely clears Excel out of RAM, freeing up RAM for other applications.

✔ Tips

- Closing all document windows is not the same as quitting. The only way to remove Excel from RAM is to quit. I tell you about closing document windows in **Chapter 4**.

- Quitting Excel also instructs Excel to save preference settings.

To quit Excel

Choose Excel > Quit Excel (**Figure 8**) or press ⌘⌘Q. Here's what happens:

- ◆ If any documents are open, they close.

- ◆ If an open document contains unsaved changes, a dialog appears (**Figure 9**) so you can save the changes. I explain how to save documents in **Chapter 4**.

- ◆ The Excel application closes.

✔ Tip

- As you've probably guessed, Excel automatically quits when you restart, shut down, or log out of your computer.

QUITTING EXCEL

Excel Workbooks, Templates, & Wizards

The documents you create and save using Excel are *workbook* files. A workbook is an Excel document that can contain worksheets and charts.

Excel offers three ways to create workbook files:

◆ A *blank workbook file* is an empty workbook file with Excel's default settings. You must enter and format all workbook contents.

◆ A workbook file based on a *template* contains the values, formulas, formatting, custom toolbars, and macros included in a template file.

◆ A *wizard*, such as the List Wizard, creates a workbook file by prompting you for information to be entered in the workbook.

✔ Tips

■ Basing a workbook on a template can save a lot of time if you often need to create a standard document—such as a monthly report or invoice—repeatedly. I explain how to create templates in **Chapter 4**.

■ I tell you more about Excel workbook files in **Chapter 4**. I cover the List Wizard in **Chapter 10**.

Figure 10
The File menu.

Figure 11 Click the arrow beside a category you want to view to display subcategories within it. Then, when you click a subcategory, previews of the documents within it appear.

Figure 12 Use the View pop-up menu...

Figure 13 ...to change the way templates are listed.

The Project Gallery

The Project Gallery (**Figure 5**) offers an easy way to create documents with Microsoft Office applications.

To open the Project Gallery

Choose File > Project Gallery (**Figure 10**) or press Shift ⌃ ⌘ P.

✔ Tip

■ By default, the Project Gallery automatically appears when you launch Excel by opening its application icon.

To display templates & wizards in a specific category

1. On the left side of the window, click the arrow beside a category you want to view. A list of subcategories appears beneath it (**Figure 11**).

2. Click on the name of a subcategory to display previews of the templates or wizards within it (**Figure 11**).

To customize the Project Gallery's display

Use the pop-up menus at the bottom of the Project Gallery window to set options:

◆ View menu options (**Figure 12**) let you switch between Catalog view (**Figures 5 and 11**) and List view (**Figure 13**).

◆ Show menu options (**Figure 14**) let you specify the type of documents you want to show.

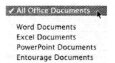

Figure 14
The Show pop-up menu enables you to show a specific type of Office document.

Creating Workbooks

You can create a new workbook file with the Project Gallery or with the New command.

To create an empty workbook

1. Choose File > Project Gallery (**Figure 10**) to display the Project Gallery window (**Figure 5**).

2. In the Category list, select Blank Documents.

3. In the preview area, select Excel Workbook.

4. Click OK.

or

Choose File > New Workbook (**Figure 10**) or press ⌘ ⌘ N.

or

Click the New button on the Standard toolbar.

An empty workbook window appears (**Figure 15**).

To create a workbook based on a template

1. Choose File > Project Gallery (**Figure 10**) to display the Project Gallery window (**Figure 5**).

2. In the Category list, select the category for the template you want to use.

3. In the preview area, select the preview for the template you want to use (**Figure 11**).

4. Click OK.

A workbook based on the template that you selected appears (**Figure 16**). Follow the instructions in the template to replace place-holder values with your values.

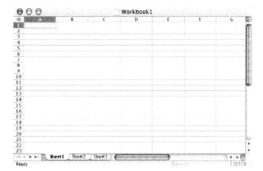

Figure 15 An empty workbook window.

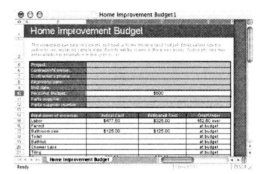

Figure 16 A workbook based on a template.

Cell reference in Name box of formula bar

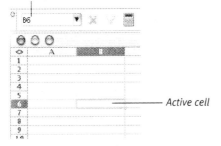

— Active cell

Figure 17 The reference for an active cell appears in the formula bar.

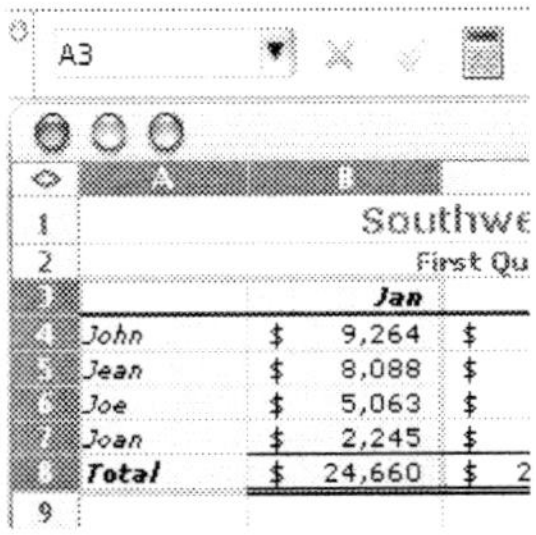

Figure 18 In this illustration, the range *A3:B8* is selected.

Activating & Selecting Cells

Worksheet information is entered into cells. A *cell* is the intersection of a column and a row. Each little "box" in the worksheet window is a cell.

Each cell has a unique *address* or *reference*. The reference uses the letter(s) of the column and the number of the row. Thus, cell *B6* would be at the intersection of column *B* and row *6*. The reference for the active cell appears in the Name box at the left end of the formula bar (**Figure 17**).

To enter information in a cell, you must make that cell *active*. A cell is active when there is a dark or colored border called the *cell pointer* around it. When a cell is active, anything you type is entered into it.

To use Excel commands on a cell or its contents, you must *select* the cell. The active cell is also a selected cell. If desired, however, you can select multiple cells or a *range* of cells. This enables you to use commands on all selected cells at once. A range (**Figure 18**) is a rectangular selection of cells defined by the top-left and bottom-right cell references.

✔ Tips

- Although the active cell is always part of a selection of multiple cells, it is never highlighted like the rest of the selection. You should, however, see a dark or colored border (the cell pointer) around it (**Figure 18**).

- Although you can select multiple cells, only one cell—the one referenced in the Name box (**Figure 18**)—is active.

- The column and row headings for selected cells appear bold (**Figures 17** and **18**).

- Using the scroll bars does not change the active or selected cell(s). It merely changes your view of the worksheet's contents.

To activate a cell

Use the mouse pointer to click in the cell you want to make active.

or

Press the appropriate keystroke (**Table 1**) to move the cell pointer to the cell you want to make active.

To select a range of cells with the mouse

1. Position the mouse pointer in the first cell you want to select (**Figure 19**).

2. Press the mouse button down and drag to highlight all the cells in the selection (**Figure 20**).

or

1. Click in the first cell of the range you want to select.

2. Hold down [Shift] and click in the last cell of the range. Everything between the first and second clicks is selected. (This technique is known as "Shift-Click.")

To go to a cell or range of cells

1. Choose Edit > Go To or press [F5] to display the Go To dialog (**Figure 21**).

2. Enter the reference for the cell you want to activate or the range that you want to select in the Reference text box.

3. Click OK.

   If you entered a single cell reference, the cell is activated. If you entered a range reference, the range is selected.

✔ Tip

■ To specify a reference for a range, enter the addresses of the first and last cells of the range, separated with a colon (:). For example, **Figure 18** shows *A3:B8* selected and **Figure 20** shows *A4:E7* selected.

Table 1

Keys for Moving the Cell Pointer	
KEY	**MOVEMENT**
↑	Up one cell
↓	Down one cell
→	Right one cell
←	Left one cell
Tab	Right one cell
Shift Tab	Left one cell
Home	First cell in row
Page Up	Up one window
Page Down	Down one window
⌘ Home	Cell A1
⌘ End	Cell at intersection of last column and last row containing data

Figure 19 To select cells, begin in one corner of the range...

Figure 20 ...press the mouse button down, and drag to the opposite corner of the range.

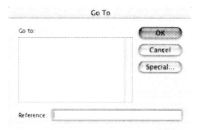

Figure 21 The Go To dialog lets you move to any cell quickly.

ACTIVATING & SELECTING CELLS

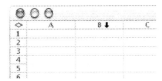

Figure 22 Click a column heading to select the column.

Figure 23 Click a row heading to select the row.

Figure 24 Click the Select All button to select all cells in the worksheet.

To select an entire column

1. Position the mouse pointer on the heading for the column you want to select. The mouse pointer turns into an arrow pointing down (**Figure 22**).

2. Click once. The column is selected.

To select an entire row

1. Position the mouse pointer on the heading for the row you want to select. The mouse pointer turns into an arrow pointing to the right (**Figure 23**).

2. Click once. The row is selected.

To select multiple columns or rows

1. Position the mouse pointer on the first column or row heading.

2. Press the mouse button down, and drag along the headings until all the desired columns or rows are selected.

✔ Tip

- When selecting multiple columns or rows, be careful to position the mouse pointer on the heading and not between two headings! If you drag the border of two columns, you will change a column's width rather than make a selection.

To select the entire worksheet

1. Position the mouse pointer on the Select All button in the upper-left corner of the worksheet window. The mouse pointer turns into an arrow pointing into the worksheet (**Figure 24**).

2. Click once.

or

Press ⌘ A.

The worksheet is selected.

SELECTING COLUMNS & ROWS

To select multiple ranges

1. Use any selection technique to select the first cell or range of cells (**Figure 25**).
2. Hold down (⌘) and drag to select the second cell or range of cells (**Figure 26**).
3. Repeat step 2 until all desired ranges are selected.

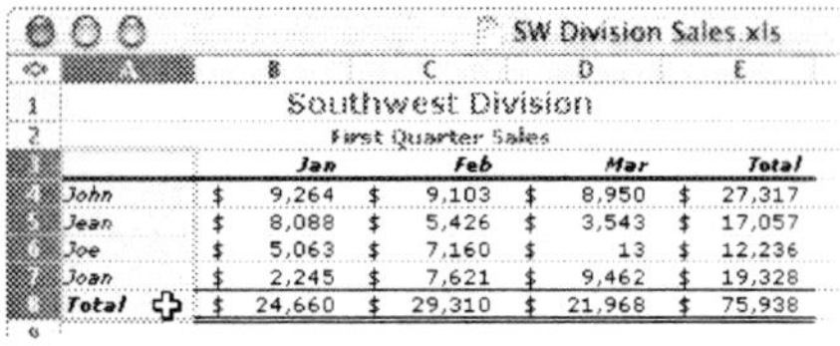

	Southwest Division			
	First Quarter Sales			
	Jan	Feb	Mar	Total
John	$ 9,264	$ 9,103	$ 8,950	$ 27,317
Jean	$ 8,088	$ 5,426	$ 3,543	$ 17,057
Joe	$ 5,063	$ 7,160	$ 13	$ 12,236
Joan	$ 2,245	$ 7,621	$ 9,462	$ 19,328
Total	$ 24,660	$ 29,310	$ 21,968	$ 75,938

Figure 25 To select two ranges of cells, start by selecting the first range, ...

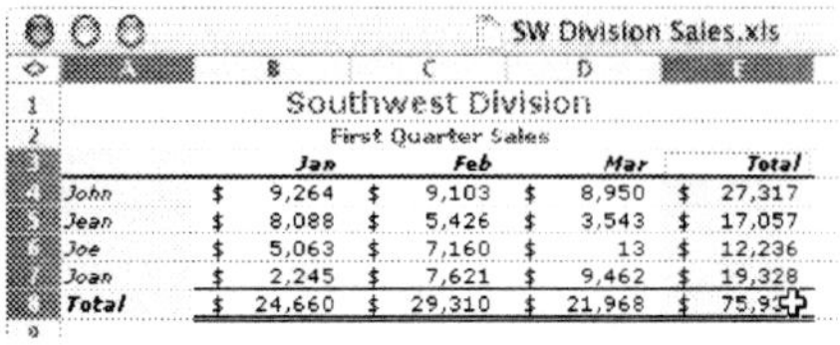

	Southwest Division			
	First Quarter Sales			
	Jan	Feb	Mar	Total
John	$ 9,264	$ 9,103	$ 8,950	$ 27,317
Jean	$ 8,088	$ 5,426	$ 3,543	$ 17,057
Joe	$ 5,063	$ 7,160	$ 13	$ 12,236
Joan	$ 2,245	$ 7,621	$ 9,462	$ 19,328
Total	$ 24,660	$ 29,310	$ 21,968	$ 75,938

Figure 26 ...then hold down (⌘) and select the second range.

✔ Tips

- Selecting multiple ranges can be tricky. It takes practice. Don't be frustrated if you can't do it on the first few tries!
- To add ranges that are not visible in the worksheet window, be sure to use the scroll bars to view them. Using the keyboard to move to other cells while selecting multiple ranges will remove the selections you've made so far or add undesired selections.
- Do not click in the worksheet window or use the movement keys while multiple ranges are selected unless you are finished working with them. Doing so will deselect all the cells.

To deselect cells

Click anywhere in the worksheet.

or

Press any of the keys in **Table 1**.

✔ Tip

- Remember, at least one cell must be selected at all times—that's the active cell.

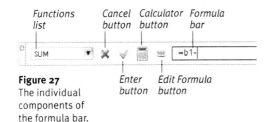

Functions
list

Cancel   Calculator   Formula
button   button   bar

Figure 27
The individual
components of
the formula bar.

Enter   Edit Formula
button   button

Entering Values & Formulas

To enter a value or formula into a cell, begin by
making the cell active. As you type or click to
enter information, the information appears in
both the cell and in the formula bar just above
the window's title bar. You complete the entry
by pressing (Return) or (Enter) or clicking the
Enter button ✓ on the formula bar.

While you are entering information into a cell,
the formula bar is *active*. You can tell that it's
active because the Name box on the left end of
the formula bar turns into a Functions list and
two additional buttons appear between it and
the cell contents area (**Figure 27**).

There are two important things to remember
when the formula bar is active:

◆   Anything you type or click on may be
    included in the active cell.

◆   Some Excel options and menu commands
    are unavailable.

You deactivate the formula bar by accepting or
cancelling the current entry.

✔ Tips

■   Pressing (Return) or (Enter) to complete a
    formula entry accepts the entry and moves
    the cell pointer one cell down. Clicking the
    Enter button ✓ accepts the entry without
    moving the cell pointer.

■   To cancel an entry before it has been
    completed, press (Esc) or click the Cancel
    button ✗ on the formula bar. This re-
    stores the cell to the way it was before you
    began.

■   If you include formatting notation like dollar
    signs, commas, and percent symbols when
    you enter numbers, you may apply format-
    ting styles. I tell you more about formatting
    the contents of cells in **Chapter 6**.

Values

As discussed at the beginning of this chapter, a value is any text, number, date, or time you enter into a cell. Values are constant—they don't change unless you change them.

To enter a value

1. Activate the cell in which you want to enter the value.

2. Type in the value. As you type, the information appears in two places: the active cell and the formula bar, which becomes active (**Figure 28**).

3. To complete and accept the entry (**Figure 29**), press [Return] or [Enter] or click the Enter button ✓ on the formula bar.

✔ Tips

- Although you can often use the arrow keys or other movement keys in **Table 1** to complete an entry by moving to another cell, it's a bad habit because it won't always work.

- By default, Excel aligns text against the left side of the cell and aligns numbers against the right side of the cell. I explain how to change alignment in **Chapter 6**.

- Don't worry if the data you put into a cell doesn't seem to fit. You can always change the column width or use the AutoFit Text feature to make it fit. I tell you how in **Chapter 6**.

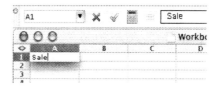

Figure 28 As data is entered into a cell, it appears in the cell and in the formula bar.

Figure 29 A completed entry. The insertion point is gone.

Table 2

Basic Mathematical Operators Understood by Excel		
OPERATOR	USE	EXAMPLE
+	Addition	=A1+B10
-	Subtraction	=A1-B10
-	Negation	=-A1
*	Multiplication	=A1*B10
/	Division	=A1/B10
^	Exponential	=A1^3
%	Percentage	=20%

Table 3

How Excel Evaluates Expressions		
ASSUMPTIONS		
A1=5 B10=7 C3=4		
FORMULA	EVALUATION	RESULT
=A1+B10*C3	=5+7*4	33
=C3*B10+A1	=4*7+5	33
=(A1+B10)*C3	=(5+7)*4	48
=A1+10%	=5+10%	5.1
=(A1+10)%	=(5+10)%	0.15
=A1^2-B10/C3	=5^2-7/4	23.25
=(A1^2-B10)/C3	=(5^2-7)/4	4.5
=A1^(2-B10)/C3	=5^(2-7)/4	0.00008

Formula Basics

Excel makes calculations based on formulas you enter into cells. When you complete the entry of a formula, Excel displays the results of the formula rather than the formula you entered.

Here are some important things to keep in mind when writing formulas:

◆ If a formula uses cell references to refer to other cells and the contents of one or more of those cells changes, the result of the formula changes, too.

◆ All formulas begin with an equal (=) sign. This is how Excel knows that a cell entry is a formula and not a value.

◆ Formulas can contain any combination of values, references, operators (**Table 2**), and functions. I tell you about using operators in formulas in this chapter and about using functions in **Chapter 5**.

◆ Formulas are not case sensitive. This means that *=A1+B10* is the same as *=a1+b10*. Excel automatically converts characters in cell references and functions to uppercase.

When calculating the results of expressions with a variety of operators, Excel makes calculations in the following order:

1. Negation

2. Expressions in parentheses

3. Percentages

4. Exponentials

5. Multiplication or division

6. Addition or subtraction

Table 3 shows some examples of formulas and their results to illustrate this. As you can see, the inclusion of parentheses can really make a difference when you write a formula!

FORMULA BASICS

✔ Tips

- Do not use the arrow keys or other movement keys to complete an entry by moving to another cell. Doing so may add cells to the formula!
- Whenever possible, use references rather than values in formulas. This way, you won't have to rewrite formulas when values change. **Figures 30** and **31** illustrate this.
- A reference can be a cell reference, a range reference, or a cell or range name. I tell you about name references a little later in this chapter and in **Chapter 13**.
- To add a range of cells to a formula, type the first cell in the range followed by a colon (:) and then the last cell in the range. For example, *B1:B10* references the cells from *B1* straight down through *B10*.
- If you make a syntax error in a formula, Excel tells you (**Figures 32** and **33**). If the error is one of the common errors programmed into Excel's Formula AutoCorrect feature, Excel offers to correct the formula for you (**Figure 33**). Otherwise, you will have to troubleshoot the formula and correct it yourself.
- I tell you how to edit formulas in **Chapter 3** and how to include functions in formulas in **Chapter 5**.

Sales 1000
Cost 400
Profit 600
=1000-400
Commission 90
=600*15%

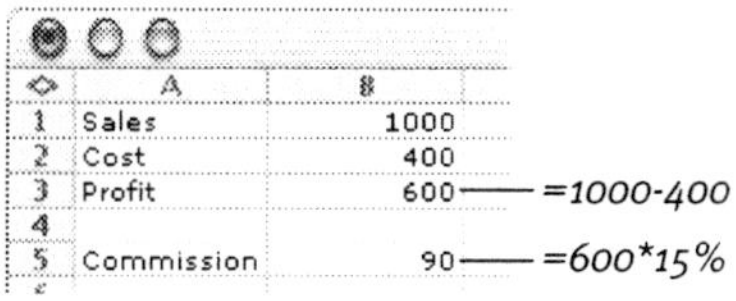

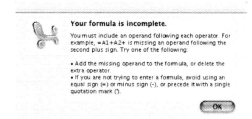

Figure 30 If any of the values change, the formulas will need to be rewritten!

Sales 1000
Cost 400
Profit 600
=B1-B2
Rate 15%
Commission 90
=B3*B5

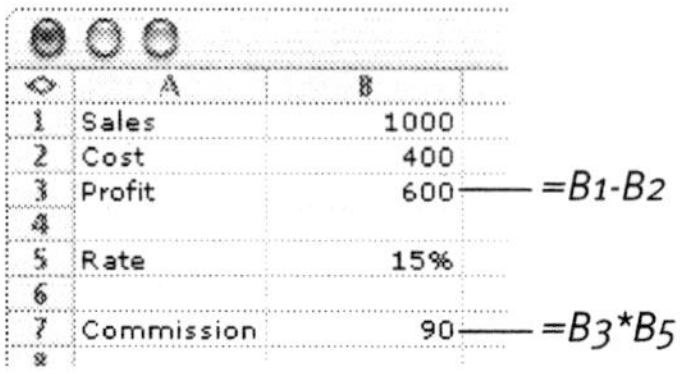

Figure 31 But if the formulas reference cells containing the values, when the values change, the formulas will not need to be rewritten to show correct results.

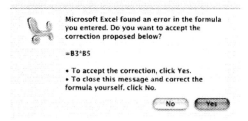

Your formula is incomplete.
You must include an operand following each operator. For example, =A1+A2+ is missing an operand following the second plus sign. Try one of the following:
• Add the missing operand to the formula, or delete the extra operator.
• If you are not trying to enter a formula, avoid using an equal sign (=) or minus sign (-), or precede it with a single quotation mark (').
OK

Figure 32 Excel tells you when a formula has a syntax error and provides information to help you.

Microsoft Excel found an error in the formula you entered. Do you want to accept the correction proposed below?
=B3*B5
• To accept the correction, click Yes.
• To close this message and correct the formula yourself, click No.
No
Yes

Figure 33 If the syntax error is one of the common formula errors Excel knows about, Excel offers to fix it for you.

Figure 34
To enter a formula, type it into a cell.

Figure 35
A completed formula entry.

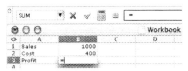

Figure 36 To enter the formula =B1-B2, type = to begin the formula, ...

Figure 37 ...click cell B1 to add its reference to the formula, ...

Figure 38 ...type - to tell Excel to subtract, ...

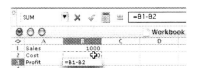

Figure 39 ...click cell B2 to add its reference to the formula, ...

Figure 40 ...and finally, click the Enter button to complete the formula.

To enter a formula by typing

1. Activate the cell in which you want to enter the formula.

2. Type in the formula. As you type, the formula appears in two places: the active cell and the formula bar (**Figure 34**).

3. To complete the entry (**Figure 35**), press [Return] or [Enter] or click the Enter button ✓ on the formula bar.

To enter a formula by clicking

1. Activate the cell in which you want to enter the formula.

2. Type an equal (=) sign to begin the formula (**Figure 36**).

3. To enter a cell reference, click on the cell you want to reference (**Figures 37** and **39**).

    or

    To enter a constant value or operator, type it in (**Figure 38**).

4. Repeat step 3 until the entire formula appears in the formula bar.

5. To complete the entry (**Figure 40**), press [Return] or [Enter] or click the Enter button ✓ on the formula bar.

✔ Tips

- If you click a cell reference without typing an operator, Excel assumes you want to add that reference to the formula.

- Be careful where you click when writing a formula! Each click adds a reference to the formula. If you add an incorrect reference, press [Delete] until it has been deleted or click the Cancel button ✖ on the formula bar to start the entry from scratch. I tell you more about editing a cell's contents in **Chapter 3**.

- You can add a range of cells to a formula by dragging over the cells.

ENTERING FORMULAS

The Calculator

Excel's Calculator feature offers another way to enter formulas into cells. It displays a familiar interface—like a standard pocket calculator (**Figure 41**)—for building formulas. As you click or type to enter formula components into the Calculator, it displays the result of the formula in a text box. Clicking OK in the Calculator completes the formula and enters it into the worksheet cell.

To enter a formula with the Calculator

1. Activate the cell in which you want to enter the formula.

2. Click the Calculator button ⬚ on the formula bar. The Calculator appears (**Figure 41**).

3. Enter the formula into the top text box using any combination of the following techniques:

▲ Enter cell references by clicking or dragging over the cells or typing in the cell references.

▲ Enter numbers by clicking the number buttons or typing the number characters.

▲ Enter operators by clicking the operator buttons or typing the operator characters.

As you enter the formula's components, the results of the calculation appear in the Answer text box (**Figure 42**).

4. Click OK or press ⟨Return⟩. The completed formula is entered into the worksheet cell and the Calculator disappears.

✔ Tips

■ You can also use the Calculator to enter complex formulas that include functions. I explain how in my discussion of functions in **Chapter 5**.

Figure 41
The Calculator offers a familiar interface for entering formulas.

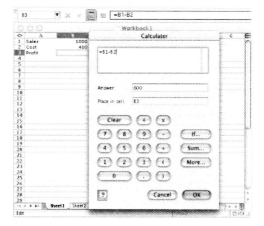

Figure 42 As you enter the formula in the Calculator, the results appear in the Answer text box.

■ You can also edit formulas with the Calculator. Select the cell containing the formula, click the Calculator button to display the formula in the Calculator, modify the formula as desired, and click OK.

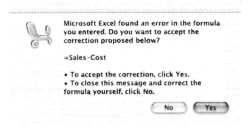

Figure 43 The Formula AutoCorrect feature can even help you fix incorrectly entered name references.

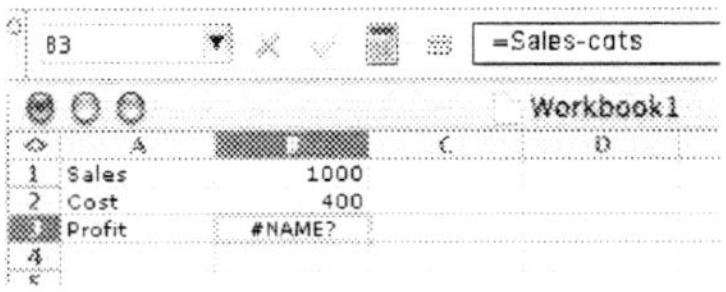

Figure 44 If a name reference in a formula is not correct, a *#NAME?* error appears in the cell.

Figure 45 To use Natural Language Formulas, simply type the formula using cell references based on adjacent cells.

Figure 46 When you complete the formula, the result appears in the cell.

Natural Language Formulas

Excel's Natural Language Formulas feature enables you to write formulas using references automatically derived from the column or row headings for cells.

For example, the formula in **Figure 35** references the cells immediately to the right of the cells containing the text *Sales* and *Cost*. Excel can recognize the text as labels or *names* for the cells beside them, thus allowing it to understand the formula *=Sales-Cost*.

✔ Tips

- Although the names feature has been part of Excel for years, Excel's ability to recognize names without you manually defining or creating them was added in Excel 98. I tell you more about names in **Chapter 13**.

- If you enter an incorrect name reference in a formula, one of two things happens:

  ▲ Excel's Formula AutoCorrect feature offers to fix it (**Figure 43**)—if Excel can guess what name you meant to type.

  ▲ A *#NAME?* error appears in the cell (**Figure 44**).

To enter a formula using Natural Language Formulas

1. Activate the cell in which you want to enter the formula.

2. Type in the formula, using the text labels above or beside cells to identify them (**Figure 45**).

3. To complete the entry (**Figure 46**), press ⸢Return⸣ or ⸢Enter⸣ or click the Enter button ✓ on the formula bar.

EDITING WORKSHEETS

Editing Worksheets

Microsoft Excel offers a number of features and techniques that you can use to modify your worksheets.

◆ Use standard editing techniques and the Clear command to change or clear the contents of cells.

◆ Use Insert and Edit menu commands to insert or delete cells, columns, and rows.

◆ Use Edit menu commands, the fill handle, and drag-and-drop editing to copy cells from one location to another, including cells containing formulas.

◆ Use the fill handle and Fill submenu commands to copy cell contents to multiple cells or create a series.

◆ Modify formulas so they are properly updated by Excel when copied.

◆ Use Edit menu commands and drag-and-drop editing to move cells from one location to another.

◆ Undo, redo, and repeat multiple actions.

This chapter covers all of these techniques.

Editing Cell Contents

You can use standard editing techniques to edit the contents of cells either as you enter values or formulas or after you have completed an entry. You can also clear a cell's contents, leaving the cell empty.

To edit as you enter

1. If necessary, click to position the blinking insertion point cursor in the cell (**Figure 1**) or formula bar (**Figure 2**).

2. Press ⟨Delete⟩ to delete the character to the left of the insertion point.

   or

   Type the characters that you want to insert at the insertion point.

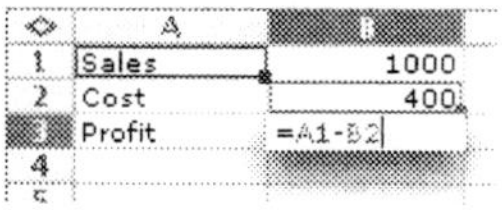

To edit a completed entry

1. Double-click the cell containing the incorrect entry to activate it for editing.

2. If the cell contains a value, follow the instructions in the previous section to insert or delete characters as desired.

   or

   If the cell contains a formula, color-coded Range Finder frames appear, to graphically identify cell references (**Figures 3** and **5**). There are three ways to edit cell references:

   ▲ Edit the reference as discussed in the previous section.

   ▲ Drag a frame border to move the frame over another cell. As shown in **Figure 4**, the mouse pointer turns into a grasping hand as you drag.

   ▲ Drag a frame handle to expand or contract it so the frame includes more or fewer cells. As shown in **Figure 6**, the mouse pointer turns into a square with arrows in two corners when you position it on a frame handle and drag.

Figure 1 To edit a cell's contents while entering information, click to reposition the insertion point in the cell...

Figure 2 ...or in the formula bar and make changes as desired.

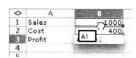

Figure 3 The Range Finder frames clearly indicate the problem with this formula.

Figure 4 You can drag a Range Finder frame to correct the cell reference. In this example, the RangeFinder frame on cell A1 is dragged to cell B1.

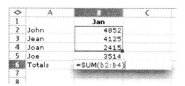

Figure 5 In this example, the Range Finder indicates that the range of cells in the formula excludes a cell.

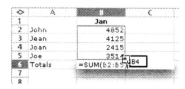

Figure 6 You can drag a Range Finder frame handle to expand the range and correct the reference in the formula.

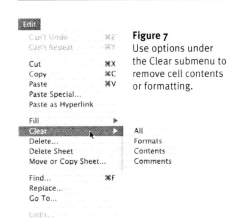

Figure 7
Use options under the Clear submenu to remove cell contents or formatting.

To clear cell contents

1. Select the cell(s) you want to clear.

2. Choose Edit > Clear > Contents (**Figure 7**).

   or

   Press ⸢Control⸥⸢B⸥ or ⸢Delete⸥.

✔ Tips

- Another way to clear the contents of just one cell is to select the cell, press ⸢Delete⸥, and then press ⸢Return⸥ or ⸢Enter⸥.

- Do not press ⸢Spacebar⸥ to clear a cell's contents! Doing so inserts a space character into the cell. Although the contents seem to disappear, they are just replaced by an invisible character.

- Clearing a cell is very different from deleting a cell. When you clear a cell, the cell remains in the worksheet—only its contents are removed. When you delete a cell, the entire cell is removed from the worksheet and other cells shift to fill the gap. I tell you about inserting and deleting cells next.

- The Contents command clears only the values or formulas entered into a cell. The other Clear submenu commands (**Figure 7**) work as follows:

  ▲ **All** clears everything, including formatting and comments.

  ▲ **Formats** clears only cell formatting.

  ▲ **Comments** clears only cell comments.

  I tell you about formatting cells in **Chapter 6** and about adding cell comments in **Chapter 11**.

CLEARING CELL CONTENTS

Inserting & Deleting Cells

Excel offers an Insert command and a Delete command to insert and delete columns, rows, or cells.

◆ When you use the Insert command, Excel shifts cells down or to the right to make room for the new cells.

◆ When you use the Delete command, Excel shifts cells up or to the left to fill the gap left by the missing cells.

Figures 8, **11**, and **14** show examples of how inserting a column or deleting a row affects the addresses or references of the cells in a worksheet. Fortunately, Excel is smart enough to know how to adjust cell references in formulas so that the formulas you write remain correct.

To insert a column or row

1. Select a column or row (**Figure 9**).

2. Choose Insert > Columns or Insert > Rows (**Figure 10**).

   or

   Choose Insert > Cells (**Figure 10**) or press Control I .

   The column (**Figure 11**) or row is inserted.

✔ Tips

■ To insert multiple columns or rows, in step 1, select the number of columns or rows you want to insert. For example, if you want to insert three columns before column *B*, select columns *B*, *C*, and *D*.

■ If a complete column or row is not selected when you choose the Cells command or press Control I in step 2, the Insert dialog appears (**Figure 17**). Select the appropriate radio button (Entire row or Entire column) for what you want to insert, then click OK. I tell you about inserting cells a little later in this chapter.

	A	B	C	D
1		Jan	Feb	Mar
2	John	4852	1254	3451
3	Jean	4125	2415	3684
4	Joan	2415	3154	3269
5	Joe	3514	3214	3742
6				

Figure 8 A simple worksheet.

	A	B	C	D
1		Jan	Feb	Mar
2	John	4852	1254	3451
3	Jean	4125	2415	3684
4	Joan	2415	3154	3269
5	Joe	3514	3214	3742

Figure 9 Selecting a column.

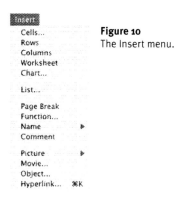

Insert

Cells...
Rows
Columns
Worksheet
Chart...

List...

Page Break
Function...
Name   ▶
Comment

Picture   ▶
Movie...
Object...
Hyperlink... ⌘K

Figure 10
The Insert menu.

	A	B	C	D	E
1			Jan	Feb	Mar
2	John		4852	1254	3451
3	Jean		4125	2415	3684
4	Joan		2415	3154	3269
5	Joe		3514	3214	3742

Figure 11 An inserted column.

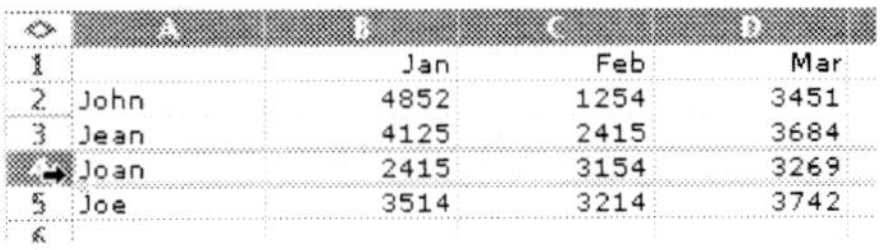

Figure 12 Selecting a row.

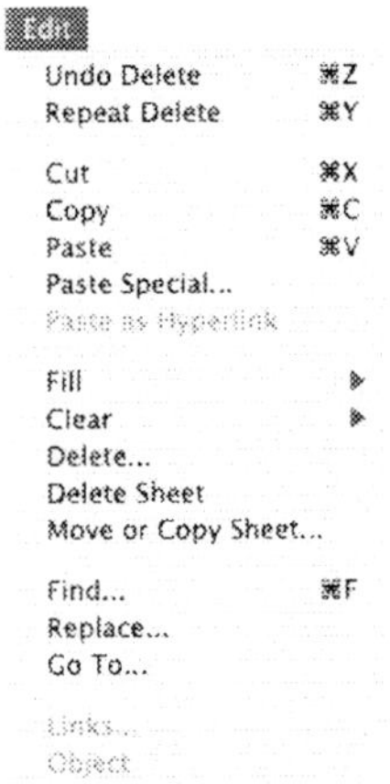

Figure 13
The Edit menu.

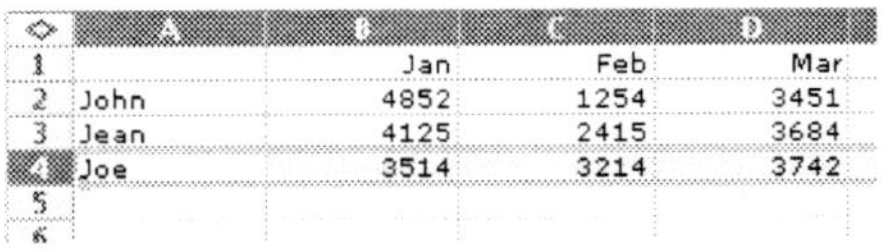

Figure 14 The row selected in **Figure 12** is deleted.

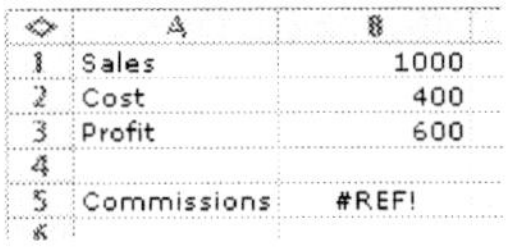

Figure 15 In this example, I deleted a row containing a value referenced in the formula in *B5*. Because Excel can't find one of the references it needs, it displays a #REF! error.

To delete a column or row

1. Select a column or row (**Figure 12**).

2. Choose Edit > Delete (**Figure 13**) or press Control K.

   The column or row (**Figure 14**)—along with all of its contents—disappears.

✔ Tips

- To delete more than one column or row at a time, in step 1, select all of the columns or rows you want to delete.

- If a complete column or row is not selected when you choose the Delete command or press Control K in step 2, the Delete dialog appears (**Figure 19**). Select the appropriate radio button (Entire row or Entire column) for what you want to delete, then click OK.

- If you delete a column or row that contains referenced cells, the formulas that reference the cells may display a #REF! error message (**Figure 15**). This means that Excel can't find a referenced cell. If this happens, you'll have to rewrite any formulas in cells displaying the error.

DELETING COLUMNS & ROWS

To insert cells

1. Select a cell or range of cells (**Figure 16**).

2. Choose Insert > Cells (**Figure 10**) or press `Control` `I`.

3. In the Insert dialog that appears (**Figure 17**), select the appropriate radio button to tell Excel how to shift the selected cells to make room for new cells—Shift cells right or Shift cells down.

4. Click OK.

   The cell(s) are inserted (**Figure 18**).

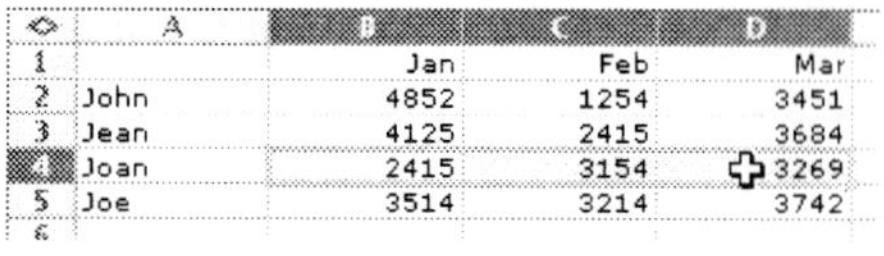

✔ Tip

- Excel always inserts the number of cells that is selected when you use the Insert command (**Figures 16** and **18**).

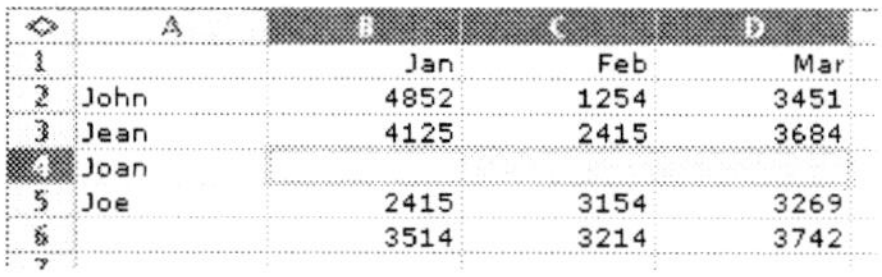

To delete cells

1. Select a cell or range of cells to delete (**Figure 16**).

2. Choose Edit > Delete (**Figure 13**) or press `Control` `K`.

3. In the Delete dialog that appears (**Figure 19**), select the appropriate radio button to tell Excel how to shift the other cells when the selected cells are deleted—Shift cells left or Shift cells up.

4. Click OK.

   The cell(s) are deleted (**Figure 20**).

✔ Tip

- If you delete a cell that contains referenced cells, the formulas that reference the cells may display a #REF! error message (**Figure 15**). If this happens, you'll have to rewrite any formulas in cells displaying the error.

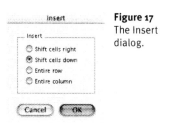

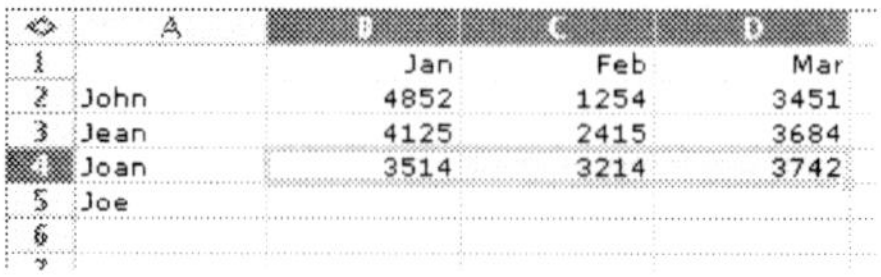

Figure 16 Selecting a range of cells.

Figure 17
The Insert dialog.

Figure 18 Here's what happens when you insert cells selected in **Figure 16**, using the Shift cells down option.

Figure 19
The Delete dialog.

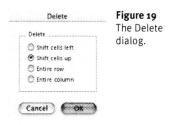

Figure 20 Here's what happens when you delete the cells selected in **Figure 16**, using the Shift cells up option.

John
Jean
Joan
Joe
John
Jean
Joan
Joe

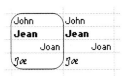

Figure 21
The Copy and Paste commands can make an exact copy.

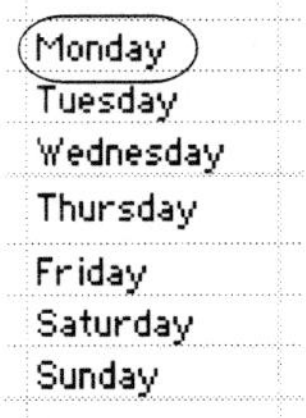

Monday
Tuesday
Wednesday
Thursday
Friday
Saturday
Sunday

Figure 22
Using the Fill handle on a cell containing the word *Monday* generates a list of the days of the week.

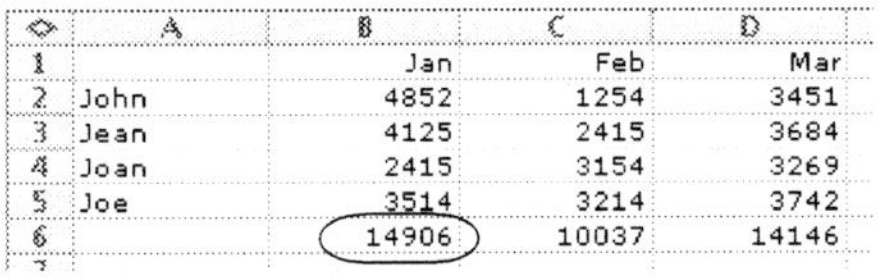

	A	B	C	D
1		Jan	Feb	Mar
2	John	4852	1254	3451
3	Jean	4125	2415	3684
4	Joan	2415	3154	3269
5	Joe	3514	3214	3742
6		14906	10037	14146
7				

Figure 23 Copying a formula that totals a column automatically writes correctly referenced formulas to total similar columns.

Copying Cells

Excel offers several ways to copy the contents of one cell to another: the Copy and Paste commands, the fill handle, and the Fill command.

How Excel copies depends not only on the method used, but on the contents of the cell(s) being copied.

- When you use the Copy and Paste commands to copy a cell containing a value, Excel makes an exact copy of the cell, including any formatting (**Figure 21**). I tell you about formatting cells in **Chapter 6**.
- When you use the fill handle or Fill command to copy a cell containing a value, Excel either makes an exact copy of the cell, including any formatting, or creates a series based on the original cell's contents (**Figure 22**).
- When you copy a cell containing a formula, Excel copies the formula, changing any relative references in the formula so they're relative to the destination cell(s) (**Figure 23**).

✔ Tip

- Copy cells that contain formulas whenever possible to save time and ensure consistency.

Copying with Copy & Paste

The Copy and Paste commands in Excel work very much the way they do in other applications. Begin by selecting the source cells and copying them to the Clipboard. Then select the destination cells and paste the Clipboard contents in.

To copy with Copy & Paste

1. Select the cell(s) you want to copy (**Figure 24**).

2. Choose Edit > Copy (**Figure 13**), press ⌃⌘C, or click the Copy button 🗐 on the Standard toolbar.

   An animated marquee appears around the selection (**Figure 25**).

3. Select the cell(s) in which you want to paste the selection (**Figure 26**). If more than one cell has been copied, you can select either the first cell of the destination range or the entire range.

4. Choose Edit > Paste (**Figure 27**), press ⌃⌘V or Enter, or click the Paste button 📋 on the Standard toolbar.

   The originally selected cells are copied to the new location (**Figure 28**).

✔ Tips

- If the destination cells contain information, Excel may overwrite them without warning you.

- If you choose the Paste command, press ⌃⌘V, or click the Paste button 📋 , the marquee remains around the copied range, indicating that it is still in the Clipboard and may be pasted elsewhere. The marquee disappears automatically as you work, but if you want to remove it manually, press Esc.

Figure 24
Begin by selecting the cell(s) you want to copy.

Figure 25
A marquee appears around the selection when it has been copied to the Clipboard.

Figure 26
Select the destination cell(s).

Figure 27
The Edit menu with the Paste command available. The Paste command is only available when something has been cut or copied to the Clipboard.

Figure 28
The contents of the copied cells appear in the destination cells.

- The Edit menu's Paste Special command (**Figure 27**) offers additional options over the regular Paste command. For example, you can use it to paste only the formatting of a copied selection, convert formulas in the selection into values, or add the contents of the source cells to the destination cells.

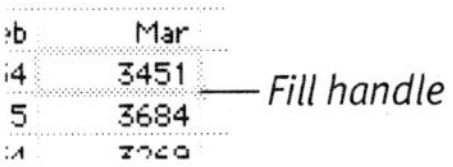

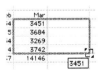

Figure 29 The fill handle on a single cell.

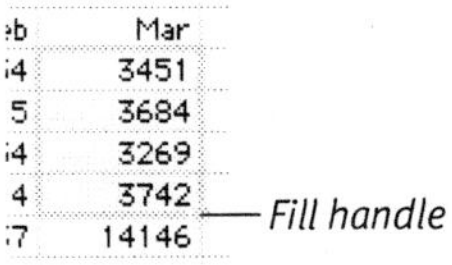

·b	Mar
·4	3451
5	3684
·4	3269
4	3742 — *Fill handle*
·7	14146

Figure 30 The fill handle on a range of cells.

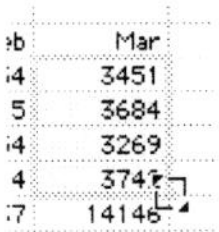

·b	Mar
·4	3451
5	3684
·4	3269
4	374?
·7	14146

Figure 31 When the mouse pointer is over the fill handle, it turns into a box with triangles in two corners.

·b	Mar	
·4	3451	
5	3684	
·4	3269	
4	3742	
·7	14146	3451

Figure 32 As you drag the fill handle, a dark border indicates the destination cell(s).

·b	Mar	
·4	3451	3451
5	3684	3684
·4	3269	3269
4	3742	3742
·7	14146	

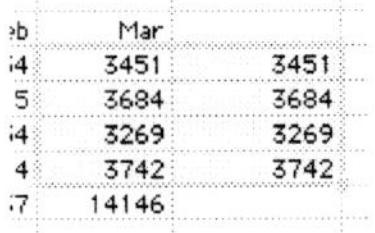

Figure 33 The destination cells fill with the contents of the source cells.

The Fill Handle

The *fill handle* is a small black or colored box in the lower-right corner of the cell pointer (**Figure 29**) or selection (**Figure 30**). You can use the fill handle to copy the contents of one or more cells to adjacent cells.

To copy with the fill handle

1. Select the cell(s) containing the information you want to copy (**Figure 30**).

2. Position the mouse pointer on the fill handle. The mouse pointer turns into a box with triangles in two corners (**Figure 31**).

3. Press the mouse button down and drag to the adjacent cells. A gray border surrounds the source and destination cells (**Figure 32**).

4. When all the destination cells are surrounded by the gray border, release the mouse button. The cells are filled (**Figure 33**).

✔ Tips

-   You can use the fill handle to copy any number of cells. The destination cells, however, must be adjacent to the original cells.

-   When using the fill handle, you can only copy in one direction (up, down, left, or right) at a time.

-   If the destination cells contain information, Excel may overwrite them without warning you.

The Fill Command

The Fill command works a lot like the fill handle in that it copies information to adjacent cells. But rather than dragging to copy, you select the source and destination cells at the same time and then use the Fill command to complete the copy. The Fill submenu offers several options for copying to adjacent selected cells:

◆ **Down** copies the contents of the top cell(s) in the selection to the selected cells beneath it.

◆ **Right** copies the contents of the left cell(s) in the selection to the selected cells to the right of it.

◆ **Up** copies the contents of the bottom cell(s) in the selection to the selected cells above it.

◆ **Left** copies the contents of the right cell(s) in the selection to the selected cells to the left of it.

¦b	Mar
¦4	3451
5	3684
¦4	3269
4	3742
¦7	14146

Figure 34 To use the Fill command, begin by selecting the source and destination cells.

Figure 35
The Fill submenu on the Edit menu.

To copy with the Fill command

1. Select the cell(s) you want to copy along with the adjacent destination cell(s) (**Figure 34**).

2. Choose the appropriate command from the Fill submenu under the Edit menu (**Figure 35**): Down, Right, Up, Left.

   The cells are filled as specified (**Figure 33**).

✔ Tip

■ You must select both the source and destination cells when using the Fill command. If you select just the destination cells, Excel won't copy the correct cells.

Figure 36 To create an AutoFill series, start by entering the first value in a cell.

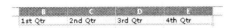

Figure 37 Drag the fill handle to include all cells that will be part of the series.

Figure 38 Excel creates the series automatically.

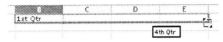

Figure 39 To use the Series command, select the source and destination cells.

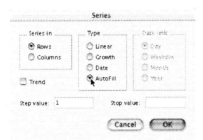

Figure 40 Select the AutoFill radio button in the Series dialog.

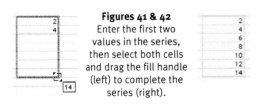

Figures 41 & 42 Enter the first two values in the series, then select both cells and drag the fill handle (left) to complete the series (right).

Series & AutoFill

A *series* is a sequence of cells that forms a logical progression. Excel's AutoFill feature can generate a series of numbers, months, days, dates, and quarters.

To create a series with the fill handle

1. Enter the first item of the series in a cell (**Figure 36**). Be sure to complete the entry by pressing Return or Enter or clicking the Enter button on the formula bar.

2. Position your mouse pointer on the fill handle and drag. All the cells that will be part of the series are surrounded by a gray border and a yellow box indicates the value that will be in the last cell in the range (**Figure 37**).

3. Release the mouse button to complete the series (**Figure 38**).

To create a series with the Series command

1. Enter the first item in the series in a cell (**Figure 36**).

2. Select all cells that will be part of the series, including the first cell (**Figure 39**).

3. Choose Edit > Fill > Series (**Figure 35**).

4. In the Series dialog that appears (**Figure 40**), select the AutoFill radio button.

5. Click OK to complete the series (**Figure 38**).

✔ Tip

- To generate a series that skips values, enter the first two values of the series in adjoining cells, then use the fill handle or Series command to create the series, including both cells as part of the source (**Figures 41** and **42**).

Copying Formulas

You copy a cell containing a formula the same way you copy any other cell in Excel: with the Copy and Paste commands, with the fill handle, or with the Fill command. These methods are discussed earlier in this chapter.

Generally speaking, Excel does not make an exact copy of a formula. Instead, it copies the formula based on the kinds of references used within it. If relative references are used, Excel changes them based on the location of the destination cell in relation to the source cell. You can see an example of this in **Figures 43** and **44**.

✔ Tips

- You'll find it much quicker to copy formulas rather than to write each and every formula from scratch.

- Not all formulas can be copied with accurate results. For example, you can't copy a formula that sums up a column of numbers to a cell that should represent a sum of cells in a row (**Figure 45**).

- I explain the various types of cell references—relative, absolute, and mixed—beginning on the next page.

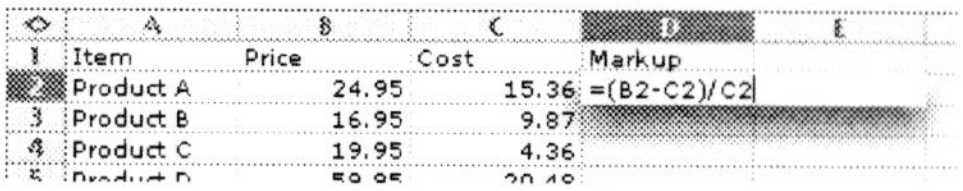

Figure 43 Here's a formula to calculate markup percentage. If the company has 763 products, would you want to write the same basic formula 762 more times? Of course not!

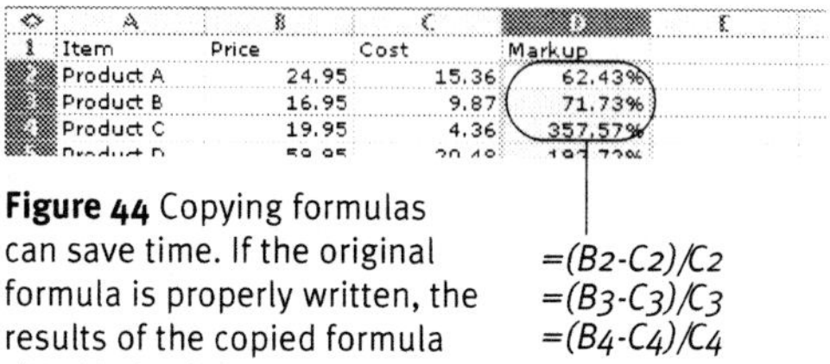

Figure 44 Copying formulas can save time. If the original formula is properly written, the results of the copied formula should also be correct.

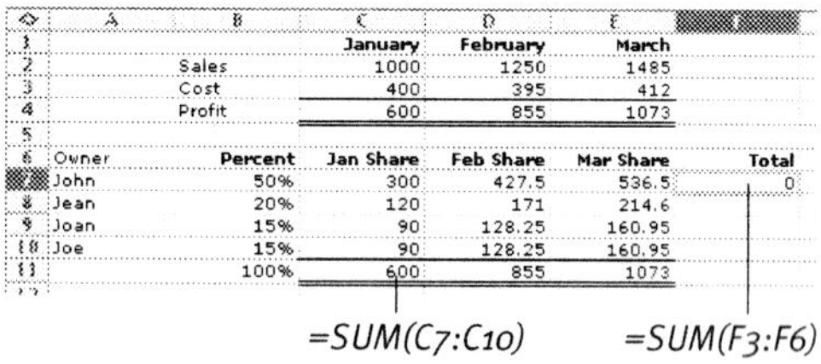

$$=(B2-C2)/C2$$
$$=(B3-C3)/C3$$
$$=(B4-C4)/C4$$

$$=SUM(C7:C10) \qquad =SUM(F3:F6)$$

Figure 45 In this illustration, the formula in cell $C11$ was copied to cell $F7$. This doesn't work because the two cells don't add up similar ranges. The formula in cell $F7$ would have to be rewritten from scratch. It could then be copied to $F8$ through $F10$. (I tell you about the SUM function in **Chapter 5**.)

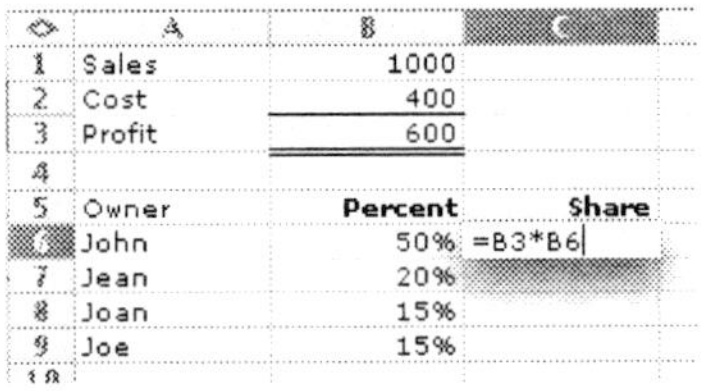

Relative vs. Absolute Cell References

Figure 46 This formula correctly calculates a partner's share of profit.

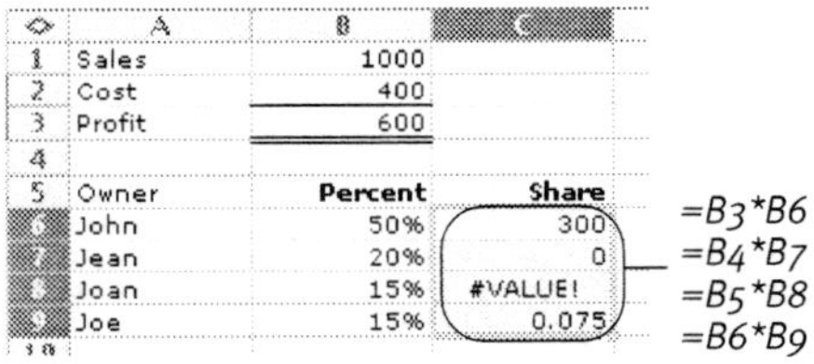

$=B3*B6$
$=B4*B7$
$=B5*B8$
$=B6*B9$

Figure 47 But when the formula is copied for the other partners, the relative reference to cell *B3* is changed, causing incorrect results and an error message!

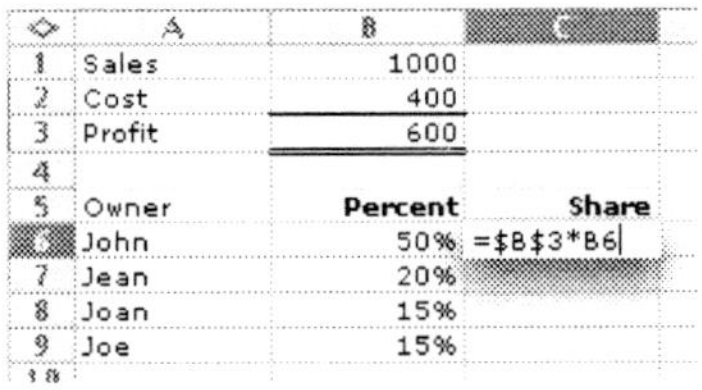

Figure 48 Rewrite the original formula so it includes an absolute reference to cell *B3*, which all of the formulas must reference.

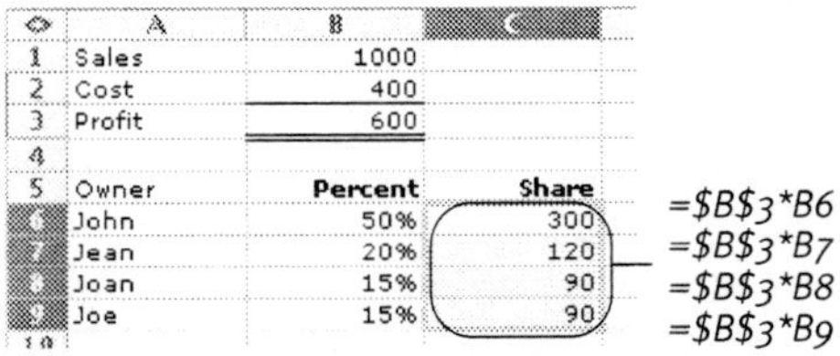

$=\$B\$3*B6$
$=\$B\$3*B7$
$=\$B\$3*B8$
$=\$B\$3*B9$

Figure 49 When the formula is copied for the other partners, only the relative reference (to the percentages) changes. The results are correct.

There are two primary types of cell references:

◆ A *relative cell reference* is the address of a cell relative to the cell the reference is in. For example, a reference to cell *B1* in cell *B3*, tells Excel to look at the cell two cells above *B3*. Most of the references you use in Excel are relative references.

◆ An *absolute cell reference* is the exact location of a cell. To indicate an absolute reference, enter a dollar sign ($) in front of the column letter(s) and row number of the reference. An absolute reference to cell *B1*, for example, would be written *$B$1*.

As **Figures 46** and **47** illustrate, relative cell references change when you copy them to other cells. Although in many cases, you might want the references to change, sometimes you don't. That's when you use absolute references (**Figures 48** and **49**).

✔ Tips

■ Here's a trick for remembering the meaning of the notation for absolute cell references: in your mind, replace the dollar sign with the word *always*. Then you'll read *$B$1* as *always B always 1—always B1*!

■ If you're having trouble understanding how these two kinds of references work and differ, don't worry. This is one of the most difficult spreadsheet concepts you'll encounter. Try creating a worksheet like the one illustrated on this page and working your way through the figures one at a time. Pay close attention to how Excel copies the formulas you write!

RELATIVE VS. ABSOLUTE CELL REFERENCES

To include an absolute cell reference in a formula

1. Enter the formula by typing or clicking as discussed in **Chapter 2**.

2. Insert a dollar sign before the column and row references for the cell reference you want to make absolute (**Figure 50**).

    or

    With the insertion point on the cell reference that you want to make absolute, press ⌃ ⌘ T to have Excel insert the dollar signs automatically.

3. Complete the entry by pressing Return or Enter.

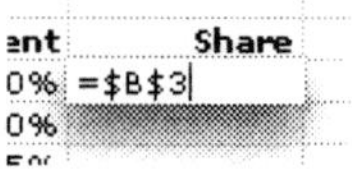

✔ Tips

■ You can edit an existing formula to include absolute references by inserting dollar signs where needed or using the ⌃ ⌘ T shortcut on a selected reference. I tell you how to edit cell contents earlier in this chapter.

■ Do not use a dollar sign in a formula to indicate currency formatting. I tell you how to apply formatting to cell contents, including currency format, in **Chapter 6**.

Mixed References

Once you've mastered the concept of relative vs. absolute cell references, consider the third type of reference: a *mixed cell reference*.

In a mixed cell reference, either the column or row reference is absolute while the other reference remains relative. Thus, you can use cell references like *A$1* or *$A1*. Use this when a column reference must remain constant but a row reference changes or vice versa. **Figure 51** shows a good example.

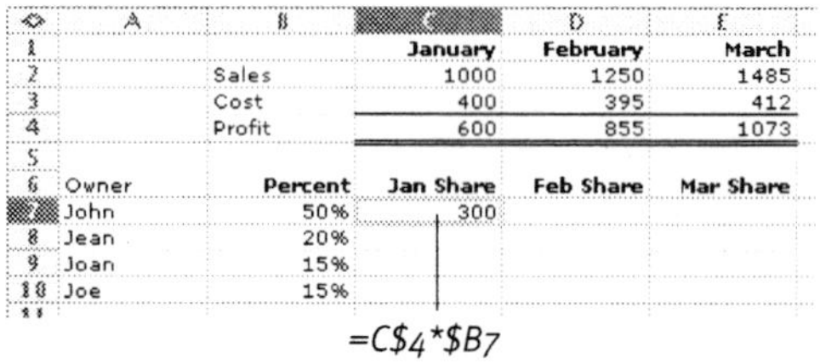

ent   Share
0% =$B$3|
0%

Figure 50 Either include the dollar signs as you type or press ⌃ ⌘ T when the insertion point is in a cell reference.

◇	A	B	C	D	E
1			January	February	March
2		Sales	1000	1250	1485
3		Cost	400	395	412
4		Profit	600	855	1073
5					
6	Owner	Percent	Jan Share	Feb Share	Mar Share
7	John	50%	300		
8	Jean	20%			
9	Joan	15%			
10	Joe	15%			
11					

$$=C\$4*\$B7$$

Figure 51 The formula in cell *C7* includes two different kinds of mixed references. It can be copied to cells *C8* through *C10* and *C7* through *E10* for correct results in all cells. Try it and see for yourself!

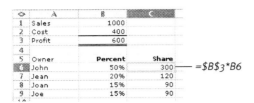

Figure 52 Note the formula in cell *C6*.

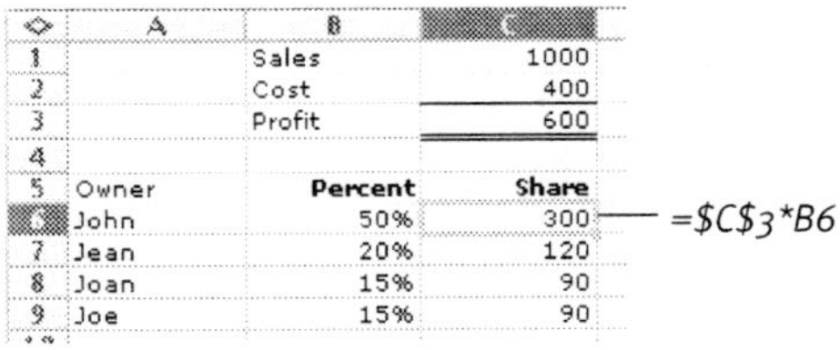

Figure 53 See how it changes when one of the cells it references moves?

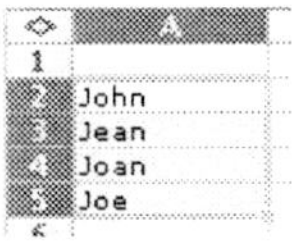

Figure 54
Select the cell(s)
you want to move.

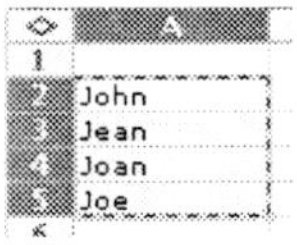

Figure 55
When you use the Cut command, a marquee appears around the selection but the selected cells do not disappear.

Figure 56
Select the destination cell(s).

Figure 57
When you use the Paste command, the selection moves.

Moving Cells

Excel offers two ways to move the contents of one cell to another: the Cut and Paste commands and dragging the border of a selection. Either way, Excel moves the contents of the cell.

✔ Tip

■ When you move a cell, Excel searches the worksheet for any cells that contain references to it and changes the references to reflect the cell's new location (**Figures 52** and **53**).

To move with Cut & Paste

1. Select the cell(s) you want to move (**Figure 54**).

2. Choose Edit > Cut (**Figure 13**), press ⌃ ⌘ X, or click the Cut button ✄ on the Standard toolbar.

   An animated marquee appears around the selection (**Figure 55**).

3. Select the cell(s) to which you want to paste the selection (**Figure 56**).

4. Choose Edit > Paste (**Figure 27**), press ⌃ ⌘ V or Enter, or click the Paste button 📋 on the Standard toolbar.

   The cell contents are moved to the new location (**Figure 57**).

✔ Tip

■ Consult the tips at the bottom of page 44 for Paste command warnings and tips.

To move with drag & drop

1. Select the cell(s) you want to move (**Figure 54**).

2. Position the mouse pointer on the border of the selection. It turns into a hand (**Figure 58**).

3. Press the mouse button down and drag toward the new location. As you move the mouse, a gray border the same shape as the selection moves along with it and a yellow box indicates the range where the cells will move (**Figure 59**).

4. Release the mouse button. The selection moves to its new location (**Figure 57**).

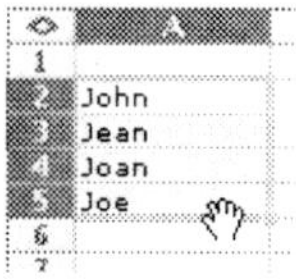

✔ Tips

- If you try to drag a selection to cells already containing information, Excel warns you with a dialog or Office Assistant balloon (**Figure 60**). If you click OK to complete the move, the destination cells will be overwritten with the contents of the cells you are moving.

- To copy using drag and drop, hold down Option as you press the mouse button down. The mouse pointer turns into a hand with a tiny plus sign (+) inside it (**Figure 61**). When you release the mouse button, the selection is copied.

- To insert cells using drag and drop, hold down Shift as you press the mouse button down. As you drag, a gray bar moves along with the mouse pointer and a yellow box indicates where the cells will be inserted (**Figure 62**). When you release the mouse button, the cells are inserted (**Figure 63**).

Figure 58
When you move the mouse pointer onto the border of a selection, it turns into a hand.

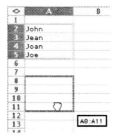

Figure 59
As you drag, a gray border moves along with the mouse pointer.

Do you want to replace the contents of the destination cells?

Cancel   OK

Figure 60 Excel warns you when you will overwrite cells with a selection you drag.

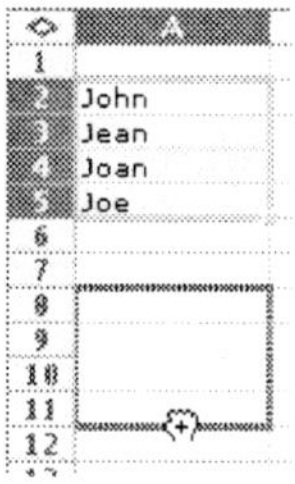

Figure 61
Hold down Option to copy a selection by dragging it. A plus sign appears inside the mouse pointer.

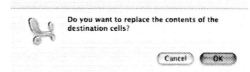

Figure 62 Hold down Shift to insert a selection between other cells. A bar indicates where the cells will be inserted.

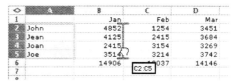

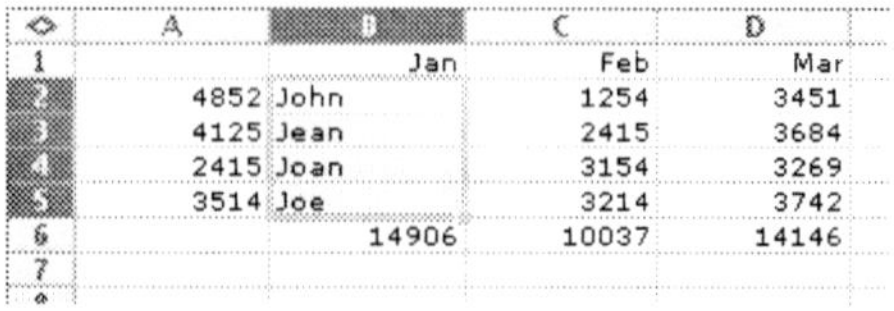

Figure 63 This makes it possible to rearrange the cells in a worksheet.

MOVING WITH DRAG & DROP

Figure 64
Choose Office
Clipboard from
the View menu.

Figure 65
The Office Clipboard,
with nothing on it.

Figure 66
The Office Clipboard
with an Excel chart, an
Excel worksheet, and
some Word text.

The Office Clipboard

The Office Clipboard enables you to "collect
and paste" multiple items. You simply display
the Office Clipboard, then copy or cut cells,
text, or objects as usual. But instead of the
Clipboard contents being replaced each time
you use the Copy or Cut command, all items
are stored on the Office Clipboard (**Figure 66**).
You can then paste any of the items on the
Office Clipboard into your Excel document.

✔ Tips

- The Office Clipboard works with all Microsoft Office applications—not just Excel—
  so you can store items from different types
  of Office documents.

- This feature is also known as *Collect and
  Paste*.

To add items to the Office Clipboard

1. If necessary, choose View > Office Clipboard
   (**Figure 64**) to display the Office Clipboard
   (**Figure 65**).

2. Select the text, cell(s), or object you want
   to copy.

3. Choose Edit > Copy (**Figure 13**), press
   ⌃ ⌘ C, or click the Copy button 🗋 on
   the Standard toolbar.

   The selection is added to the Office
   Clipboard.

4. Repeat steps 2 and 3 for each item you
   want to add to the Office Clipboard.
   Figure 66 shows what it might look like
   with multiple items added.

ADDING ITEMS TO THE OFFICE CLIPBOARD

To use Office Clipboard items

1. If necessary, choose View > Office Clipboard (**Figure 64**) to display the Office Clipboard.

Then:

2. Drag the item you want to use from the Office Clipboard window into the worksheet window.

Or then:

2. In the worksheet window, select the cell(s) where you want to place the Office Clipboard item.

3. In the Office Clipboard window, click the item you want to paste into the document (**Figure 66**).

4. Click the Paste button at the bottom of the Office Clipboard (**Figure 67**).

✔ Tips

- You can select multiple Office Clipboard items by holding down [Shift] while clicking each one.

- If more than one item in the Office Clipboard is selected, clicking the Paste Selected button pastes them all in, in the order they were selected.

- Choosing Paste All from the Paste All & Clear All pop-up menu at the bottom of the Office Clipboard (**Figure 67**) pastes all items into the document.

To remove Office Clipboard items

1. In the Office Clipboard window, select the item(s) you want to remove.

2. Click the Clear button at the bottom of the Office Clipboard (**Figure 67**).

or

Choose Clear All from the Paste All & Clear All pop-up menu at the bottom of the Office Clipboard (**Figure 67**) to remove all items.

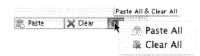

Figure 67 Use the Paste All & Clear All pop-up menu at the bottom of the Office Clipboard to either paste or remove all Office Clipboard items.

Undoing, Redoing, & Repeating Actions

Excel's Edit menu offers a trio of commands that enable you to undo, redo, or repeat the last thing you did.

◆ **Undo** (**Figure 13**) reverses your last action. Excel supports multiple levels of undo, enabling you to reverse more than just the very last action.

◆ **Redo** (**Figure 27**) reverses the Undo command. This command is only available if the last thing you did was use the Undo command.

◆ **Repeat** (**Figure 13**) performs your last action again. This command is only available when you performed any action other than use the Undo or Redo command.

✔ Tips

■ The exact wording of these commands on the Edit menu (**Figures 13** and **27**) varies depending on the last action performed. The Undo command is always the first command under the Edit menu; the Redo or Repeat command (whichever appears on the menu) is always the second command under the Edit menu.

■ The Redo and Repeat commands are never both available at the same time.

■ Think of the Undo command as the Oops command—anytime you say "Oops," you'll probably want to use it.

To undo the last action

Choose Edit > Undo (**Figures 13** or **35**) or press ⌃ ⌘ Z.

or

Click the Undo button on the Standard toolbar.

To undo multiple actions

Choose Edit > Undo (**Figures 13** or **35**) or press ⌃ ⌘ Z repeatedly.

or

Click the triangle beside the Undo button on the Standard toolbar to display a pop-up menu of recent actions. Drag down to select all the actions that you want to undo (**Figure 68**). Release the mouse button to undo all selected actions.

To reverse the last undo

Choose Edit > Redo (**Figures 27** or **35**) or press ⌃ ⌘ Y.

or

Click the Redo button on the Standard toolbar.

To reverse multiple undos

Choose Edit > Redo (**Figures 27** or **35**) or press ⌃ ⌘ Y repeatedly.

or

Click the triangle beside the Redo button on the Standard toolbar to display a pop-up menu of recently undone actions. Drag down to select all the actions that you want to redo (**Figure 69**). Release the mouse button to reverse all selected undos.

To repeat the last action

Choose Edit > Repeat (**Figure 13**) or press ⌃ ⌘ Y.

Figure 68 You can use the Undo button's menu to select multiple actions to undo.

Figure 69 You can also use the Redo button's menu to select multiple actions to redo.

WORKING WITH FILES

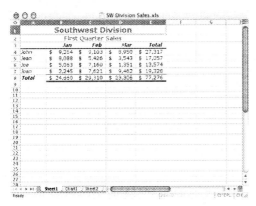

Figure 1 Here's a worksheet.

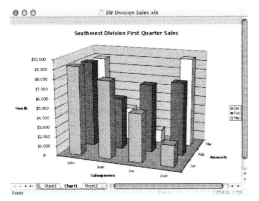

Figure 2 And here's a chart sheet in the same workbook file.

Excel Files

Microsoft Excel document files are called *workbooks*.

◆ Each workbook file includes multiple sheets.

◆ Workbook files appear in document windows.

◆ Workbook files can be saved on disk and reopened for editing and printing.

This chapter, explains how to perform a variety of tasks with workbook sheets, windows, and files.

Workbook Sheets

Excel workbook files can include up to 255 individual *sheets*, which are like pages in the workbook. Each workbook, by default, includes three sheets named *Sheet1* through *Sheet3*.

In Excel, there are two kinds of sheets:

◆ A *worksheet* (**Figure 1**) is for entering information and performing calculations. You can also embed charts in a worksheet.

◆ A *chart sheet* (**Figure 2**) is for creating charts that aren't embedded in a worksheet.

✔ Tips

■ Use the multiple sheet capabilities of workbook files to keep sheets for the same project together. This is an excellent way to organize related work.

■ I tell you about worksheets throughout this book and about charts and chart sheets in **Chapter 8**.

To switch between sheets

Click the sheet tab at the bottom of the workbook window (**Figure 3**) for the sheet you want.

or

Press (Option)(←) or (Option)(→) to scroll through all of the sheets in a workbook, one at a time.

✔ Tips

- If the sheet tab for the sheet you want is not displayed, use the tab scrolling buttons (**Figure 4**) to scroll through the sheet tabs.

- To display more or fewer sheet tabs, drag the tab split box (**Figure 5**) to increase or decrease the size of the sheet tab area. As you change the size of the sheet tab area, you'll also change the size of the horizontal scroll bar at the bottom of the workbook window.

To select multiple sheets

1. Click the sheet tab for the first sheet you want to select.

2. Hold down (⌃ ⌘) and click the sheet tab(s) for the other sheet(s) you want to select. The sheet tabs for each sheet you include in the selection turn white (**Figure 6**).

✔ Tips

- To select multiple adjacent sheets, click the sheet tab for the first sheet, then hold down (Shift) and click on the sheet tab for the last sheet you want to select. All sheet tabs in between also become selected.

- Selecting multiple sheets makes it quick and easy to print, delete, edit, format, or perform other tasks with more than one sheet at a time.

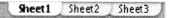

Figure 3 Use sheet tabs to move from sheet to sheet in a workbook.

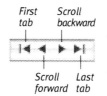

Figure 4 Use the sheet tab scrolling buttons to view sheet tabs that are not displayed.

First tab *Scroll backward* *Scroll forward* *Last tab*

Figure 5 Drag the tab split box to change the size of the sheet tab area and display more or fewer sheet tabs.

Figure 6 To select multiple sheets, hold down (⌃ ⌘) while clicking each sheet tab.

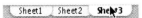

Figure 7 Begin by selecting the sheet you want the new sheet to be inserted before.

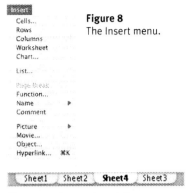

Figure 8
The Insert menu.

Figure 9 An inserted worksheet.

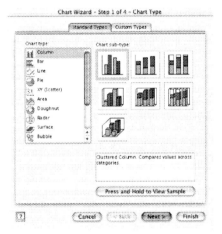

Figure 10 The first step of the Chart Wizard.

Figure 11 The last step of the Chart Wizard enables you to insert the chart as a new sheet.

Figure 12 An inserted chart sheet.

To insert a worksheet

1. Click the tab for the sheet you want to insert a new sheet before (**Figure 7**).

2. Choose Insert > Worksheet (**Figure 8**).

   A new worksheet is inserted before the one you originally selected (**Figure 9**).

✔ Tip

■ By default, the new worksheet is named with the word *Sheet* followed by a number. I tell you how to rename sheets on the next page.

To insert a chart sheet

1. Click the tab for the sheet you want to insert a new sheet before (**Figure 7**).

2. Choose Insert > Chart (**Figure 8**).

3. The Chart Wizard - Step 1 of 4 dialog appears (**Figure 10**). Follow the steps in the Chart Wizard (as discussed in **Chapter 8**) to create a chart.

4. In the Chart Wizard - Step 4 of 4 dialog (**Figure 11**), select the As new sheet radio button and enter a name for the sheet beside it. Then click Finish.

   A new chart sheet is inserted before the worksheet you originally selected (**Figure 12**).

INSERTING SHEETS

To delete a sheet

1. Click on the sheet tab for the sheet you want to delete to select it.

2. Choose Edit > Delete Sheet (**Figure 13**).

3. A warning dialog (**Figure 14**) or Office Assistant balloon appears. Click OK to confirm that you want to delete the sheet.

✔ Tips

- The appearance of the Edit menu (**Figure 13**) varies depending on the type of sheet.

- As the dialog in **Figure 14** warns, sheets are permanently deleted. That means even the Undo command won't get a deleted sheet back.

- If another cell in the workbook contains a reference to a cell on the sheet you've deleted, that cell will display a #REF! error message. The formula in that cell will have to be rewritten.

To rename a sheet

1. Click on the sheet tab for the sheet you want to rename to make it active.

2. Choose Format > Sheet > Rename (**Figure 15**) or double-click the sheet tab.

3. The sheet tab becomes highlighted (**Figure 16**). Enter a new name for the sheet (**Figure 17**) and press [Return] or [Enter] to save it.

   The sheet tab displays the new name (**Figure 18**).

✔ Tips

- The appearance of the Format menu (**Figure 15**) varies depending on the type of sheet.

- Sheet names can be up to 31 characters long and can contain any character except a colon (:) or mathematical operator.

Figure 13
The Edit menu.

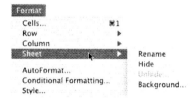

Figure 14 When you delete a sheet, Excel warns you that it will be permanently deleted.

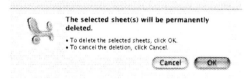

Figure 15 The Sheet submenu under the Format menu.

Figure 16 Double-click the sheet tab to select its name.

Figure 17 Enter a new name for the sheet.

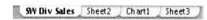

Figure 18 Press [Return] to save the new name.

DELETING & RENAMING SHEETS

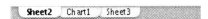

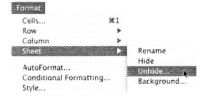

Figure 19 When you hide a sheet, its tab disappears.

Figure 20 When a sheet is hidden, the Unhide command is available on the Sheet submenu.

Figure 21
The Unhide dialog lists all hidden sheets.

To hide a sheet

1. Select the sheet(s) you want to hide (**Figure 18**).

2. Choose Format > Sheet > Hide (**Figure 15**).

   The sheet and its sheet tab disappear (**Figure 19**), just as if the sheet were deleted! But don't worry—the sheet still exists in the workbook file.

✔ Tips

- You cannot hide a sheet if it is the only sheet in a workbook.

- Don't confuse this command with the Hide command under the Window menu. These commands do two different things! I tell you about the Window menu's Hide command later in this chapter.

To unhide a sheet

1. Choose Format > Sheet > Unhide (**Figure 20**).

2. In the Unhide dialog that appears (**Figure 21**), select the sheet you want to unhide.

3. Click OK.

   The sheet and its sheet tab reappear.

✔ Tips

- You can only unhide one sheet at a time.

- If the Unhide command is gray (**Figure 15**), no sheets are hidden.

- Don't confuse this command with the Unhide command under the Window menu. I tell you about the Window menu's Unhide command later in this chapter.

To move or copy a sheet

1. Select the tabs for the sheet(s) you want to move or copy.

2. Choose Edit > Move or Copy Sheet (**Figure 13**). The Move or Copy dialog appears (**Figure 22**).

3. Use the To book pop-up menu (**Figure 23**) to choose the workbook you want to move or copy the sheet(s) to.

4. Use the Before sheet scrolling list to choose the sheet you want the sheet(s) to be copied before.

5. If you want to copy or duplicate the sheet rather than move it, turn on the Create a copy check box.

6. Click OK.

✔ Tips

- To move or copy sheets to another workbook, make sure that workbook is open (but not active) before you choose the Move or Copy Sheet command. Otherwise, it will not be listed in the To book pop-up menu (**Figure 23**).

- If you choose (new book) from the To book pop-up menu (**Figure 23**), Excel creates a brand new, empty workbook file and places the selected sheet(s) into it.

- You can use the Move or Copy Sheet command to change the order of sheets in a workbook. Just make sure the current workbook is selected in the To book pop-up menu (**Figure 23**). Then select the appropriate sheet from the Before sheet scrolling list or select (move to end).

- You can also move or copy a sheet within a workbook by dragging. To move the sheet, simply drag the sheet tab to the new position (**Figure 24**). To copy the sheet, hold down Option while dragging the sheet tab (**Figure 25**).

Figure 22
Use the Move or Copy dialog to pick a destination for the selected sheet(s) and tell Excel to copy them rather than move them.

Figure 23
The To book pop-up menu lists all of the workbooks that are currently open.

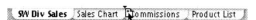

Figure 24 You can also drag a sheet tab to move it...

Figure 25 ...or hold down Option while dragging a sheet tab to copy it.

WORKBOOK WINDOWS

Figure 26
The Window menu offers commands for working with—you guessed it—windows.

Window
Zoom Window
Minimize Window   ⌘M
Bring All to Front
New Window
Arrange...
Hide
Unhide
Split
Freeze Panes
✓ 1 SW Division Sales.xls
2 Profit Sharing.xls
3 Site Activity.xls
4 Mailing List.xls

Workbook Windows

Like most Mac OS programs, Excel allows you to have more than one document window open at a time. You can manipulate Excel's workbook windows a number of ways:

◆ Activate a window so you can work with its contents.

◆ Create a new window for a workbook so you can see two sheets from the same workbook at once.

◆ Arrange windows so you can see and work with more than one at a time.

◆ Minimize and hide windows to get them out of the way.

◆ Display minimized or hidden windows to work with them.

◆ Change a window's magnification so you can see more of its contents or see its contents more clearly.

◆ Split a window so you can see and work with two or more parts of a sheet at a time. This is particularly handy when you need to work with two sections of a large worksheet at once.

◆ Close windows when you're finished working with them.

✔ Tip

■ I explain how to create a new workbook in **Chapter 2** and how to open an existing workbook later in this chapter.

To activate another window

Choose the name of the window you want to make active from the list of open windows at the bottom of the Window menu (**Figure 26**).

To create a new window

1. Activate the workbook for which you want to create another window.

2. Choose Window > New Window (**Figure 26**).

   A new window for that workbook appears (**Figure 27**) and the new window's name appears on the Window menu (**Figure 28**).

✔ Tips

■ Opening another window for a document is not the same as opening a separate copy of the document. Any change you make in one window will also appear in the other window.

■ If more than one window is open for a workbook and you close one of them, the workbook does not close—just that window. I tell you about closing windows later in this section.

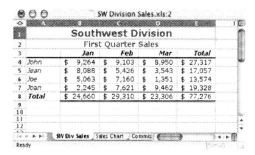

Figure 27 When you open more than one window for a file, the window number appears in the title bar...

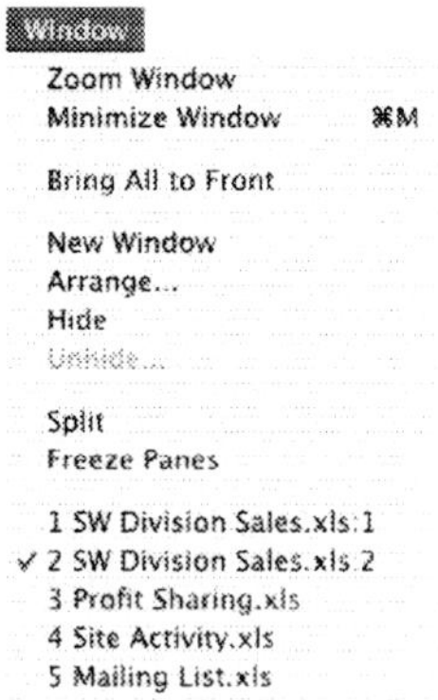

Figure 28 ...and both windows are listed on the Window menu.

CREATING NEW WINDOWS

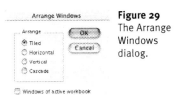

Figure 29
The Arrange Windows dialog.

To arrange windows

1. Choose Window > Arrange (**Figure 26**).

2. In the Arrange Windows dialog that appears (**Figure 29**), select an Arrange option. **Figures 30** through **33** illustrate all of them.

3. To arrange only the windows of the active workbook, turn on the Windows of active workbook check box.

4. Click OK.

✔ Tips

- To work with one of the arranged windows, click in it to make it active.

- The window with the colored buttons on the left side of the title bar is the active window. (In Mac OS X, windows that are not active have translucent title bars.)

- To make one of the arranged windows full size again, click on it to make it active and then click the window's zoom box. The window fills the screen while the other windows remain arranged behind it. Click the zoom box again to shrink it back down to its arranged size.

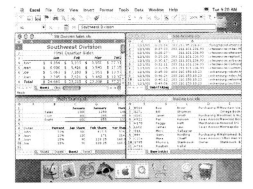

Figure 30 Tiled windows.

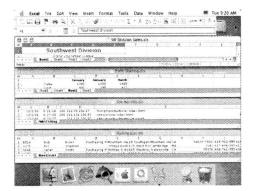

Figure 31 Horizontally arranged windows.

Figure 32 Vertically arranged windows.

Figure 33 Cascading windows.

ARRANGING WINDOWS

To minimize a window

1. Activate the window you want to minimize.

2. Choose Window > Minimize Window (**Figure 26**), press ⌃ ⌘ M, or click the window's minimize button.

    The window shrinks into the Dock (**Figure 34**).

To display a minimized window

Click the icon for the window in the Dock (**Figure 34**).

The window expands from the Dock and becomes the active window.

To hide a window

1. Activate the window you want to hide.

2. Choose Window > Hide (**Figure 26**).

✔ Tips

- Hiding a window is not the same as closing it. A hidden window remains open, even though it is not listed at the bottom of the Window menu. I tell you about closing windows later in this chapter.

- Hiding a window is not the same as hiding a sheet in a workbook. Hiding a window hides the entire workbook; hiding a sheet hides just one sheet of the workbook. I tell you about hiding sheets earlier in this chapter.

To unhide a window

1. Choose Window > Unhide (**Figure 35**).

2. In the Unhide dialog that appears (**Figure 36**), choose the window you want to unhide.

3. Click OK.

✔ Tip

- If the Unhide command is gray (**Figures 26** and **28**), no windows are hidden.

Figure 34 A minimized document window appears in the Dock.

Figure 35 When a window is hidden, the Unhide command is available on the Window menu.

Figure 36 Use the Unhide dialog to select the window you want to unhide.

MINIMIZING & HIDING WINDOWS

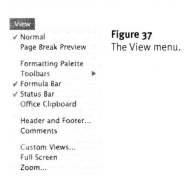

Figure 37
The View menu.

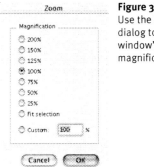

Figure 38
Use the Zoom dialog to set the window's magnification.

Figure 39
You can also choose a magnification option from the Zoom pop-up menu on the Standard toolbar.

112| ▼

Figure 40 You can enter a custom zoom percentage in the Zoom box on the Standard toolbar.

To change a window's magnification

1. Choose View > Zoom (**Figure 37**).

2. In the Zoom dialog that appears (**Figure 38**), select the radio button for the magnification you want.

3. Click OK.

or

1. Click the arrow beside the Zoom box on the Standard toolbar to display a menu of magnifications (**Figure 39**).

2. Choose the magnification you want from the menu.

✔ Tips

■ To zoom selected cells so they fill the window, select the Fit selection radio button in the Zoom dialog (**Figure 38**) or choose the Selection command on the Zoom pop-up menu (**Figure 39**).

■ You can enter a custom magnification in the Zoom dialog (**Figure 38**) by selecting the Custom radio button and entering a value of your choice.

■ You can enter a custom magnification in the Zoom box on the Standard toolbar by clicking the value in the box to select it, typing in a new value (**Figure 40**), and pressing [Return] or [Enter].

■ Custom zoom percentages must be between 10% and 400%.

■ Zooming the window using techniques discussed here does not affect the way a worksheet will print.

■ A "zoomed" window's sheet works just like any other worksheet.

■ When you save a workbook, the magnification settings of its sheets are saved. When you reopen the workbook, the sheets appear with the last used zoom magnification percentage.

CHANGING WINDOW MAGNIFICATION

To split a window

1. Select the cell immediately below and to the right of where you want the split(s) to occur (**Figure 41**).

2. Choose Window > Split (**Figure 26**). The window splits at the location you specified (**Figure 42**).

or

1. Position the mouse pointer on the split bar at the top of the vertical scroll bar or right end of the horizontal scroll bar. The mouse pointer turns into a double line with arrows coming out of it (**Figure 43**).

2. Press the mouse button down and drag. A split bar moves with the mouse pointer (**Figure 44**).

3. Release the mouse button. The window splits at the bar (**Figure 45**).

To adjust the size of panes

1. Position the mouse pointer on a split bar.

2. Press the mouse button down and drag until the split bar is in the desired position.

3. Release the mouse button. The split moves.

To remove a window split

Choose Window > Remove Split (**Figure 46**).

or

Double-click a split bar.

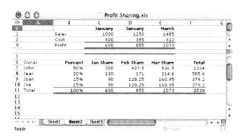

Figure 45 When you release the mouse button, the window splits.

Figure 41 Position the cell pointer where you want the split to occur.

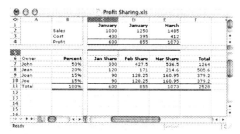

Figure 42 When you choose the Split command, the window splits.

Figure 43
Position the mouse pointer on the split bar at the end of the scroll bar.

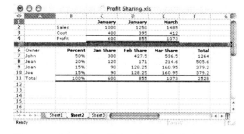

Figure 44 Drag the split bar into the window.

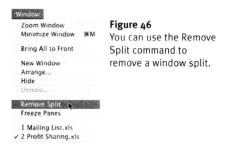

Figure 46 You can use the Remove Split command to remove a window split.

Figure 47
The File menu.

To close a window

Click the window's close button.

or

Choose File > Close (**Figure 47**) or press ⌘⌘W.

✔ Tips

- If the file you are closing has unsaved changes, Excel warns you (**Figure 48**). Click Save to save changes. I tell you about saving files next.

- To close all open windows, hold down Shift and choose File > Close All (**Figure 49**).

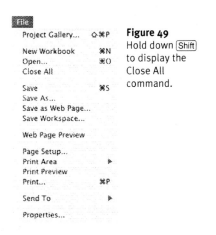

Figure 48 When you attempt to close an unsaved document, Excel warns you and gives you an opportunity to save it.

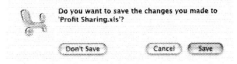

Figure 49
Hold down Shift to display the Close All command.

Saving Files

As you work with a file, everything you do is stored in only one place: *random access memory* or *RAM*. The contents of RAM are a lot like the light in a lightbulb—as soon as you turn it off or pull the plug, it's gone. Your hard disk provides a much more permanent type of storage area. You use the Save command to copy the workbook file in RAM to disk.

✔ Tip

■ It's a very good idea to save documents frequently as you work. This ensures that the most recent versions are always saved to disk in the event of a computer problem.

To save a workbook file for the first time

1. Choose File > Save or File > Save As (**Figure 47**), press ⌘⌘S, or click the Save button 🖫 on the Standard toolbar to display the Save As dialog sheet (**Figure 50**).

2. Click the triangle beside the Where pop-up menu to expand the dialog so it shows the file hierarchy (**Figure 51**).

3. Navigate to the folder in which you want to save the file:

   ▲ Use the Where pop-up menu (**Figure 52**) to select a different location.

   ▲ Double-click a folder to open it.

   ▲ Click the New Folder button to create a new folder within the current folder. Enter the name for the folder in the New Folder dialog (**Figure 53**) and click the Create button.

4. Enter a name for the file in the Save As text box.

5. Click Save.

   The file is saved to disk. Its name appears in the window's title bar (**Figure 54**).

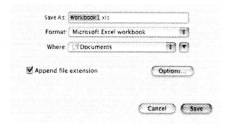

Figure 50 The Save As dialog sheet with the file name suggested by Excel. This is the collapsed version of the dialog.

Figure 51 Clicking the triangle beside the Where menu expands the dialog to show the file hierarchy.

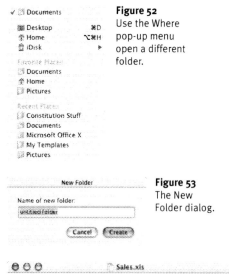

Figure 52 Use the Where pop-up menu open a different folder.

Figure 53 The New Folder dialog.

Figure 54 The File's name appears in the title bar, along with a tiny Excel workbook file icon.

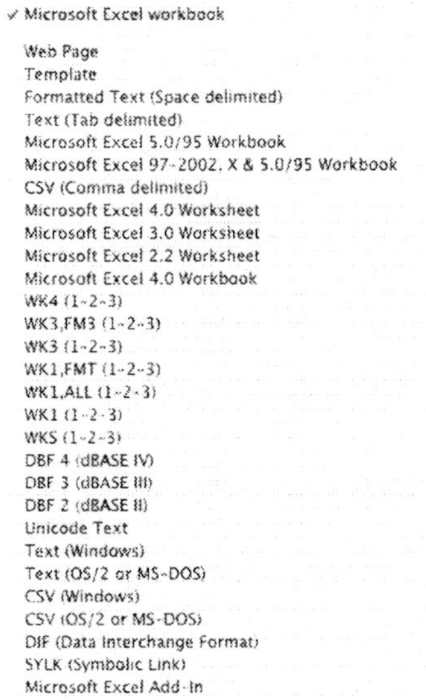

✓ Microsoft Excel workbook

Web Page
Template
Formatted Text (Space delimited)
Text (Tab delimited)
Microsoft Excel 5.0/95 Workbook
Microsoft Excel 97-2002, X & 5.0/95 Workbook
CSV (Comma delimited)
Microsoft Excel 4.0 Worksheet
Microsoft Excel 3.0 Worksheet
Microsoft Excel 2.2 Worksheet
Microsoft Excel 4.0 Workbook
WK4 (1-2-3)
WK3,FM3 (1-2-3)
WK3 (1-2-3)
WK1,FMT (1-2-3)
WK1,ALL (1-2-3)
WK1 (1-2-3)
WKS (1-2-3)
DBF 4 (dBASE IV)
DBF 3 (dBASE III)
DBF 2 (dBASE II)
Unicode Text
Text (Windows)
Text (OS/2 or MS-DOS)
CSV (Windows)
CSV (OS/2 or MS-DOS)
DIF (Data Interchange Format)
SYLK (Symbolic Link)
Microsoft Excel Add-In

Figure 55
Use the Format pop-up menu to save the document as a template or another type of file.

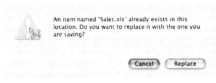

An item named "Sales.xls" already exists in this location. Do you want to replace it with the one you are saving?

(Cancel) (Replace)

Figure 56 Excel double-checks to make sure you want to overwrite a file with the same name.

✔ Tips

■ You can use the Format pop-up menu in the Save As dialog (**Figure 55**) to specify a format for the file or active sheet. This enables you to save the document as a template or in a format that can be opened and read by other versions of Excel or other applications.

■ If you save a file with the same name and same disk location as another file, a dialog appears, asking if you want to replace the file (**Figure 56**).

   ▲ Click the Replace button to replace the file already on disk with the file you are saving.

   ▲ Click the Cancel button to return to the Save As dialog where you can enter a new name or specify a new disk location.

To save changes to a file

Choose File > Save (**Figure 47**), press ⌃ ⌘ S, or click the Save button 💾 on the Standard toolbar.

The file is saved with the same name in the same location on disk.

To save a file with a different name or in a different location

1. Choose File > Save As (**Figure 47**).

2. Follow steps 2 and/or 3 on the previous page to select a new disk location and/or enter a different name for the file.

3. Click the Save button.

Opening Existing Files

Once a file has been saved on disk, you can reopen it to read it, modify it, or print it.

To open an existing file

1. Choose File > Open (**Figure 47**), press ⌘O, or click the Open button 📂 on the Standard toolbar.

2. Use the Open dialog that appears (**Figure 57**) to locate the file that you want to open:

   ▲ Use the From pop-up menu (**Figure 52**) to select a different location.

   ▲ Double-click a folder to open it.

3. Select the file that you want to open and click the Open button.

   or

   Double-click the file that you want to open.

✔ Tips

■ To view only specific types of files in the Open dialog, select a format from the Show pop-up menu (**Figure 58**).

■ If you select All Readable Documents from the Show pop-up menu (**Figure 58**), you can open just about any kind of file. Be aware, however, that a file in an incompatible format may not appear the way you expect when opened.

■ You can use the Find File button in the Open dialog to search for a file based on criteria you specify.

■ To open a copy of a file rather than the original, choose Copy from the Open pop-up menu (**Figure 59**).

■ To add a folder to your Favorite Places list, select it in the Open dialog (**Figure 57**) and click the Add to Favorites button.

Figure 57 The Open dialog.

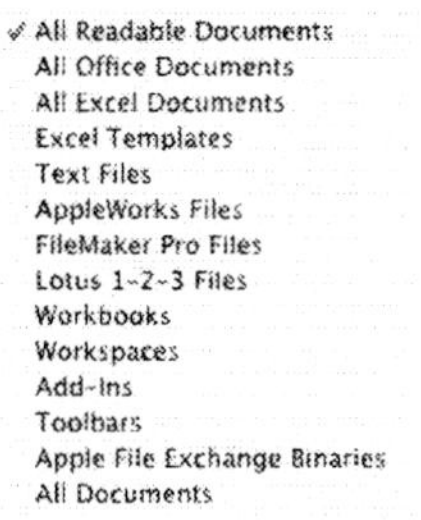

Figure 58
You can narrow down or expand the list of files shown by choosing an option from the Show pop-up menu.

✓ All Readable Documents
All Office Documents
All Excel Documents
Excel Templates
Text Files
AppleWorks Files
FileMaker Pro Files
Lotus 1-2-3 Files
Workbooks
Workspaces
Add-Ins
Toolbars
Apple File Exchange Binaries
All Documents

✓ Original
Copy
Read-Only

Figure 59 You can open a copy of a document rather than the original by choosing Copy from the Open pop-up menu.

USING FUNCTIONS IN FORMULAS

◇	A	B	C
1	**Product Inventory**		
2			
3	**Product Code**	**Department**	**Qty**
4	VGU56X	Electronics	47
5	EZJ124S	Baby Clothes	129
6	IXQ2422U	Lingerie	234
7	IGN116C	Lingerie	117
8	GKS255F	Junior Clothes	455
9	FPK813O	Misses Clothes	356
10	JCY35K	Women's Accessories	459
11	GTL103G	Junior Clothes	329
12	WDH36Y	Computers	151
13			
14			

Figure 1 Using the SUM function makes it easier to add up a range of numbers.

Function name   *Arguments*

SUM(number1,number2,...)

Figure 2 The parts of a function. Bold components are required.

✔ Tips

■ If a function comes at the beginning of a formula, it must begin with an equal sign (=).

■ Some arguments are optional. In the SUM function, for example, you can have only one argument, like a reference to a single range of cells.

Functions

A function is a predefined formula for making a specific kind of calculation. Functions make it quicker and easier to write formulas.

For example, say you need to add up a column of numbers like the one in **Figure 1**. It's perfectly acceptable to write a formula using cell references separated by the addition operator (+) like this:

$$=C4+C5+C6+C7+C8+C9+C10+C11+C12$$

But rather than enter a lengthy formula, you can use the SUM function to add up the same numbers like this:

$$=SUM(C4:C12)$$

The SUM function is only one of over 200 functions built into Excel. I list all functions in **Appendix B**.

Anatomy of a Function

As shown in **Figure 2**, each function has two main parts.

◆ The *function name* determines what the function does.

◆ The *arguments* determine what values or cell references the function should use in its calculation. Arguments are enclosed in parentheses and, if there's more than one, separated by commas.

Arguments

The argument component of a function can consist of any of the following:

- **Numbers (Figure 3).** Like any other formula, however, the result of a function that uses values for arguments will not change unless the formula is changed.

- **Text (Figure 4).** Excel includes a number of functions just for text. I tell you about them later in this chapter.

- **Cell references (Figures 4** through **8).** This is a practical way to write functions, since when you change cell contents, the results of functions that reference them change automatically.

- **Formulas (Figures 6** and **7).** This lets you create complex formulas that perform a series of calculations at once.

- **Functions (Figures 7** and **8).** When a function includes another function as one of its arguments, it's called *nesting functions*.

- **Error values (Figure 8).** You may find this useful to "flag" errors or missing information in a worksheet.

- **Logical values.** Some function arguments require TRUE or FALSE values.

 =Date(2001,6,30)

Figure 3 This example uses numbers as arguments for the DATE function.

	A	B	C	D
1		Rates		
2	Over $400	15%		
3	Up to $400	10%		
4				
5		Sales	Amt. Due	Comment
6	John	443.16	66.47	Good Work!
7	Jean	512.84	76.93	Good Work!
8	Joe	328.69	32.87	Try harder.
9	Joan	401.98	60.30	Good Work!

=IF(B6>400,"Good Work!","Try Harder")

Figure 4 This example uses cell references, numbers, and text as arguments for the IF function.

	A	B	
1		Rates	
2	Over $400	15%	
3	Up to $400	10%	
4			
5		Sales	
6	John	443.16	
7	Jean	512.84	
8	Joe	328.69	
9	Joan	401.98	
10	Total	1686.7	

Figure 5
This example shows two different ways to use cell references as arguments for the SUM function.

=SUM(B6:B9) or
=SUM(B6,B7,B8,B9)

	A	B	C
1		Sales	Amt. Due
2	John	443.16	66.47
3	Jean	512.84	
4	Joe	328.69	
5	Joan	401.98	
6	Total	1686.7	

Figure 6 This example uses a formula as an argument for the ROUND function.

=ROUND(B2*15%,2)

	A	B	C
1		Rates	
2	Over $400	15%	
3	Up to $400	10%	
4			
5		Sales	Amt. Due
6	John	443.16	66.47
7	Jean	512.84	
8	Joe	328.69	
9	Joan	401.98	
10	Total	1686.7	

=ROUND(IF(B6>400,B6*B2,B6*B3),2)

Figure 7 This example uses the ROUND and IF functions to calculate commissions based on a rate that changes according to sales.

	A	B	
1		Sales	
2	John	443.16	
3	Jean	512.84	
4	Joe		
5	Joan	401.98	
6	Total	#N/A	

=IF(COUNTBLANK(B4:B7)>0,
#N/A,SUM(B4:B7))

Figure 8 This example uses three functions (IF, COUNTBLANK, and SUM), cell references, and error values to either indicate missing information or add a column of numbers.

ARGUMENTS

You've entered too many arguments for this function.

To get help with entering arguments for the function, click OK to close this message. Then, on the formula bar, click the equal sign button (located to the left of the equal sign in your formula).

OK

Figure 9 If you don't enter parentheses correctly, Excel can get confused.

Your formula is missing a parenthesis--) or (.

Check the formula, and then add the parenthesis in the appropriate place.

OK

Figure 10 Sometimes, Excel knows just what the problem is.

Microsoft Excel found an error in the formula you entered. Do you want to accept the correction proposed below?

=IF(COUNTBLANK(B2:B5)>0,#N/A,SUM(B2:B5))

• To accept the correction, click Yes.
• To close this message and correct the formula yourself, click No.

No   Yes

Figure 11 The Formula AutoCorrect feature can fix common formula errors for you.

Figure 12 You can type in a function just like you type in any other formula.

Figure 13 When you complete the entry, the cell containing the function displays the result of the formula.

Entering Functions

Excel offers several ways to enter a function:

◆ typing

◆ typing and clicking

◆ using the Formula Palette

◆ using the Calculator

There is no "best" way—use the methods that you like most.

✔ Tips

■ Function names are not case sensitive. *Sum* or *sum* is the same as *SUM*. Excel converts all function names to uppercase characters.

■ Do not include spaces when writing formulas.

■ When writing formulas with nested functions, it's important to properly match parentheses. Excel helps you by boldfacing or coloring parentheses as you type them. If parentheses don't match, Excel either displays an error message (**Figures 9** and **10**) or offers to correct the error for you (**Figure 11**). Sometimes Excel will simply fix the error without displaying a message.

To enter a function by typing

1. Begin the formula by typing an equal sign (=).

2. Type in the function name.

3. Type an open parenthesis character.

4. Type in the value or cell reference for the first argument.

5. If entering more than one argument, type each of them in with commas between them.

6. Type a closed parenthesis character (**Figure 12**).

7. Press ⟨Return⟩ or ⟨Enter⟩ or click the Enter button ✓ on the formula bar.

   The result of the function is displayed in the cell (**Figure 13**).

To enter a function by typing & clicking

1. Begin the formula by typing an equal sign (=).

2. Type in the function name.

3. Type an open parenthesis character.

4. Type in a value or click on the cell whose reference you want to include as the first argument (**Figure 14**).

5. If entering more than one argument, type a comma, then type in a value or click on the cell for the next reference (**Figure 15**). Repeat this step for each argument in the function.

6. Type a closed parenthesis character (**Figure 16**).

7. Press [Return] or [Enter] or click the Enter button ✓ on the formula bar.

    The result of the function is displayed in the cell (**Figure 13**).

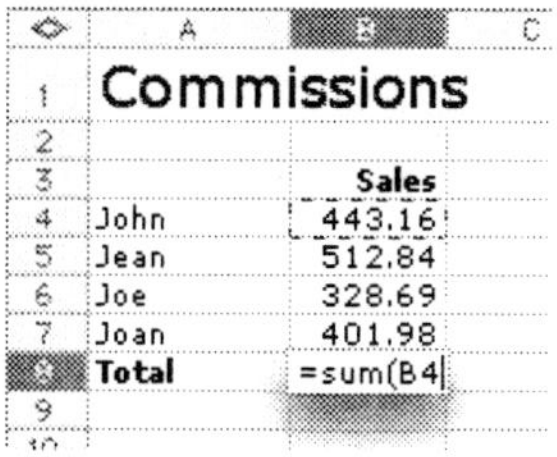

✔ Tips

■ To include a range by clicking, in step 4 or 5 above, drag the mouse pointer over the cells you want to include (**Figure 17**).

■ Be careful where you click or drag when entering a function or any formula. Each click or drag may add references to the formula! If you click on a cell by mistake, you can press [Delete] to delete each character of the incorrectly added reference or click the Cancel button ✖ on the formula bar to start over from scratch.

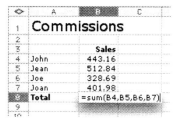

Figure 14
After typing the beginning of the function, you can click on cell references for arguments.

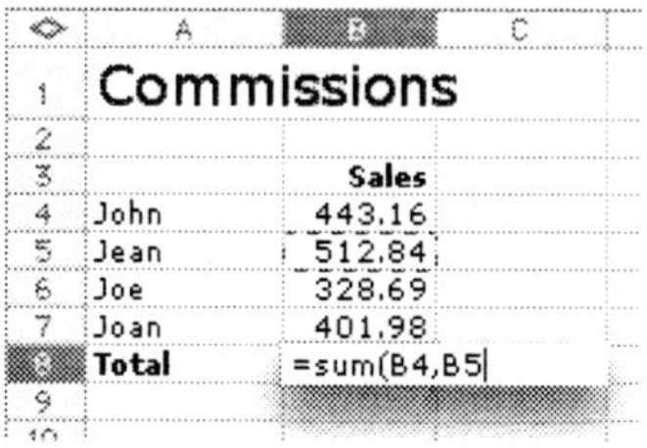

Figure 15
Type a comma before clicking to enter additional cell references for arguments.

Figure 16
Be sure to type a closed parenthesis character at the end of the function.

Figure 17
You can always enter a range in a formula by dragging, even when the range is an argument for a function.

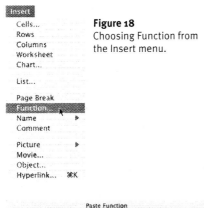

Figure 18
Choosing Function from the Insert menu.

Figure 19 The Paste Function dialog.

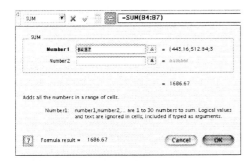

Figure 20 The Formula Palette.

Figure 21
The Functions pop-up menu at the far left end of the formula bar.

To enter a function with the Formula Palette

1. Choose Insert > Function (**Figure 18**) or click the Paste Function button fx on the Standard toolbar.

2. In the Paste Function dialog that appears (**Figure 19**), click to select a category in the Function category list on the left side of the dialog.

3. Click to select a function from the Function name scrolling list on the right side of the dialog. You may have to use the scroll bar to locate the function name you want.

4. Click OK.

   The Formula Palette appears beneath the formula bar (**Figure 20**). It provides information about the function you selected and may include one or more entries for the argument(s).

5. Enter a value or cell reference in the appropriate text box for each required argument.

6. When you are finished entering function arguments, click OK.

   The Formula Palette closes and the result of the function is displayed in the cell (**Figure 13**).

✔ Tips

- You can also open the Formula Palette by clicking the Edit Formula button on the formula bar. (This enables you to use the Formula Palette to enter or edit any formula, even if it doesn't include a function.) To paste a function into the Formula Palette, choose a specific function or More Functions from the Functions pop-up menu at the far left end of the formula bar (**Figure 21**).

Continued on next page...

USING THE FORMULA PALETTE

Continued from previous page.

- Another way to open the Formula Palette is with the Calculator (**Figure 22**). In step 1, click the Calculator button 🔳 on the formula bar to display the Calculator. Then click the More button. Follow steps 2 through 6 to complete the formula. I explain how to use the Calculator to enter the SUM and IF functions later in this chapter.

- Ready for one more way to open the Formula Palette? Choose More Functions from the AutoSum pop-up menu on the Standard toolbar (**Figure 23**). Then follow steps 2 through 6 to complete the formula.

- In step 2, if you're not sure what category a function is in, select All. The Function name scrolling list displays all the functions Excel has to offer.

- In step 5, you can click or drag in the worksheet window to enter a cell reference or range. To see obstructed worksheet cells, click the Hide Formula Palette button 🔳 to collapse the Formula Palette (**Figure 24**). When you're finished selecting the cell or range, click the Display Formula Palette button 🔳 to expand the Formula Palette and continue working with it.

- In step 5, you can enter a function as an argument by clicking in the argument's text box and choosing a specific function or More Functions from the Functions pop-up menu at the far left end of the formula bar (**Figure 21**). Although the Formula Palette only shows function options for one function at a time, you can view and edit the entire formula in the formula bar (**Figure 25**).

- As you enter arguments in the Formula Palette, the calculated value of your entries appears at the bottom of the Formula Palette (**Figure 20**).

Figure 22
Clicking the More button in the Calculator also displays the Formula Palette.

Figure 23
The AutoSum button has a menu of functions.

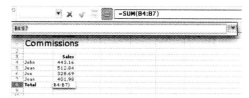

Figure 24 You can collapse the Formula Palette to see and select cell references in the worksheet window.

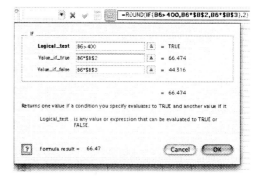

Figure 25 Only one function's options appear in the Formula Palette at a time, but you can view and edit the entire formula in the formula bar.

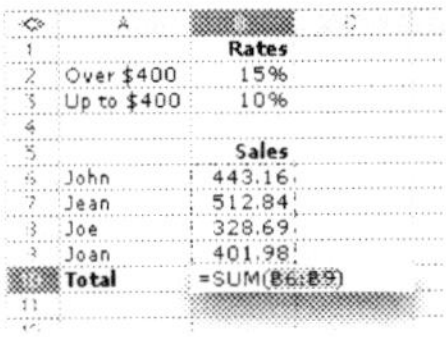

Figure 26
When you click the AutoSum button, Excel writes a formula, guessing which cells you want to sum.

Math & Trig Functions

Excel's math and trig functions perform standard mathematical and trigonometric calculations. On the next few pages, I tell you about the most commonly used ones, starting with one so popular it even has its own toolbar button: SUM.

The SUM function

The SUM function (**Figure 5**) adds up numbers. It uses the following syntax:

SUM(number1,number2,...)

Although the SUM function can accept up to 30 arguments separated by commas, only one is required.

To use the AutoSum button

1. Select the cell below the column or to the right of the row of numbers you want to add.

2. Click the AutoSum button Σ on the Standard toolbar once.

   Excel examines the worksheet and makes a "guess" about which cells you want to add. It writes the corresponding formula and puts a marquee around the range of cells it used (**Figure 26**).

3. If the range in the formula is incorrect, type or select the correct range. Since the reference for the range of cells is selected in the formula, anything you type or select will automatically replace it.

4. When the formula is correct, press (Return) or (Enter), click the Enter button ✓ on the formula bar, or click the AutoSum button Σ on the Standard toolbar a second time.

   The formula is entered and its results appear in the cell.

To use the AutoSum button on multiple cells

1. Select a range of cells adjacent to the columns or rows you want to add (**Figure 27**).
2. Click the AutoSum button Σ once.

   Excel writes the formulas in the cells you selected (**Figure 28**).

or

1. Select the cells containing the columns you want to add (**Figure 29**).
2. Click the AutoSum button Σ once.

   Excel writes all the formulas in the row of cells immediately below the ones you selected (**Figure 30**).

or

1. Select the cells containing the columns and rows you want to add, along with the empty row beneath them and the empty column to the right of them (**Figure 31**).
2. Click the AutoSum button Σ once.

   Excel writes all the formulas in the bottom and rightmost cells (**Figure 32**).

✔ Tip

- Be sure to check the formulas Excel writes when you use the AutoSum button Σ. Excel is smart, but it's no mind-reader. The cells it includes may not be the ones you had in mind!

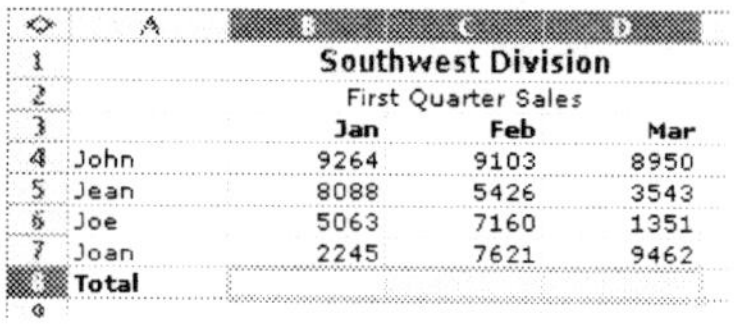

	A	B	C	D
1		Southwest Division		
2		First Quarter Sales		
3		Jan	Feb	Mar
4	John	9264	9103	8950
5	Jean	8088	5426	3543
6	Joe	5063	7160	1351
7	Joan	2245	7621	9462
8	Total			
9				

Figure 27 Select the cells adjacent to the columns (or rows) of cells that you want to add.

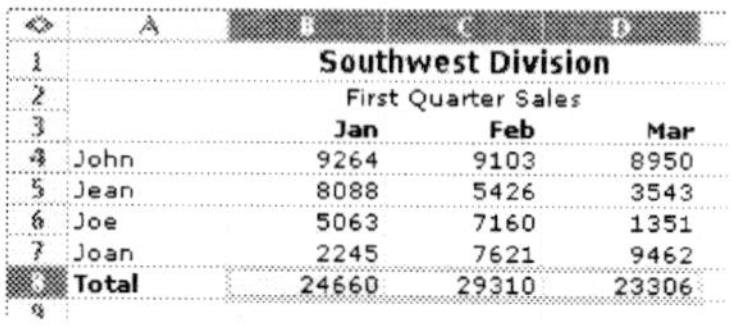

	A	B	C	D
1		Southwest Division		
2		First Quarter Sales		
3		Jan	Feb	Mar
4	John	9264	9103	8950
5	Jean	8088	5426	3543
6	Joe	5063	7160	1351
7	Joan	2245	7621	9462
8	Total	24660	29310	23306
9				

Figure 28 When you click the AutoSum button, Excel enters the appropriate formulas in the cells.

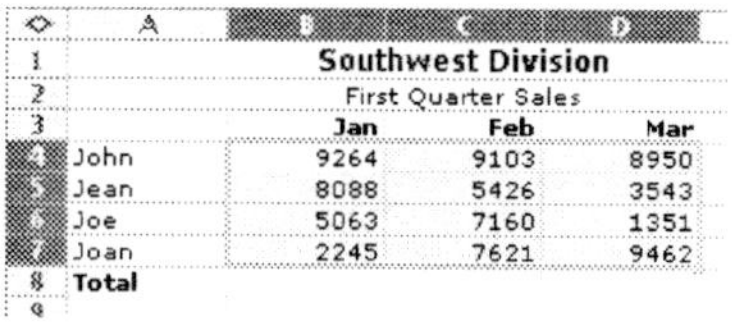

	A	B	C	D
1		Southwest Division		
2		First Quarter Sales		
3		Jan	Feb	Mar
4	John	9264	9103	8950
5	Jean	8088	5426	3543
6	Joe	5063	7160	1351
7	Joan	2245	7621	9462
8	Total			
9				

Figure 29 Select the cells containing the columns that you want to add.

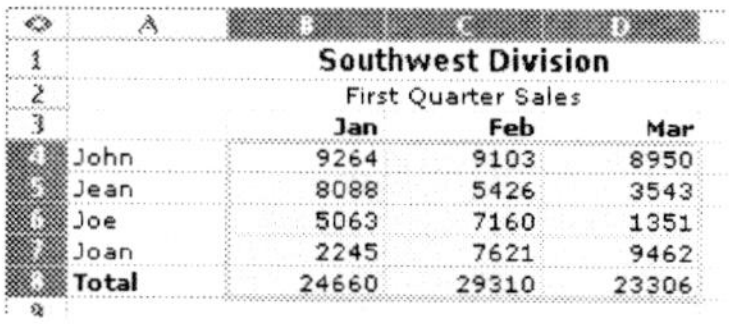

	A	B	C	D
1		Southwest Division		
2		First Quarter Sales		
3		Jan	Feb	Mar
4	John	9264	9103	8950
5	Jean	8088	5426	3543
6	Joe	5063	7160	1351
7	Joan	2245	7621	9462
8	Total	24660	29310	23306
9				

Figure 30 When you click the AutoSum button, Excel enters the appropriate formulas in the cells beneath the selected cells.

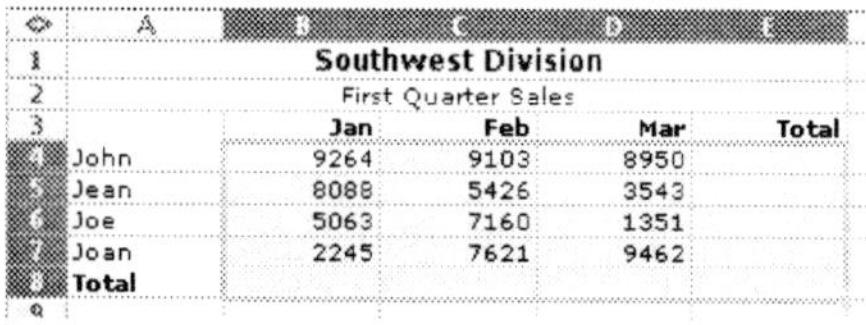

	A	B	C	D	E
1		Southwest Division			
2		First Quarter Sales			
3		Jan	Feb	Mar	Total
4	John	9264	9103	8950	
5	Jean	8088	5426	3543	
6	Joe	5063	7160	1351	
7	Joan	2245	7621	9462	
8	Total				
9					

Figure 31 Select the cells you want to add, along with the cells in which you want the totals to appear.

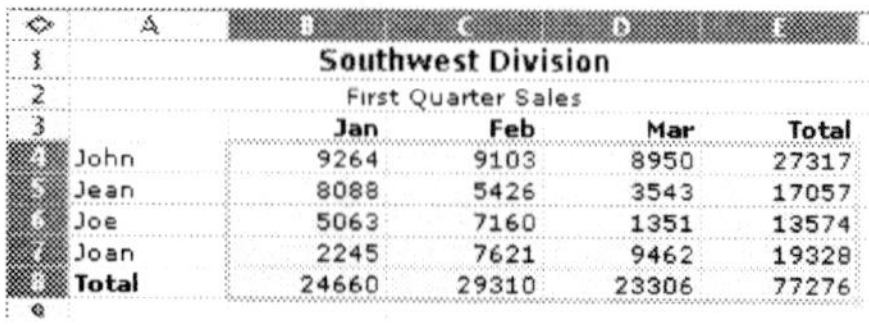

	A	B	C	D	E
1		Southwest Division			
2		First Quarter Sales			
3		Jan	Feb	Mar	Total
4	John	9264	9103	8950	27317
5	Jean	8088	5426	3543	17057
6	Joe	5063	7160	1351	13574
7	Joan	2245	7621	9462	19328
8	Total	24660	29310	23306	77276
9					

Figure 32 When you click the AutoSum button, Excel enters the appropriate formulas in the empty cells of the selection.

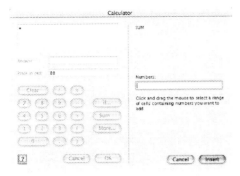

Figure 33 When you click the Sum button in the Calculator dialog, the dialog expands.

Figure 34 As you drag your mouse to select cells, the cell reference appears in the Calculator.

Figure 35
The SUM function formula appears in the Calculator's top text box.

To enter the SUM function with the Calculator

1. Select the cell in which you want to enter the SUM function formula.

2. Click the Calculator button ▦ on the formula bar to display the Calculator (**Figure 22**).

3. Click the Sum button. The Calculator dialog expands to offer a Numbers text box (**Figure 33**).

4. Use the mouse to select the cells you want to include as arguments for the SUM function:

   ▲ Click to include individual cells.

   ▲ Drag to include ranges of cell.

   As you click or drag, the references appear in the Numbers text box (**Figure 34**).

5. When you are finished entering references, click the Insert button. The Calculator collapses and the completed formula appears in its top text box (**Figure 35**).

6. Click OK. The formula results appear in the selected cell.

The PRODUCT function

The PRODUCT function (**Figure 36**) multiplies its arguments much like the SUM function adds them. It uses the following syntax:

PRODUCT(number1,number2,...)

Although the PRODUCT function can accept up to 30 arguments separated by commas, only one is required.

The ROUND function

The ROUND function (**Figure 37**) rounds a number to the number of decimal places you specify. It uses the following syntax:

ROUND(number,num_digits)

Both arguments are required. The num_digits argument specifies how many decimal places the number should be rounded to. If 0, the number is rounded to a whole number. If less than 0, the number is rounded on the left side of the decimal point (**Figure 38**).

✔ Tips

- Rather than make a calculation in one cell and round it in another as shown in **Figures 37** and **38**, combine the two formulas in one cell (**Figure 39**).

- The ROUNDUP function works like the ROUND function, but it always rounds up to the next higher number. The num_digits argument is not required; if omitted, the number is rounded to the next highest whole number.

- The ROUNDDOWN function works just like the ROUNDUP function, but it always rounds down.

	A	B	C	D	E	F
1	Item	Cost	Markup	Qty	Value	
2	Product A	1.54	115%	152	269.192	=PRODUCT(B2:D2)
3	Product B	3.58	250%	142	1270.9	=PRODUCT(B3,C3,D3)
4						

Figure 36 Two ways to use the PRODUCT function. The formulas in column *E* are shown in column *F*.

	A	B	C	D	E	F
1		Sales	Rate	Amount Due	Rounded	
2	John	14528.16	15%	2179.224	2179.22	=ROUND(D2,2)
3	Jean	45284.48	20%	9056.896	9056.9	=ROUND(D3,2)
4	Joe	36547.19	15%	5482.0785	5482.08	=ROUND(D4,2)
5	Joan	27582.43	15%	4137.3645	4137.36	=ROUND(D5,2)

Figure 37 Use the ROUND function to round numbers to the number of decimal places you specify. The formulas in column *E* are shown in column *F*.

	A	E	F	G
1		Total	Rounded	
2	Sales	154258.7	154300	=ROUND(E2,-2)
3	Cost	50043.07		

Figure 38 You can also use the ROUND function to round numbers to the left of the decimal point. The formula in cell *F2* is shown in cell *G2*.

	A	B	C	D	E
1		Sales	Rate	Amount Due	
2	John	14528.16	15%	2179.22	=ROUND(B2*C2,2)
3	Jean	45284.48	20%	9056.9	=ROUND(B3*C3,2)
4	Joe	36547.19	15%	5482.08	=ROUND(B4*C4,2)
5	Joan	27582.43	15%	4137.36	=ROUND(B5*C5,2)

Figure 39 You can also use the ROUND function to round the results of another formula or function. The formulas in column *D* are shown in column *E*.

PRODUCT & ROUND FUNCTIONS

◇	A	B	C	D	E
1	Number	Even		Odd	
2	159.487	160	=EVEN(A2)	161	=ODD(A2)
3	1647.1	1648	=EVEN(A3)	1649	=ODD(A3)
4	-14.48	-16	=EVEN(A4)	-15	=ODD(A4)

Figure 40 Use the EVEN and ODD functions to round a number up to the next even or odd number. The formulas in columns B and D are shown in columns C and E.

◇	A	B	C
1	Number	Integer	
2	159.487	159	=INT(A2)
3	1647.1	1647	=INT(A3)
4	-14.48	-15	=INT(A4)

Figure 41 Use the INT function to round a number down to the next whole number. The formulas in column B are shown in column C.

◇	A	B	C
1	Number	Absolute Value	
2	159.487	159.49	=ABS(A2)
3	1647.1	1647.1	=ABS(A3)
4	-14.48	14.48	=ABS(A4)

Figure 42 Use the ABS function to get the absolute value of a number. The formulas in column B are shown in column C.

The EVEN & ODD functions

The EVEN function (**Figure 40**) rounds a number up to the next even number. It uses the following syntax:

EVEN(number)

The number argument, which is required, is the number you want to round.

The ODD function works exactly the same way, but rounds a number up to the next odd number.

The INT function

The INT function (**Figure 41**) rounds a number down to the nearest whole number or integer. It uses the following syntax:

INT(number)

The number argument, which is required, is the number you want to convert to an integer.

The ABS function

The ABS function (**Figure 42**) returns the absolute value of a number—it leaves positive numbers alone but turns negative numbers into positive numbers. (Is that high school math coming back to you yet?) It uses the following syntax:

ABS(number)

The number argument, which is required, is the number you want to convert to an absolute value.

EVEN, ODD, INT, & ABS FUNCTIONS

The SQRT function

The SQRT function (**Figure 43**) calculates the square root of a number. It uses the following syntax:

SQRT(number)

The number argument, which is required, is the number you want to find the square root of.

✔ Tip

■ You'll get a #NUM! error message if you try to use the SQRT function to calculate the square root of a negative number (**Figure 43**). Prevent the error by using the ABS function in the formula (**Figure 44**).

The PI function

The PI function (**Figure 45**) returns the value of , accurate up to 15 digits. It uses the following syntax:

PI()

The RAND function

The RAND (**Figure 46**) function generates a random number greater than or equal to 0 and less than 1 each time the worksheet is calculated. It uses the following syntax:

RAND()

✔ Tips

■ Although neither the PI nor RAND function has arguments, if you fail to include the parentheses, you'll get a #NAME? error.

■ To generate a random number between two numbers (low and high), write a formula like this:

=RAND()*(high-low)+low

See **Figure 46** for some examples.

■ The calculated value of a formula using the RAND function will change each time the worksheet is recalculated.

	A	B	C
1	Number	Square Root	
2	36	6	=SQRT(A2)
3	22	4.690416	=SQRT(A3)
4	-10	#NUM!	=SQRT(A4)

Figure 43 Use the SQRT function to find the square root of a number.

	A	B	C
1	Number	Square Root	
2	36	6	=SQRT(ABS(A2))
3	22	4.690416	=SQRT(ABS(A3))
4	-10	3.162278	=SQRT(ABS(A4))

Figure 44 By combining the SQRT and ABS functions, you can prevent #NUM! errors when calculating the square root of a negative number. The formulas in column *B* are shown in column *C*.

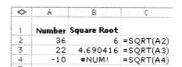

3.14159265358979

Figure 45 The PI function calculates to 14 decimal places.

	A	B	C	D
1	Low	High	Random	
2	0	1	0.16594	=RAND()
3	0	1000	545.3868	=RAND()*(B3-A3)+A3
4	36	42	36.13255	=RAND()*(B4-A4)+A4
5	3458	4835	4084.431	=RAND()*(B5-A5)+A5

Figure 46 The RAND function can be used alone or as part of a formula to generate a random number within a range. The formulas in column *C* are shown in column *D*.

SQRT, PI, & RAND FUNCTIONS

	A	B	C
1		**Radians**	
2	Entry	1	
3			
4	Convert to Degrees	57.29577951	=DEGREES(B2)
5			
6	Sine	0.841470985	=SIN(D2)
7	Arcsine	1.570796327	=ASIN(D2)
8	Cosine	0.540302306	=COS(D2)
9	Arccosine	0	=ACOS(D2)
10	Tangent	1.557407725	=TAN(D2)
11	Arctangent	0.785398163	=ATAN(D2)
12			
13		**Degrees**	
14	Entry	45	
15			
16	Convert to Radians	0.785398163	=RADIANS(D2)
17			
18	Sine	0.707106781	=SIN(RADIANS(D2))
19	Arcsine	0.903339111	=ASIN(RADIANS(D2))
20	Cosine	0.707106781	=COS(RADIANS(D2))
21	Arccosine	0.667457216	=ACOS(RADIANS(D2))
22	Tangent	1	=TAN(RADIANS(D2))
23	Arctangent	0.66577375	=ATAN(RADIANS(D2))

Figure 47 This example shows several trig functions in action. The formulas for column *B* are shown in column *C*.

The RADIANS & DEGREES functions

The RADIANS function converts degrees to radians. The DEGREES function converts radians to degrees. They use the following syntax:

RADIANS(angle)
DEGREES(angle)

The angle argument, which is required, is the angle you want converted. Use degrees in the RADIANS function and radians in the DEGREES function. Both are illustrated in **Figure 47**.

The SIN function

The SIN function (**Figure 47**) calculates the sine of an angle. It uses the following syntax:

SIN(number)

The number argument, which is required, is the angle, in radians, for which you want the sine calculated.

The COS function

The COS function (**Figure 47**) calculates the cosine of an angle. It uses the following syntax:

COS(number)

The number argument, which is required, is the angle, in radians, for which you want the cosine calculated.

The TAN function

The TAN function (**Figure 47**) calculates the tangent of an angle. It uses the following syntax:

TAN(number)

The number argument, which is required, is the angle, in radians, for which you want the tangent calculated.

✔ Tip

- To calculate the arcsine, arccosine, or arctangent of an angle, use the ASIN, ACOS, or ATAN function (**Figure 47**). Each works the same as its counterpart.

RADIANS, DEGREES, SIN, COS, & TAN FUNCTIONS

Statistical Functions

Excel's statistical functions make it easy to perform complex statistical analyses. Here's a handful of the functions I think you'll use most.

✔ Tips

- Excel's AVERAGE function does not include empty cells when calculating the average for a range of cells.

- Although the AVERAGE, MEDIAN, MODE, MIN and MAX functions can each accept up to 30 arguments separated by commas, only one argument is required.

- You can use the AutoSum button's menu on the Standard toolbar (**Figure 23**) to enter a function using the AVERAGE, COUNT, MAX, and MIN functions.

	A	B	C
1	*Product Inventory*		
2			
3	**Item Name**	**Price**	
4	Dogzilla	14.99	
5	Oceanic	15.99	
6	Delayed Impact	8.99	
7	Mask of Zero	24.99	
8	Genus II	19.99	
9	Eisenhower	19.99	
10	Men in White	22.99	
11	Loaded Weapon	13.99	
12			
13	**Average**	17.74	=AVERAGE(B4:B11)
14	**Median**	17.99	=MEDIAN(B4:B11)
15	**Mode**	19.99	=MODE(B4:B11)
16	**Minimum**	8.99	=MIN(B4:B11)
17	**Maximum**	24.99	=MAX(B4:B11)

Figure 48 This example shows a few of Excel's statistical functions at work. The formulas for column *B* are shown in column *C*.

The AVERAGE function

The AVERAGE function (**Figure 48**) calculates the average or mean of its arguments. It uses the following syntax:

AVERAGE(number1,number2,...)

The MEDIAN function

The MEDIAN function (**Figure 48**) calculates the median of its arguments. The median is the "halfway point" of the numbers—half the numbers have higher values and half have lower values. The MEDIAN function uses the following syntax:

MEDIAN(number1,number2,...)

The MODE function

The MODE function (**Figure 48**) returns the mode of its arguments. The mode is the most common value. The MODE function uses the following syntax:

MODE(number1,number2,...)

If there are no repeated values, Excel returns a #NUM! error.

◇	A	B	C
1			
2		6/30/99	
3		154.69	
4		chocolate	
5			
6		-475.699	
7		45	
8		ice cream	
9		$ 75.00	
10			
11	Blank Cells	5	=COUNT(B2:B9)
12	Values	7	=COUNTA(B2:B9)
13			

Figure 49 This example of the COUNT and COUNTA functions illustrates that while the COUNT function counts only cells containing numbers (including dates and times), the COUNTA function counts *all* non-blank cells. The formulas in column *B* are shown in column *C*.

The MIN & MAX functions

The MIN function (**Figure 48**) returns the minimum value of its arguments while the MAX function returns the maximum value of its arguments. They use the following syntax:

MIN(number1,number2,...)

MAX(number1,number2,...)

The COUNT & COUNTA functions

The COUNT function counts how many numbers are referenced by its arguments. The COUNTA function counts how many values are referenced by its arguments. Although this may sound like the same thing, it isn't—COUNT includes only numbers or formulas resulting in numbers while COUNTA includes any non-blank cell. **Figure 49** shows an example that clarifies the difference.

The COUNT and COUNTA functions use the following syntax:

COUNT(number1,number2,...)

COUNTA(number1,number2,...)

Although either function can accept up to 30 arguments separated by commas, only one is required.

MIN, MAX, COUNT, & COUNTA FUNCTIONS

The STDEV & STDEVP functions

Standard deviation is a statistical measurement of how much values vary from the average or mean for the group. The STDEV function calculates the standard deviation based on a random sample of the entire population. The STDEVP function calculates the standard deviation based on the entire population. **Figure 50** shows an example of each.

The STDEV and STDEVP functions use the following syntax:

STDEV(number1,number2,...)

STDEVP(number1,number2,...)

Although either function can accept up to 30 arguments separated by commas, only one is required.

✔ Tip

- To get accurate results from the STDEVP function, the arguments must include data for the entire population.

◇	A	B	C
1	*Product Inventory*		
2			
3	**Item Name**	**Price**	
4	Dogzilla	14.99	
5	Oceanic	15.99	
6	Delayed Impact	8.99	
7	Mask of Zero	24.99	
8	Genus II	19.99	
9	Eisenhower	19.99	
10	Men in White	22.99	
11	Loaded Weapon	13.99	
12			
13	**Average**	17.74	=AVERAGE(B4:B11)
14	**STDEV**	5.2304	=STDEV(B4:B11)
15	**STDVP**	4.8926	=STDEVP(B4:B11)

Figure 50 In this example, the STDEV function assumes that the range is a random sample from a larger population of information. The STDEVP function assumes that the same data is the entire population. That's why the results differ. The formulas in column *B* are shown in column *C*.

◇	A	B	C
1	**Depreciation Comparison**		
2			
3	Cost	$ 5,000.00	
4	Salvage Value	$ 250.00	
5	Life (in years)	5	
6			
7	Year	1	
8	Straight Line	$950.00	=SLN(B3,B4,B5)
9	Declining Balance	$2,255.00	=DB(B3,B4,B5,B7)
10	Double Declining Bala	$2,000.00	=DDB(B3,B4,B5,B7)
11	Sum of the Year's Digi	$1,583.33	=SYD(B3,B4,B5,B7)

Figure 51 A simple worksheet lets you compare different methods of depreciation using the SLN, DB, DDB, and SYD functions. The formulas in column *B* are shown in column *C*.

Financial Functions

Excel's financial functions enable you to calculate depreciation, evaluate investment opportunities, or calculate the monthly payments on a loan. On the next few pages, I tell you about a few of the functions I think you'll find useful.

The SLN function

The SLN function (**Figure 51**) calculates straight line depreciation for an asset. It uses the following syntax:

SLN(cost,salvage,life)

Cost is the acquisition cost of the asset, salvage is the salvage or scrap value, and life is the useful life expressed in years or months. All three arguments are required.

The DB function

The DB function (**Figure 51**) calculates declining balance depreciation for an asset. It uses the following syntax:

DB(cost,salvage,life,period,month)

The cost, salvage, and life arguments are the same as for the SLN function. Period, which must be expressed in the same units as life, is the period for which you want to calculate depreciation. These first four arguments are required. Month is the number of months in the first year of the asset's life. If omitted, 12 is assumed.

The DDB function

The DDB function (**Figure 51**) calculates the double-declining balance depreciation for an asset. It uses the following syntax:

DDB(cost,salvage,life,period,factor)

The cost, salvage, life, and period arguments are the same as for the DB function and are required. Factor is the rate at which the balance declines. If omitted, 2 is assumed.

The SYD function

The SYD function (**Figure 51**) calculates the sum-of-years' digits depreciation for an asset. It uses the following syntax:

SYD(cost,salvage,life,period)

The cost, salvage, life, and period arguments are the same as for the DB and DDB functions. All arguments are required.

SLN, DB, DDB, & SYD FUNCTIONS

The PMT function

The PMT function calculates the periodic payment for an annuity based on constant payments and interest rate. This function is commonly used for two purposes: to calculate the monthly payments on a loan and to calculate the monthly contribution necessary to reach a specific savings goal.

The PMT function uses the following syntax:

PMT(rate,nper,pv,fv,type)

Rate is the interest rate per period, nper is the total number of periods, and pv is the present value or current worth of the total payments. These three arguments are required. The fv argument is the future value or balance desired at the end of the payments. If omitted, 0 is assumed. Type indicates when payments are due: use 0 for payments at the end of the period and 1 for payments at the beginning of the period. If omitted, 0 is assumed.

To calculate loan payments

1. Enter the text and number values shown in **Figure 52** in a worksheet. If desired, use your own amounts.

2. Enter the following formula in cell *B5*: =*PMT(B2/12,B3,B1)*

   This formula uses only the first three arguments of the PMT function. The rate argument is divided by 12 to arrive at a monthly interest rate since the number of periods is expressed in months and payments will be made monthly (all time units must match).

3. Press [Return] or [Enter] or click the Enter button ✓ on the formula bar.

   The result of the formula appears in the cell as a negative number (**Figure 53**) because it is an outgoing cash flow. (A minus sign or parentheses indicates a negative number.)

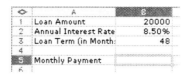

◇	A	B
1	Loan Amount	20000
2	Annual Interest Rate	8.50%
3	Loan Term (in Month:	48
4		
5	Monthly Payment	
6		

Figure 52 A basic structure for a worksheet that calculates loan payments.

◇	A	B
1	Loan Amount	20000
2	Annual Interest Rate	8.50%
3	Loan Term (in Month:	48
4		
5	Monthly Payment	($492.97)
6		

Figure 53 The loan payment worksheet after entering a formula with the PMT function.

◇	A	B
1	Loan Amount	25000
2	Annual Interest Rate	8.50%
3	Loan Term (in Month:	48
4		
5	Monthly Payment	($616.21)
6		

Figure 54 Playing "what-if." In this example, I increased the loan amount to see how much more the monthly payment would be.

✔ Tips

- If you prefer, you can use the Formula Palette to write the formula in step 2. Be sure to include the formula *B2/12* in the rate text box. Leave the fv and type text boxes blank.

- You can calculate loan payments without creating a whole worksheet—simply enter values rather than cell references as arguments for the PMT function. But using cell references makes it easy to play "what-if"— see how payments change when the loan amount, rate, and number of periods change. **Figure 54** shows an example.

	A	B	C	D
1	Loan Amount	20000		
2	Annual Interest Rate	8.50%		
3	Loan Term (in Month:	48		
4				
5	Monthly Payment	($492.97)		
6				
7	Payment Number	Beg Balance	Interest	Principal
8	1			
9	2			
10	3			
11	4			

Figure 55 To create an amortization table, start with this simple worksheet.

	A	B	C	D
1	Loan Amount	20000		
2	Annual Interest Rate	8.50%		
3	Loan Term (in Month:	48		
4				
5	Monthly Payment	($492.97)		
6				
7	Payment Number	Beg Balance	Interest	Principal
8	1	20000	141.67	$351.30
9	2	$19,648.70		
10	3			
11	4			

Figure 56 Add formulas to calculate interest, principal, and beginning balance.

	A	B	C	D
1	Loan Amount	20000		
2	Annual Interest Rate	8.50%		
3	Loan Term (in Month:	48		
4				
5	Monthly Payment	($492.97)		
6				
7	Payment Number	Beg Balance	Interest	Principal
8	1	20000	141.67	$351.30
9	2	$19,648.70	139.18	$353.79
10	3	$19,294.92	136.67	$356.30
11	4	$18,938.62	134.15	$358.82
12	5	$18,579.81	131.61	$361.36
13	6	$18,218.45	129.05	$363.92
14	7	$17,854.53	126.47	$366.50
15	8	$17,488.04	123.87	$369.10
16	9	$17,118.94	121.26	$371.71
17	10	$16,747.24	118.63	$374.34
18	11	$16,372.90	115.97	$377.00
19	12	$15,995.90	113.3	$379.67
20	13	$15,616.24	110.62	$382.35
21	14	$15,233.89	107.91	$385.06
22	15	$14,848.84	105.18	$387.79
23	16	$14,461.05	102.43	$390.54
24	17	$14,070.51	99.67	$393.30
25	18	$13,677.22	96.88	$396.09
26	19	$13,281.13	94.07	$398.90
27	20	$12,882.23	91.25	$401.72
28	21	$12,480.52	88.4	$404.57

Figure 57 Then copy the formulas down each column for all months of the loan term.

To create an amortization table

1. Create a loan payment worksheet following the steps on the previous page.
2. Enter text and number values for headings as shown in **Figure 55**. Make sure there is a row with a payment number for each month of the loan term in cell *B3*.
3. In cell *B8*, enter *=B1*.
4. In cell *C8*, enter the following formula: *=ROUND(B8*$B$2/12,2)*

   This formula calculates the interest for the period and rounds it to two decimal places.
5. In cell *D8*, enter the following formula: *=-$B$5-C8*

   This formula calculates the amount of principal paid for the current month.
6. In cell *B9*, enter the following formula: *=ROUND(B8-D8,2)*

   This formula calculates the current month's beginning balance, rounded to two decimal places.

   At this point, your worksheet should look like the one in **Figure 56**.
7. Use the fill handle to copy the formula in cell *B9* down the column for each month.
8. Use the fill handle to copy the formulas in cells *C8* and *D8* down the columns for each month.

   Your amortization table is complete. It should look like the one in **Figure 57**.

✔ Tips

- If desired, you can add column totals at the bottom of columns *C* and *D* to total interest (you may be shocked) and principal (which should match cell *B1*).
- I tell you more about using the fill handle in **Chapter 3**.

To calculate contributions to reach a savings goal

1. Enter the text and number values shown in **Figure 58** in a worksheet. If desired, use your own amounts.

2. Enter the following formula in cell *B5*: *=PMT(B2/12,B3,,B1)*

   This formula uses the first four arguments of the PMT function, although the pv argument is left blank—that's why there are two commas after *B3*. The rate argument is divided by 12 to arrive at a monthly interest rate.

3. Press Return or Enter or click the Enter button on the formula bar.

   The result of the formula is expressed as a negative number (**Figure 59**) because it is an outgoing cash flow. (A minus sign or parentheses indicates a negative number.)

✔ Tips

- If you prefer, you can use the Formula Palette to write the formula in step 2. Be sure to include the formula *B2/12* in the rate text box. Leave the pv and type text boxes blank.
- You can calculate the amount of a monthly contribution to reach a savings goal without creating a whole worksheet—simply enter values rather than cell references as arguments for the PMT function. But using cell references makes it easy to play "what-if"—see how contributions change when the desired amount, rate, and number of periods change. **Figure 60** shows an example.
- To force an outgoing cash flow to be expressed as a positive number, simply include a minus sign (-) right after the equals sign (=) at the beginning of the formula.

	A	B
1	Desired Amount	30000
2	Annual Interest Rate	4.90%
3	Months	120
4		
5	Monthly Contribution	
6		

Figure 58 A basic structure for a worksheet to calculate contributions to reach a savings goal.

	A	B
1	Desired Amount	30000
2	Annual Interest Rate	4.90%
3	Months	120
4		
5	Monthly Contribution	($194.23)
6		

Figure 59 The PMT function calculates the monthly contribution.

	A	B
1	Desired Amount	50000
2	Annual Interest Rate	4.90%
3	Months	120
4		
5	Monthly Contribution	($323.72)
6		

Figure 60 Change one value and the result of the formula changes.

◇	A	B
1	Monthly Payment	150
2	Annual Interest Rate	8.50%
3	Number of Months	12
4		
5	Future Value	($1,871.81)
6		=FV(B@/12,B3,B1)
7		

Figure 61 Use the FV function to calculate the future value of constant cash flows, like those of periodic payroll savings deductions. The formula in cell *B5* is shown in cell *B6*.

◇	A	B
1	Initial Investment	-25000
2		
3	Monthly Cash In	200
4	Annual Interest Rate	9%
5	Number of Months	360
6		
7	Present Value	($24,856.37)
8		=PV(B4/12,B5,B3)
9		

Figure 62 This example uses the PV function to determine whether an investment is a good one. (It isn't because the present value is less than the initial investment.) The formula in cell *B7* is shown in cell *B8*.

◇	A	B
1	Year 1	-500
2	Year 2	150
3	Year 3	100
4	Year 4	125
5	Year 5	135
6	Year 6	200
7		
8	Internal Rate of Return:	12%
9		=IRR(B1:B6)
10		

Figure 63 This worksheet calculates the internal rate of return of an initial $500 investment that pays out cash over the next few years. The formula in cell *B8* is shown in cell *B9*.

The FV function

The FV function (**Figure 61**) calculates the future value of an investment with constant cash flows and a constant interest rate. It uses the following syntax:

FV(**rate,nper,pmt**,pv,type)

Rate is the interest rate per period, nper is the total number of periods, and pmt is the amount of the periodic payments. These three arguments are required. The pv argument is the present value of the payments. Type indicates when payments are due: use 0 for payments at the end of the period and 1 for payments at the beginning of the period. If either optional argument is omitted, 0 is assumed.

The PV function

The PV function (**Figure 62**) calculates the total amount that a series of payments in the future is worth now. It uses the following syntax:

PV(**rate,nper,pmt**,fv,type)

The rate, nper, pmt, and type arguments are the same in the FV function. Only the first three are required. The fv argument is the amount left after the payments have been made. If omitted, 0 is assumed.

The IRR function

The IRR function (**Figure 63**) calculates the internal rate of return for a series of periodic cash flows. It uses the following syntax:

IRR(**values**,guess)

The values argument, which is required, is a range of cells containing the cash flows. The guess argument, which is optional, is for your guess of what the result could be. Although seldom necessary, guess could help Excel come up with an answer when performing complex calculations.

FV, PV, & IRR FUNCTIONS

Logical Functions

You can use Excel's logical functions to evaluate conditions and act accordingly. Here's the most useful one: IF.

The IF function

The IF function evaluates a condition and returns one of two different values depending on whether the condition is met (true) or not met (false). It uses the following syntax:

IF(logical_test,value_if_true,value_if_false)

The logical_test argument is the condition you want to meet. This argument is required. The value_if_true and value_if_false arguments are the values to return if the condition is met or not met. If omitted, the values TRUE and FALSE are returned.

The following example uses the IF function to calculate commissions based on two different commission rates.

To use the IF function

1. Create a worksheet with text and number values as shown in **Figure 64**.

2. In cell *C6*, enter the following formula:
   =IF(B6>400,$B$2*B6,$B$3*B6)

   This formula begins by evaluating the sales amount to see if it's over $400. If it is, it moves to the value_if_true argument and multiplies the higher commission rate by the sales amount. If it isn't, it moves on to the value_if_false argument and multiplies the lower commission rate by the sales amount.

3. Press [Return] or [Enter] or click the Enter button ✓ on the formula bar to complete the formula (**Figure 65**).

4. Use the fill handle to copy the formula down the column for the rest of the salespeople (**Figure 66**).

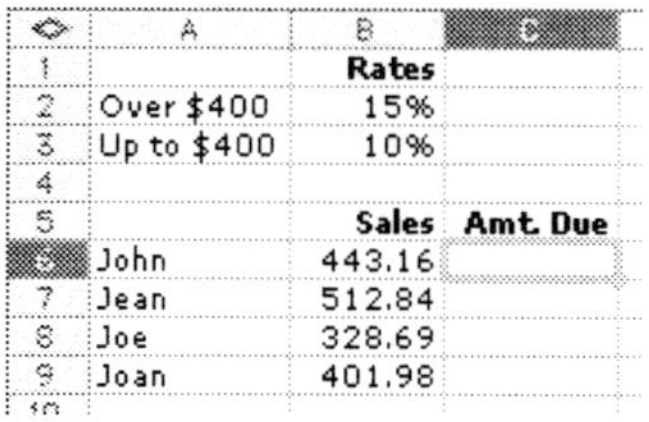

Figure 64 To try the IF function for yourself, start with a basic worksheet like this.

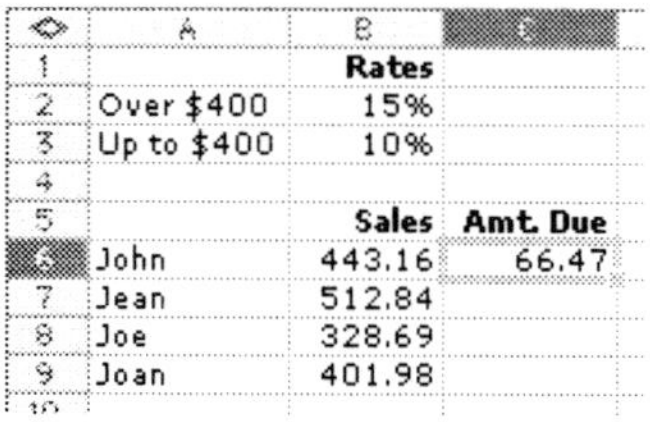

Figure 65 Enter the formula with the IF function in cell C6.

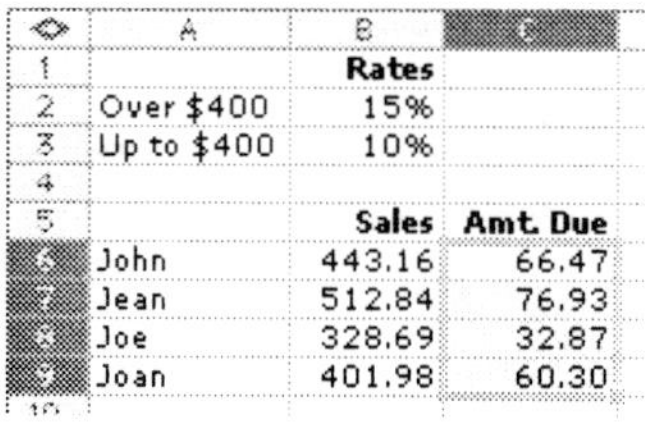

Figure 66 Then use the fill handle to copy the formula to the other cells.

IF FUNCTION

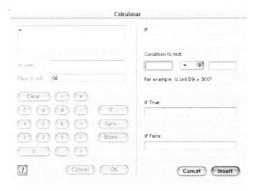

Figure 67 The Calculator expands to offer additional options for entering the IF function.

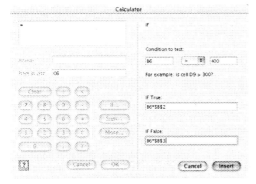

Figure 68 Use the text boxes on the right side of the Calculator dialog to enter test and result information.

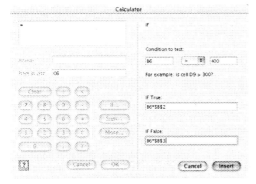

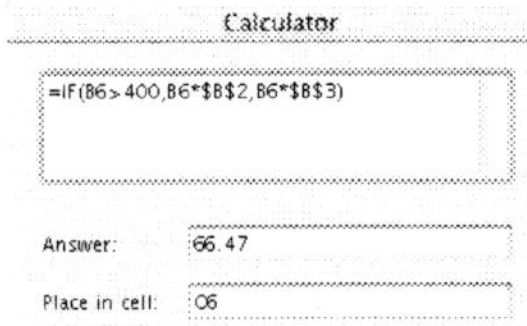

Figure 69
The completed formula appears in the big text box at the top of the Calculator.

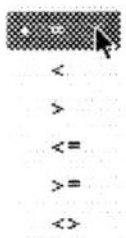

Figure 70
Be sure to use this pop-up menu to choose the correct comparison operator for the test.

To enter the IF function with the Calculator

1. Select the cell in which you want to enter the IF function formula (**Figure 64**).

2. Click the Calculator button on the formula bar to display the Calculator (**Figure 22**).

3. Click the If button. The Calculator dialog expands to offer additional options (**Figure 67**).

4. Fill in each of the text boxes to set up the test and results (**Figure 68**).

5. When you are finished entering references, click the Insert button. The Calculator collapses and the completed formula appears in its top text box (**Figure 69**).

6. Click OK. The formula results appear in the selected cell.

✔ Tips

■ In step 4, you can use the mouse to enter cell references. Just position the insertion point in the text box in which you want the cell reference to appear, then click on the cell you want to reference.

■ In step 4, be sure to use the pop-up menu in the Calculator dialog (**Figure 70**) to specify a correct comparison operator for the test.

ENTERING IF WITH THE CALCULATOR

Lookup and Reference Functions

Excel's lookup and reference functions return values based on information stored elsewhere in the workbook or in a linked worksheet.

The VLOOKUP & HLOOKUP functions

The VLOOKUP (**Figures 71** and **72**) and HLOOKUP functions return information based on data stored in a lookup table. The function attempts to match a value in one of its arguments to values in the first column (VLOOKUP) or first row (HLOOKUP) of the lookup table. If it finds a match, it returns the associated value.

The VLOOKUP and HLOOKUP functions use the following syntax:

VLOOKUP(lookup_value,table_array, col_index_num,range_lookup)

HLOOKUP(lookup_value,table_array, row_index_num,range_lookup)

Lookup_value is the value you want to match in the table. Table_array is the cell reference for the lookup table. Col_index_num or row_index_num is the number of the column or row, relative to the table, that contains the values you want returned. These three arguments are required. Range_lookup, which is not required, tells Excel what it should do if it can't match the lookup_value. There are two options for this argument: TRUE tells Excel to return the value associated with the next lowest value; FALSE tells Excel to return the #N/A error value. If omitted, TRUE is assumed.

✔ Tip

■ The first column or row of the lookup table must be sorted in ascending order for the VLOOKUP or HLOOKUP function to work properly.

	A	B	C	D
1	Item Number:	L-108		
2	Price:	13.99	=VLOOKUP(B1,A5:D12,4,FALSE)	
3				
4	**Item Number**	**Qty**	**Item Name**	**Price**
5	D-439	159	Dogzilla	14.99
6	D-845	341	Delayed Impact	8.99
7	E-473	415	Eisenhower	19.99
8	G-058	167	Genus II	19.99
9	L-108	684	Loaded Weapon IV	13.99
10	M-400	218	Men in White	22.99
11	M-482	189	Mask of Zero	24.99
12	O-571	581	Oceanic	15.99

Figure 71 This example illustrates the VLOOKUP function. When you enter an item number in cell *B1*, the formula in *B2* attempts to match it to a value in the first column of the lookup table below it *(A5:D12)*. If it finds a match, it returns the value in the fourth column of the same row as the match. The formula in cell *B2* is shown in cell *C2*.

	A	B	C	D
1	Item Number:	M-16		
2	Price:	#N/A	=VLOOKUP(B1,A5:D12,4,FALSE)	
3				
4	**Item Number**	**Qty**	**Item Name**	**Price**
5	D-439	159	Dogzilla	14.99
6	D-845	341	Delayed Impact	8.99
7	E-473	415	Eisenhower	19.99
8	G-058	167	Genus II	19.99
9	L-108	684	Loaded Weapon IV	13.99
10	M-400	218	Men in White	22.99
11	M-482	189	Mask of Zero	24.99
12	O-571	581	Oceanic	15.99

Figure 72 If the formula in *B2* doesn't find a match, it returns the *#N/A* error value, since the optional range_lookup argument is set to *FALSE*.

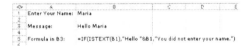

	Values			
Test	673.24	anchovy		#N/A
Blank Cell	FALSE	FALSE	TRUE	FALSE
Error other than #N/A	FALSE	FALSE	FALSE	FALSE
Any Error	FALSE	FALSE	FALSE	TRUE
Logical Value	FALSE	FALSE	FALSE	FALSE
#N/A Error	FALSE	FALSE	FALSE	TRUE
Not Text	TRUE	FALSE	TRUE	TRUE
Number	TRUE	FALSE	FALSE	FALSE
Cell Reference	TRUE	TRUE	TRUE	TRUE
Text	FALSE	TRUE	FALSE	FALSE

Figure 73 In this example, the IS functions were used (in the order shown to the right) to evaluate the contents of the cells in row 1 of the worksheet. The results of each function appear below the value.

Enter Your Name:				
Message:	You did not enter your name.			
Formula in B3:	=IF(ISTEXT(B1),"Hello "&B1,"You did not enter your name.")			

Figures 74 & 75 In this silly example, the formula in cell *B3, =IF(ISTEXT(B1),"Hello "&B1,"You did not enter your name.")*, scolds the user for not entering a name (above), then greets her by name when she does enter it (below).

Enter Your Name:	Maria			
Message:	Hello Maria			
Formula in B3:	=IF(ISTEXT(B1),"Hello "&B1,"You did not enter your name.")			

Information Functions

Excel's information functions return information about other cells.

The IS functions

Excel's IS functions (**Figure 73**) use the following syntax:

ISBLANK(value)

ISERR(value)

ISERROR(value)

ISLOGICAL(value)

ISNA(value)

ISNONTEXT(value)

ISNUMBER(value)

ISREF(value)

ISTEXT(value)

In each case, Excel tests for a different thing. The value argument is the value or cell reference to be tested.

✔ Tip

- Use an IS function in conjunction with the IF function to return a value based on the condition of a cell (**Figures 74** and **75**).

IS FUNCTIONS

Date and Time Functions

Excel's date and time functions are designed specifically to work with dates and times. I tell you about the most useful ones here.

✔ Tips

- Excel treats dates and times as serial numbers. This means that although you may enter information as a date or time—like 10/15/02 or 2:45 PM—Excel converts what you type into a number for its own internal use (see **Table 1**). A date is the number of days since January 1, 1904. A time is the portion of a day since midnight. Excel's formatting makes the number look like a date or time. I tell you about cell formatting in **Chapter 6**.

- You can change Excel's date system from the Macintosh 1904 system to the Windows 1900 system. Choose Excel > Preferences, click Calculation, and turn off the 1904 date system check box (**Figure 76**). This will change the serial numbers for dates for all worksheets in the current workbook. I tell you more about the Preferences dialog in **Chapter 15**.

- If you enter a date early in the 21st century, such as *5/15/04*, Excel assumes the year is 2004, not 1904.

The DATE function

The DATE function (**Figure 3**) returns the serial number for a date. It uses the following syntax:

=DATE(year,month,day)

The year argument is the year number, the month argument is the month number, and the day argument is the day number. All arguments are required.

Table 1

Examples of how Excel Interprets Dates and Times	
You Enter	**Excel "Sees"**
10/15/02	36082
6/30/61	21000
2:45 PM	0.61458333
10:02:35 AM	0.41846065
1/1/1904	0
12:00 AM	0

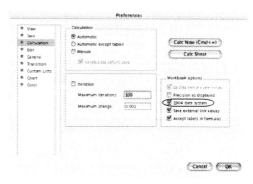

Figure 76 The Preferences dialog enables you to switch between the standard 1904 date system and the Windows 1900 date system.

◇	A	B
1	First Date	6/3/98
2	Second Date	1/14/02
3	Days Between	1321
4		=B2-B1

Figure 77 Calculating the number of days between two dates is as simple as subtracting the contents of one cell from another. The formula in cell *B3* is shown in cell *B4*.

1/14/02 15:50	=NOW()
1/14/02	=TODAY()

Figure 78 The NOW function returns the current date and time while the TODAY function returns just the current date.

◇	A	B	C
1		6/30/01	
2	Day	30	=DAY(B1)
3	Weekday	7	=WEEKDAY(B1)
4	Month	6	=MONTH(B1)
5	Year	2001	=YEAR(B1)

Figure 79 The DAY, WEEKDAY, MONTH, and YEAR functions extract portions of a date. The formulas in column *B* are shown in column *C*.

To calculate the number of days between two dates

Enter the two dates into separate cells of a worksheet, then write a formula using the subtraction operator (-) to subtract the earlier date from the later date (**Figure 77**).

or

In a worksheet cell, write a formula using the date function, like this:
=DATE(01,10,15)-DATE(01,5,8)

The NOW & TODAY functions

The NOW and TODAY functions (**Figure 78**) return the serial number for the current date and time (NOW) or current date (TODAY). Results are automatically formatted and will change each time the worksheet is recalculated or opened. They use the following syntax:

NOW()

TODAY()

Although there are no arguments, the parentheses characters must be included.

The DAY, WEEKDAY, MONTH, & YEAR functions

The DAY, WEEKDAY, MONTH, and YEAR functions (**Figure 79**) return the day of the month, the day of the week, the month number, or the year number for a serial number. They use the following syntax:

DAY(serial_number)

WEEKDAY(serial_number)

MONTH(serial_number)

YEAR(serial_number)

The serial_number argument can be a cell reference, number, or date written as text, like *10/15/01* or *15-Apr-04*.

DATE & TIME FUNCTIONS

Text Functions

Excel's text functions enable you to extract, convert, concatenate, and get information about text. I tell you about a few of the more commonly used ones here.

◇	A	B	C
1	Original Text	This IS an eXample.	
2	Lowercase	this is an example.	=LOWER(B1)
3	Uppercase	THIS IS AN EXAMPLE.	=UPPER(B1)
4	Title Case	This Is An Example.	=PROPER(B1)

Figure 80 Use the LOWER, UPPER, and PROPER functions to change the case of text. The formulas in column *B* are shown in column *C*.

The LOWER, UPPER, & PROPER functions

The LOWER, UPPER, and PROPER functions (**Figure 80**) convert text to lowercase, uppercase, and title case. They use the following syntax:

LOWER(text)

UPPER(text)

PROPER(text)

The text argument, which is required, is the text you want converted.

◇	A	B	C
1	Original Text	Mississippi	
2	First 4 characters	Miss	=LEFT(B1,4)
3	Last 4 characters	ippi	=RIGHT(B1,4)
4	4 characters starting with 3rd character	ssis	=MID(B1,3,4)

Figure 81 Use the LEFT, RIGHT, and MID functions to extract characters from text. The formulas in column *B* are shown in column *C*.

The LEFT, RIGHT, & MID functions

The LEFT, RIGHT, and MID functions (**Figure 81**) return the leftmost, rightmost, or middle characters of a text string. They use the following syntax:

LEFT(text,num_chars)

RIGHT(text,num_chars)

MID(text,start_num,num_chars)

The text argument, which is required, is the text from which characters should be extracted. The num_chars argument is the number of characters you want extracted. If omitted from the LEFT or RIGHT function, 1 is assumed. The MID function has an additional argument, start_num, which is the number of the first character from which you want to extract text. The MID function requires all arguments.

◇	A	B	C
1	Last Name	First Name	Full Name
2	Twain	Mark	Twain Mark
3			=CONCATENATE(A2," ",B2)

Figure 82 Use the CONCATENATE function to join strings of text. The formula in cell *C2* is shown in cell *C3*.

◇	A	B	C	D	E	F	G
1	Amount Due	124.95					
2	Date Due	8/16/98					
3							
4	The total amount due is $124.95. Please pay by 08/16/98.						
5							
6	="The total amount due is "&DOLLAR(B1)&". Please pay by "&TEXT(B2,"mm/dd/yy")&"."						

Figure 83 The formula in cell A4, which is: *= "The total amount due is "&DOLLAR(B1)& ". Please pay by "&TEXT(B2,"mm/dd/yy")& ". "*, writes a sentence using the contents of two cells, the concatenate operator, and two text functions.

The CONCATENATE Function

The CONCATENATE function (**Figure 82**) joins or concatenates two or more strings of text. It uses the following syntax:

CONCATENATE(text1,text2,...)

Each text argument can include single cell references, text, or numbers you want to join. The CONCATENATE function can accept up to 30 arguments, but only two are required.

✔ Tips

- Excel recognizes the ampersand character (&) as a concatenation operator in formulas. You can concatenate text by including an ampersand between cells or text strings in a formula, like this: *=B2&" "&A2*

- If you want spaces between the strings, be sure to include the space character, between double quote characters, as an argument (**Figure 82**).

- Creative use of the CONCATENATE function or operator makes it possible to give documents a personal touch. **Figure 83** shows an example.

CONCATENATING TEXT

FORMATTING CELLS

Southwest Division				
First Quarter Sales				
	Jan	Feb	Mar	Total
John	9264	9103	8950	27317
Jean	8088	5426	3543	17057
Joe	5063	7160	1351	13574
Joan	2245	7621	9462	19328
Total	24660	29310	23306	77276

Figure 1 While content should be more important than appearance, you can bet that this worksheet won't get as much attention...

Southwest Division				
First Quarter Sales				
	Jan	Feb	Mar	Total
John	$9,264	$9,103	$8,950	$27,317
Jean	8,088	5,426	3,543	17,057
Joe	5,063	7,160	1,351	13,574
Joan	2,245	7,621	9,462	19,328
Total	$24,660	$29,310	$23,306	$77,276

Figure 2 ...as this one.

Formatting Basics

To paraphrase an old Excel mentor of mine, formatting a worksheet is like putting on its makeup. The worksheet's contents may be perfectly correct, but by applying formatting, you can increase its impact to make an impression on the people who see it (**Figures 1** and **2**).

Excel offers a wide range of formatting options you can use to beautify your worksheets:

◆ **Number formatting** lets you change the appearance of numbers, dates, and times.

◆ **Alignment** lets you change the way cell contents are aligned within the cell.

◆ **Font formatting** lets you change the appearance of text and number characters.

◆ **Borders** let you add lines around cells.

◆ **Patterns** let you add color, shading, and patterns to cells.

◆ **Column and row formatting** let you change column width and row height.

You can apply formatting to cells using a variety of techniques: with Formatting Palette buttons, shortcut keys, menu commands, or the Conditional Formatting or AutoFormat features.

✔ Tip

■ Excel may automatically apply formatting to cells, depending on what you enter. For example, if you use a date function, Excel formats the results of the function as a date. You can change Excel's formatting at any time to best meet your needs.

Number Formatting

By default, Excel applies the General number format to worksheet cells. This format displays numbers just as they're entered (**Figure 3**).

Excel offers a wide variety of predefined number formatting options for different purposes:

◆ **Number** formats are used for general number display.

◆ **Currency** formats are used for monetary values.

◆ **Accounting** formats are used to line up columns of monetary values.

◆ **Date** formats are used to display dates.

◆ **Time** formats are used to display times.

◆ **Percentage** formats are used to display percentages.

◆ **Fraction** formats are used to display decimal values as fractions.

◆ **Scientific** format is used to display values in scientific notation.

◆ **Text** format is used to display cell contents as text, the way it was entered.

◆ **Special** formats include a variety of special purpose formatting options.

◆ **Custom** lets you create your own number format using formatting codes.

You can change number formatting of selected cells with options on the Formatting Palette (**Figure 5**) or in the Number tab of the Format Cells dialog (**Figures 9** through **12**).

1548.36
12458
14.2
-354.85
116.028
0.2
1.25459E+14

Figure 3
General formatting displays the numbers just as they're typed in and uses scientific notation when they're very big.

Number 1	1.5049	$	1.50
Number 2	3.504	$	3.50
	5.0089	$	5.01

Figure 4 The two columns contain identical values, but the column on the right is formatted with the Currency style. Because Excel performs calculations with the numbers underlying any formatting, the total on the right appears incorrect!

✔ Tips

■ If the integer part of a number is longer than the width of the cell or 11 digits, General number format displays it in scientific notation (**Figure 3**).

■ Number formatting changes only the appearance of a number. Although formatting may remove decimal places from displayed numbers, it does not round numbers. **Figure 4** illustrates this. Use the ROUND function, which I discuss in **Chapter 5**, to round numbers in formulas.

■ If you include characters such as dollar signs or percent symbols with a number you enter, Excel automatically assigns an appropriate built-in format to the cell.

NUMBER FORMATTING BASICS

Figure 5
The Formatting Palette offers all kinds of options for formatting worksheet cells.

Figure 6
You can choose one of the options on the Formatting Palette's Format pop-up menu to apply a predefined number format.

General	0.15	1163.2	-12.785
Number	0.15	1163.20	-12.79
Currency	$0.15	$1,163.20	-$12.79
Accounting	0.15	1,163.20	(12.79)
Date	1/1	3/9	-1/13
Time	3:36	4:48	-18:50
Percentage	15.00%	116320.00%	-1278.50%
Fraction	1/7	1163 1/5	-12 7/9
Scientific	1.50E-01	1.16E+03	-1.28E+01
Text	0.15	1163.2	-12.785
Special	00000	01163	-00013

Figure 7 Three different numbers, each with one of the Formatting Palette's number formats applied.

To apply number formatting with the Formatting Palette

To apply one of the predefined number formats in the Formatting Palette (**Figure 5**), choose it from the Format pop-up menu in the Number area (**Figure 6**):

- ◆ **General** displays the number as it was entered.

- ◆ **Number** displays the number with two decimal places.

- ◆ **Currency** displays the number as currency, with a dollar sign, commas, and two decimal places.

- ◆ **Accounting** displays the number with a comma and two decimal places. It displays negative numbers in parentheses and adjusts number position for proper column display.

- ◆ **Date** displays the number as a date in month/year format.

- ◆ **Time** displays the number as a time in hour:minute format.

- ◆ **Percentage** displays the number as a percentage with a percent symbol and two decimal places.

- ◆ **Fraction** displays the decimal part of a number as a fraction after the number.

- ◆ **Text** displays the number as entered, left-aligned in the cell, like text.

- ◆ **Special** applies whatever special formatting is currently selected in the Format Cells dialog.

- ◆ **Custom** displays the Number tab of the Format Cells dialog so you can set a custom format.

Figure 7 shows examples of these formats.

To apply number formatting with the Format Cells dialog

1. Choose Format > Cells (**Figure 8**) or press ⌃ ⌘ 1.

2. In the Format Cells dialog that appears, click the Number tab to display its options (**Figure 9**).

3. Choose a number format category from the Category scrolling list.

4. Set options in the dialog. The options vary for each category; **Figures 10, 11**, and **12** show examples. Check the Sample area to see the number in the active cell with the formatting options you selected applied.

5. Click OK to apply the formatting.

To change the number of decimal places

Click one of the Decimal buttons in the Number area of the Formatting Toolbar (**Figure 5**):

◆ **Increase Decimal** displays an additional decimal digit.

◆ **Decrease Decimal** displays one less decimal digit.

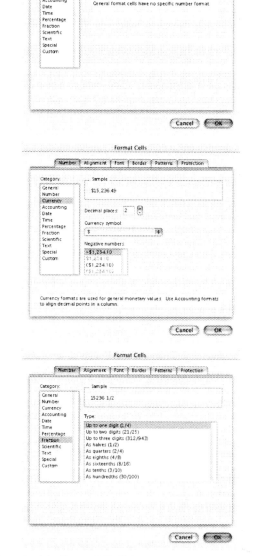

Figure 8
The Format menu offers access to most of the formatting commands discussed in this chapter.

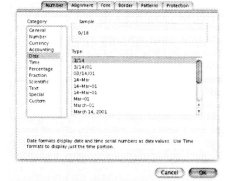

Figures 9, 10, 11, & 12 Examples of options in the Number tab of the Format Cells dialog.

APPLYING NUMBER FORMATTING

Figure 13 Examples of cells with different alignment options applied.

Jan	Feb
1,254	1,256
1,865	1,736
1,614	1,284
1,987	1,908
6,720	6,184

Figure 14 Headings sometimes look better when they're right aligned (right) rather than centered (left) over columns of numbers.

Alignment

Excel offers a wide variety of options to set the way characters are positioned within a cell (**Figure 13**):

◆ **Text Alignment** options position the text within the cell.

▲ **Horizontal** positions the text between the left and right sides of the cell or selection.

▲ **Vertical** positions the text between the top and bottom of the cell.

▲ **Indent** determines the amount of space between the cell contents and the left side of the cell.

◆ **Orientation** options control the angle at which text appears within the cell.

◆ **Text Control** options control how text appears within the cell:

▲ **Wrap text** allows word wrap between the cell's left and right sides. (This may increase the height of the cell's row.)

▲ **Shrink to fit** reduces the size of characters to fit within the cell.

▲ **Merge cells** combines multiple selected cells into one cell.

You can change alignment settings for selected cells with the Formatting Palette (**Figure 5**) or the Alignment tab of the Format Cells dialog (**Figure 15**).

✔ Tips

■ By default, within each cell, Excel left aligns text and right aligns numbers. This is called General alignment.

■ Although it's common to center headings over columns containing numbers, the worksheet may actually look better with headings right aligned. **Figure 14** shows an example.

■ Alignment is applied to cells, not cell contents. If you use the Clear Contents command or (Control)(B) shortcut to clear a cell, the formatting remains and will be applied to whatever data is next entered into it.

ALIGNMENT BASICS

To set text alignment with the Formatting Palette

1. Click the button for the Horizontal setting you want:

   ▲ **Align Left** ▤ aligns cell contents against the left side of the cell.

   ▲ **Align Center** ▤ centers cell contents between the left and right sides of the cell.

   ▲ **Align Right** ▤ aligns cell contents against the right side of the cell.

   ▲ **Justify** ▤ stretches multiple lines of text across the cell so all lines except the last fill the cell from left to right.

2. Click the button for the Vertical setting you want:

   ▲ **Top** ▤ aligns cell contents against the top of the cell.

   ▲ **Center** ▤ centers cell contents between the top and bottom of the cell.

   ▲ **Bottom** ▤ aligns cell contents against the bottom of the cell.

   ▲ **Justify** ▤ stretches multiple lines of text from the top to the bottom of the cell.

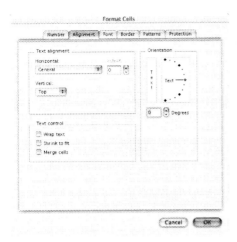

Figure 15 The Alignment tab of the Format Cells dialog.

- General
- Left (Indent)
- Center
- Right
- Fill
- Justify
- Center Across Selection

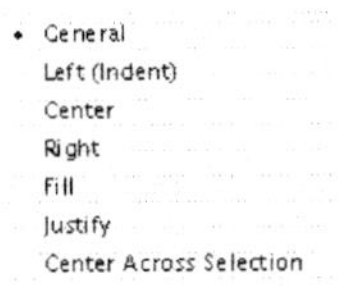

Figure 16 Options on the Horizontal pop-up menu.

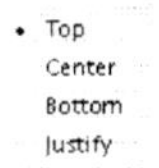

- Top
- Center
- Bottom
- Justify

Figure 17 Options on the Vertical pop-up menu.

To set alignment with the Format Cells dialog

1. Choose Format > Cells (**Figure 8**) or press ⌘ 1.

2. The Format Cells dialog appears. If necessary, click the Alignment tab to display its options (**Figure 15**).

3. Choose an option from the Horizontal (**Figure 16**) pop-up menu:
   - ▲ **General** applies default alignment.
   - ▲ **Left (Indent)** aligns cell contents against the left side of the cell. It also allows you to indent cell contents.
   - ▲ **Center** centers cell contents between the left and right sides of the cell.
   - ▲ **Right** aligns cell contents against the right side of the cell.
   - ▲ **Fill** repeats the cell contents to fill the cell.
   - ▲ **Justify** stretches multiple lines of text across the cell so all lines except the last fill the cell from left to right.
   - ▲ **Center Across Selection** centers the active cell's contents across the selected cells.

4. Choose an option from the Vertical pop-up menu (**Figure 17**):
   - ▲ **Top** aligns cell contents against the top of the cell.
   - ▲ **Center** centers cell contents between the top and bottom of the cell.
   - ▲ **Bottom** aligns cell contents against the bottom of the cell.
   - ▲ **Justify** stretches multiple lines of text from the top to the bottom of the cell.

5. Click OK.

SETTING TEXT ALIGNMENT

To indent cell contents with the Formatting Palette

In the Indent box on the Formatting Palette (**Figure 18**), enter the number of characters by which you want to indent cell contents.

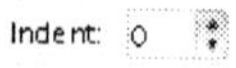

Figure 18 Enter a value in this box to set the indentation. Each unit is supposed to represent the width of one character, but I think it's wider than that. Try it and see for yourself!

To indent cell contents with the Format Cells dialog

1. Choose Format > Cells (**Figure 8**) or press ⌘ ⌘ 1 .

2. In the Format Cells dialog that appears, click the Alignment tab to display its options (**Figure 15**).

3. Choose Left (Indent) from the Horizontal pop-up menu (**Figure 16**).

4. In the Indent text box, enter the number of characters by which you want to indent cell contents (**Figure 19**).

5. Click OK.

Figure 19 To indent text, set Text alignment options like this.

To set text control options with the Formatting Palette

Turn on any valid combination of the check boxes in the bottom of the Text Alignment area of the Formatting Palette (**Figure 5**).

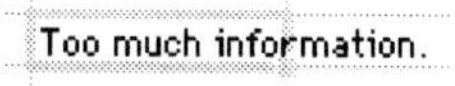

To set text control options with the Format Cells dialog

1. Choose Format > Cells (**Figure 8**) or press ⌘ ⌘ 1 .

2. In the Format Cells dialog that appears, click the Alignment tab to display its options (**Figure 15**).

3. Turn on any valid combination of the check boxes in the Text control area.

4. Click OK.

Figure 20 Select a cell with too much information.

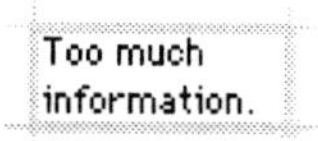

Figure 21 Here's the cell from Figure 20 with wrap text applied.

Figure 22 Here's the cell from Figure 20 with Shrink to fit applied.

✔ Tip

■ As shown in **Figures 20** through **22**, the Wrap Text and Shrink to Fit options can be used to fit cell contents within a cell.

Figure 23 Select the cells you want to merge and center.

Figure 24 The cells are merged together and the cell contents are centered in the merged cell.

✔ Tips

■ You can get similar results by choosing Center Across Selection from the Horizontal pop-up menu (**Figure 16**) in step 4 and skipping step 5. The cells, however, are not merged, so an entry into one of the adjacent cells could obscure the centered contents.

■ This technique is handy for centering worksheet titles over the cells in use.

To merge & center cells with the Formatting Palette

1. Select the cell(s) whose contents you want to center, along with the cells of the columns to the right that you want to center across (**Figure 23**).

2. Turn on the Merge cells check box in the Formatting Palette (**Figure 5**).

3. Click the Align Center button ☰ in the Horizontal area of the Formatting Palette.

The cell contents shift so they're centered between the left and right sides of the selected area (**Figure 24**).

To merge & center cells with the Format Cells dialog

1. Select the cell(s) whose contents you want to center, along with the cells of the columns to the right that you want to center across (**Figure 23**).

2. Choose Format > Cells (**Figure 8**) or press ⌃ ⌘ 1.

3. In the Format Cells dialog that appears, click the Alignment tab to display its options (**Figure 15**).

4. Choose Center from the Horizontal pop-up menu (**Figure 16**).

5. Turn on the Merge cells check box.

6. Click OK.

The cell contents shift so they're centered between the left and right sides of the selected area (**Figure 24**).

To change cell orientation with the Formatting Palette

Click the Orientation button for the type of orientation you want to apply to selected cells:

- **Rotate Text Up** ![icon] rotates the text 90° counterclockwise.

- **Angle Text Upward** ![icon] rotates the text 45° counterclockwise.

- **Horizontal Text** ![icon] (the default option) displays text horizontally within the cell.

- **Angle Text Downward** ![icon] rotates the text 45° clockwise.

- **Rotate Text Down** ![icon] rotates the text 90° clockwise.

- **Vertical Text** ![icon] keeps individual characters horizontal, but displays them in a column down the cell.

Figure 25 shows examples of each of these options.

To change cell orientation with the Format Cells dialog

1. Choose Format > Cells from the Format menu (**Figure 8**) or press ⌘⌥1.

2. In the Format Cells dialog that appears, click the Alignment tab (**Figure 15**).

3. Set options in the Orientation area (**Figure 26**) using one of these methods:

   ▲ To display text characters one above the other, click the Vertical Orientation button.

   ▲ To display text characters at an angle, drag the red diamond in the rotation area to match the angle you want.

   ▲ To display text characters at an angle, enter an angle value in the Degrees box.

4. Click OK.

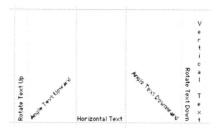

Figure 25 The Formatting Palette offers six different options for changing the orientation of a cell's contents.

Vertical Orientation button

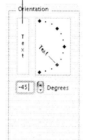

Figure 26
Set options using the Orientation area of the Format Cells dialog.

✔ Tips

- Changing the orientation of a cell's contents can change the height of the cell's row.

- You cannot set orientation options if Center Across Selection is chosen from the Horizontal pop-up menu (**Figure 16**). Choose another option before you set orientation.

- You can enter either a positive or negative value in the Degrees box (**Figure 26**).

- Rotated text appears better when printed than it does on screen.

- Rotating the text in column headings often enables you to decrease column width, thus enabling you to fit more information on screen or on paper. I tell you how to change column width later in this chapter.

	A	B	C	D	E
1		*Southwest Division*			
2		*First Quarter Sales*			
3		*Jan*	*Feb*	*Mar*	*Total*
4	John	$9,264	$9,103	$8,950	$27,317
5	Jean	8,088	5,426	3,543	17,057
6	Joe	5,063	7,160	1,351	13,574
7	Joan	2,245	7,621	9,462	19,328
8	Total	$24,660	$29,310	$23,306	$77,276

Figure 27 This example shows font, font size, and font style applied to the contents of cells.

Figure 28
You can also select individual characters within a cell...

Figure 29
...and apply formatting to them.

Font Formatting

Excel X uses 10 point Verdana as the default font or typeface for worksheets. You can apply a variety of font formatting options to cells, some of which are shown in **Figure 27**:

- ◆ **Font** is the typeface used to display characters. This includes all fonts properly installed in your system.

- ◆ **Font style** is the weight or angle of characters. Options usually include Regular, Bold, Italic, and Bold Italic.

- ◆ **Size** is the size of characters, expressed in points.

- ◆ **Underline** is character underlining. Don't confuse this with borders, which can be applied to the bottom of a cell, regardless of its contents.

- ◆ **Color** is character color.

- ◆ **Effects** are special effects applied to characters.

You can apply font formatting with the Formatting Palette, shortcut keys, and the Format Cells dialog.

✔ Tips

- ■ You can change the formatting of individual characters within a cell. Just double-click the cell to make it active, select the characters you want to change (**Figure 28**), and use the appropriate font formatting technique to change the characters (**Figure 29**).

- ■ Previous versions of Excel used 9 point Geneva as the default font. When you open a workbook created with a previous version of Excel, the default font for that file remains 9 point Geneva.

To apply font formatting with the Formatting Palette or shortcut keys

1. Select the cell(s) or character(s) you want to apply font formatting to.

2. To change the font, choose a font from the Font pop-up menu (**Figure 30**).

    or

    Click on the Font box to select its contents (**Figure 31**), type in the name of the font you want to apply (**Figure 32**), and press Return.

3. To change the character size, choose a size from the Font Size pop-up menu (**Figure 33**).

    or

    Click on the Font Size box to select its contents, type in a size, and press Return.

4. To change the character style, click any combination of Font Style buttons or press corresponding shortcut keys:

    ▲ **Bold** B (⌃ ⌘ B) makes characters appear bold.

    ▲ **Italic** *I* (⌃ ⌘ I) makes characters appear slanted.

    ▲ **Underline** U (⌃ ⌘ U) applies a single underline to characters.

    ▲ **Strikethrough** ABC puts a horizontal line through characters.

5. To change the character color, choose a color from the Font Color pop-up menu (**Figure 34**).

✔ Tips

■ Font size must be between 1 and 409 points in half-point increments. (In case you're wondering, 72 points equals 1 inch.)

■ The Automatic color option (**Figure 34**) enables Excel to automatically apply color based on other formatting options.

Figure 30
The Font menu on the Formatting Palette lists all the fonts properly installed in your system. Fonts above the line at the top of the menu are those that have been recently applied.

Figure 31 Click the font name to select it...

Figure 32 ...then type in the name of the font that you want to apply.

Figure 33
You can choose a size from the Font Size pop-up menu.

Figure 34
The Font Color pop-up menu on the Formatting Palette enables you to apply color to characters.

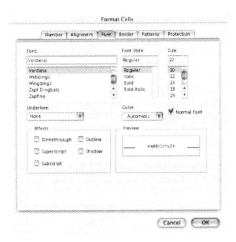

Figure 35 The Font tab of the Format Cells dialog.

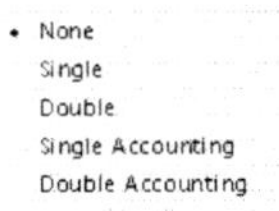

Figure 36
Excel offers several underlining options.

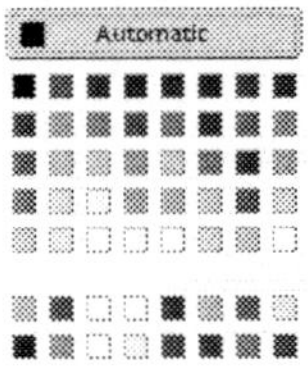

Figure 37
The Color pop-up menu in the Format Cells dialog.

To apply font formatting with the Format Cells dialog

1. Select the cell(s) or character(s) whose font you want to change.

2. Choose Format > Cells (**Figure 8**) or press ⌃⌘1.

3. In the Format Cells dialog that appears, click the Font tab to display its options (**Figure 35**).

4. Set options as desired:

   ▲ Select a font from the Font scrolling list or type a font name into the text box above the list.

   ▲ Select a style from the Font Style scrolling list or type a style name into the text box above the list.

   ▲ Select a size from the Size scrolling list or type a size into the text box above the list.

   ▲ Choose an underline option from the Underline pop-up menu (**Figure 36**).

   ▲ Choose a font color from the Color pop-up menu (**Figure 37**).

   ▲ Turn on check boxes in the Effects area to apply font effects.

5. When the sample text in the Preview area looks just the way you want, click OK.

✔ Tips

■ To return a selection to the default font, turn on the Normal font check box in the Format Cells dialog (**Figure 35**).

■ The accounting underline options in the Underline pop-up menu (**Figure 36**) stretch almost the entire width of the cell.

■ The Automatic color option (**Figure 37**) enables Excel to automatically apply color based on other formatting options.

APPLYING FONT FORMATTING

Borders

Excel offers many border styles that you can apply to separate cells or a selection of cells (**Figure 38**).

Use the Formatting Palette or the Format Cells dialog to add and format borders.

◇	A	B	C	D	E
1		Southwest Division			
2		First Quarter Sales			
3		Jan	Feb	Mar	Total
4	John	$9,264	$9,103	$8,950	$27,317
5	Jean	8,088	5,426	3,543	17,057
6	Joe	5,063	7,160	1,351	13,574
7	Joan	2,245	7,621	9,462	19,328
8	Total	$24,660	$29,310	$23,306	$77,276

Figure 38 Use borders to place lines under headings and above and below column totals.

To add borders with the Formatting Palette

1. Select the cell(s) to which you want to add borders.

2. Choose the type of border you want to apply from the Border Type pop-up menu in the Borders and Shading area of the Formatting Palette (**Figure 39**).

3. To change the style of the border, choose a style from the Line Style pop-up menu (**Figure 40**).

4. To change the color of the border, choose a color from the Border Color pop-up menu (**Figure 41**).

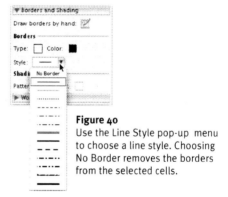

Figure 39
The Border Type pop-up menu on the Formatting Palette.

✔ Tips

■ The borders above the dividing line in the Border Type pop-up menu (**Figure 39**) apply borders to the selection as a whole, and those below the dividing line apply borders to each cell in the selection individually.

■ To remove borders from a selection, choose No Border from the Line Style pop-up menu (**Figure 40**). If the border does not disappear, it may be applied to a cell adjoining the one you selected.

■ The accounting underline options on the Underline pop-up menu in the Format Cells dialog (**Figure 36**) are not the same as borders. They do not stretch the entire width of the cell and they only appear when the cell is not blank.

Figure 40
Use the Line Style pop-up menu to choose a line style. Choosing No Border removes the borders from the selected cells.

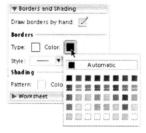

Figure 41
The Border Color pop-up menu on the Formatting Palette.

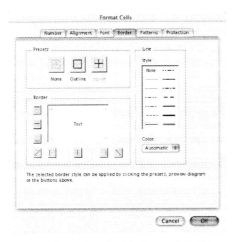

Figure 42 The Border tab of the Format Cells dialog.

To add borders with the Format Cells dialog

1. Select the cell(s) to which you want to add borders.

2. Choose Format > Cells (**Figure 8**) or press ⌘ 1.

3. In the Format Cells dialog that appears, click the Border tab to display its options (**Figure 42**).

4. Select a line style in the Line area.

5. If desired, select a color from the Color pop-up menu, which looks just like the one in **Figure 37**.

6. Set individual borders for the selected cells using one of these methods:

   ▲ Click one of the buttons in the Presets area to apply a predefined border. (None removes all borders from the selection.)

   ▲ Click a button in the Border area to add a border to the corresponding area.

   ▲ Click between the lines in the illustration in the Border area to place corresponding borders.

7. Repeat steps 4, 5, and 6 until all the desired borders for the selection are set.

8. Click OK.

✔ Tip

■ To get the borders in your worksheet to look just the way you want, be prepared to make several selections and trips to either the Type pop-up menu in the Borders and Shading area of the Formatting Palette or the Border tab of the Format Cells dialog.

ADDING BORDERS

To draw borders by hand

1. Click the Draw Border button in the Borders and Shading area of the Formatting Palette (**Figure 5**). The mouse pointer turns into a pencil tool and the Border Drawing toolbar appears (**Figure 43**).

2. Position the mouse pointer where you want the border to begin.

3. Press the mouse button and drag to draw the border. As you drag, the border appears for each cell (**Figure 44**). When the border appears as desired, release the mouse button.

4. Repeat steps 2 and 3 for each border you want to draw.

5. When you are finished, press Esc to return the mouse pointer to normal. You can hide the Border Drawing toolbar by clicking its close button.

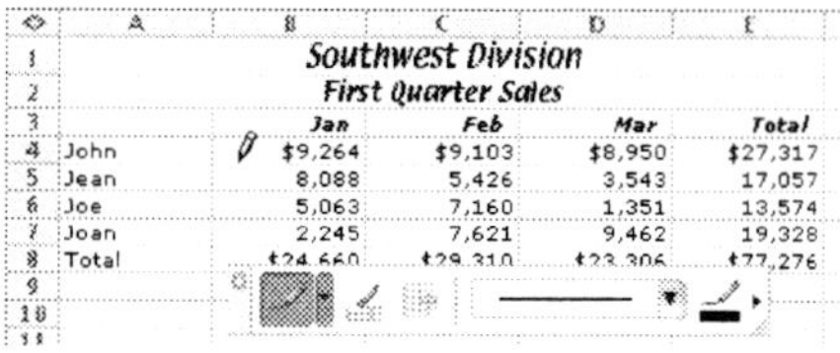

✔ Tips

- If you make a mistake while drawing a border, use the Undo command or button to remove it so you can try again.

- If you drag the pencil tool diagonally across a range of cells, a border appears around the cells.

- To remove a border, hold down Shift while dragging over the border. The pencil tool turns into an eraser tool while Shift is held down (**Figure 45**).

- You can use other options on the Border Drawing toolbar to change the border style, color, and other settings.

Figure 43 Clicking the Draw Border button turns the mouse pointer into a pencil tool and displays the Border Drawing toolbar.

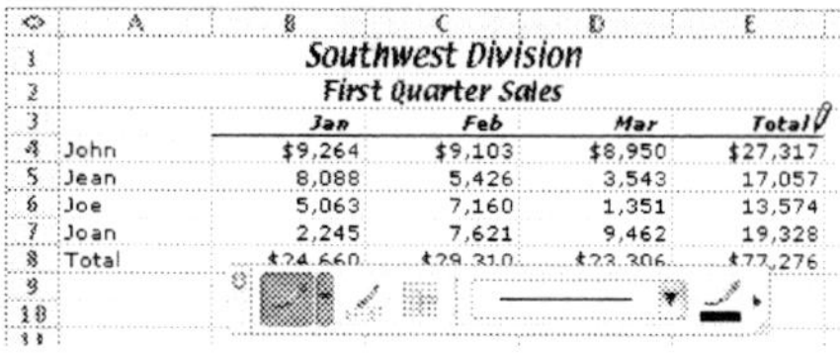

Figure 44 Drag the pencil tool to draw a border.

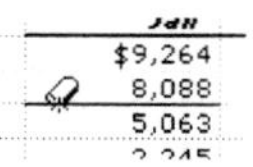

Figure 45 Hold down Shift while dragging the pencil tool to erase a border.

DRAWING BORDERS BY HAND

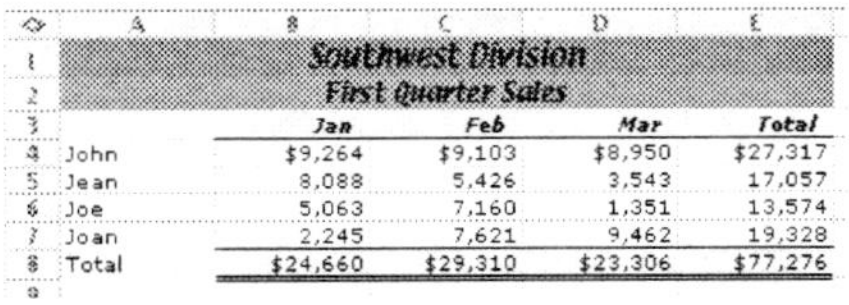

Figure 46 Use Excel's cell shading feature to add fill colors and patterns to cells.

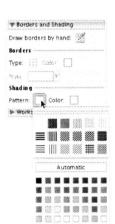

Figure 47
The Fill Color pop-up menu on the Formatting Palette.

Figure 48
The Fill Pattern pop-up menu on the Formatting Palette.

Cell Shading

Excel's shading feature lets you add color to cells (**Figure 46**), either with or without patterns. You can do this with options on the Formatting Palette or in the Format Cells dialog.

✔ Tips

■ By combining two colors with a pattern, you can create various colors and levels of shading.

■ Be careful when adding shading to cells! If the color is too dark, cell contents may not be legible.

■ To improve the legibility of cell contents in shaded cells, try making the characters bold.

■ For a different look, use a dark color for the cell and make its characters white.

To apply shading with the Formatting Palette

1. Select the cell(s) to which you want to apply shading.

2. Choose a color from the Fill Color pop-up menu (**Figure 47**).

3. To apply a pattern, choose a pattern from the top half of the Fill Pattern pop-up menu (**Figure 48**). Then, to set the pattern color, choose a color from the bottom half of the Fill Pattern pop-up menu.

✔ Tip

■ To remove colors from a selection, choose No Fill from the Fill Color pop-up menu (**Figure 47**).

APPLYING CELL SHADING

To apply shading with the Format Cells dialog

1. Select the cell(s) to which you want to apply shading.

2. Choose Format > Cells (**Figure 8**) or press Ⓒ ⌘ 1 .

3. In the Format Cells dialog that appears, click the Patterns tab to display its options (**Figure 49**).

4. Select a color from the Color palette in the Cell shading area of the dialog. This is the background color.

5. If desired, choose a foreground color and pattern from the Pattern pop-up menu (**Figure 50**).

6. When the Sample area of the dialog looks just the way you want your selection to look, click OK.

Styles

Once you get the hang of using Excel's formatting options, check out its Style feature. This advanced feature, which is beyond the scope of this book, lets you combine formats into named styles that you can apply to any cell in the workbook. This can save time and ensure consistency.

✔ Tips

■ Excel's style feature works a lot like Word's style feature.

■ To access the style feature choose Format > Style (**Figure 8**).

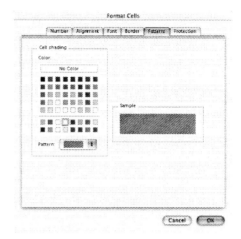

Figure 49 The Patterns tab of the Format Cells dialog.

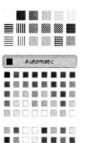

Figure 50
Use the Pattern pop-up menu to choose a pattern and a foreground color.

APPLYING CELL SHADING, STYLES

Figure 51
Conditional Formatting instructs Excel to format cells based on their contents.

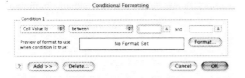

Figure 52 The Conditional Formatting dialog.

Figure 53 This condition set applies formatting to selected cells containing values greater than 5000.

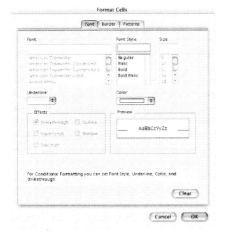

Figure 54 Formatting options for Conditional Formatting are slightly limited.

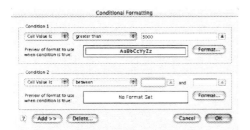

Figure 55 The Conditional Formatting dialog expands so you can add more conditions.

Conditional Formatting

Excel's Conditional Formatting feature enables you to set up special formatting that is automatically applied by Excel only when cell contents meet certain criteria.

For example, say you have a worksheet containing the total sales for each member of your company's sales staff. You want to display all sales over $5,000 in bold, blue type with a light blue background and black border. You can use Conditional Formatting to automatically apply the desired formatting in cells containing values over 5,000 (**Figure 51**).

To apply Conditional Formatting

1. Select the cells to which you want to apply Conditional Formatting.

2. Choose Format > Conditional Formatting (**Figure 8**) to display the Conditional Formatting dialog (**Figure 52**).

3. Use the pop-up menus and text boxes in the Condition 1 part of the dialog to set up the criteria for applying formatting. **Figure 53** shows an example.

4. Click the Format button to display a special version of the Format Cells dialog that offers tabs for Font, Border, and Patterns only (**Figure 54**). Use the dialog to set formatting options for cells meeting the condition.

5. To add another condition for applying the formatting, click the Add button. The dialog expands to offer an additional condition set (**Figure 55**). Repeat steps 3 and 4.

6. Repeat step 5 for each condition you want to add.

7. When you're finished specifying conditions and formatting, click OK.

APPLYING CONDITIONAL FORMATTING

121

The Format Painter

The Format Painter lets you copy cell formatting and apply it to other cells. This can help you format worksheets quickly and consistently.

To use the Format Painter

1. Select a cell with the formatting you want to copy.

2. Click the Format Painter button 🖌 on the Standard toolbar. The mouse pointer turns into a little plus sign with a paintbrush beside it and a marquee appears around the original selection (**Figure 56**).

3. Use the Format Painter pointer to select the cells you want to apply the formatting to (**Figure 57**). When you release the mouse button, the formatting is applied (**Figure 58**).

✔ Tips

- You can double-click the Format Painter button in step 1 to keep applying a copied format throughout the worksheet. Press (Esc) or click the Format Painter button again to stop applying the format and return the mouse pointer to normal.

- You can also use the Copy and Paste Special commands under the Edit menu (**Figure 59**) to copy the formatting of selected cells and paste it into other cells.

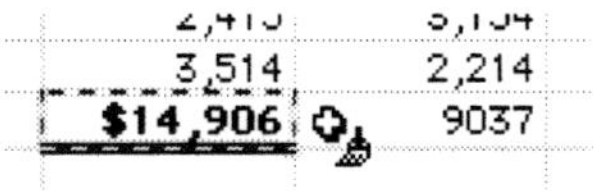

Figure 56 When you click the Format Painter button, a marquee appears around the original selection and the mouse pointer turns into the Format Painter pointer.

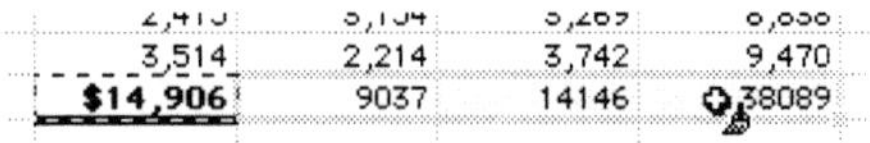

Figure 57 Drag to select the cells to which you want to copy formats.

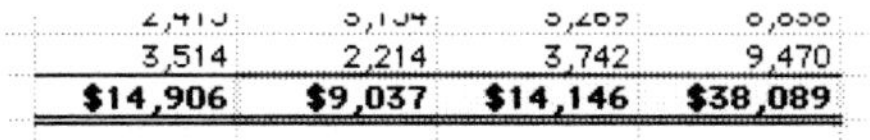

Figure 58 When you release the mouse button, the formatting is applied.

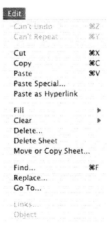

Figure 59 You can also use the Copy and Paste Special commands under the Edit menu to copy and paste formatting.

Total for all salespeople	

Figure 60 When text doesn't fit in a cell, it appears to overlap into the cell beside it...

Total for all s	14982

Figure 61 ...unless the cell beside it isn't blank.

######	

Figure 62 When a number doesn't fit in a cell, the cell fills with # signs.

$ 14,982.00	

Figure 63 You can make the number fit by making the cell wider...

$ 14,982	

Figure 64 ...or by changing the number's formatting to remove decimal places.

Column Width & Row Height

If the data you enter into a cell doesn't fit, you can make the column wider to accommodate all the characters. You can also make columns narrower to use worksheet space more efficiently. And although Excel automatically adjusts row height when you increase the font size of cells within the row, you can increase or decrease row height as desired.

Excel offers two ways to change column width and row height: with the mouse and with Format menu commands.

✔ Tips

- If text typed into a cell does not fit, it appears to overlap into the cell to its right (**Figure 60**). Even though the text may appear to be in more than one cell, all of the text is really in the cell in which you typed it. (You can see for yourself by clicking in the cell to the right and looking at the formula bar—it will not contain any part of the text!) If the cell to the right of the text is not blank, the text appears truncated (**Figure 61**). Don't let appearances fool you. The text is still all there. The missing part is just hidden by the contents of the cell beside it.

- If a number doesn't fit in a cell, the cell fills up with pound signs (#) (**Figure 62**). To display the number, make the column wider (**Figure 63**) or change the number formatting to omit symbols and decimal places (**Figure 64**). I tell you how to make columns wider on the next page and how to change number formatting earlier in this chapter.

- Setting column width or row height to 0 (zero) hides the column or row.

To change column width or row height with the mouse

1. Position the mouse pointer on the line right after the column letter(s) (**Figure 65**) or right below the row number (**Figure 66**) of the column or row you want to change. The mouse pointer turns into a line with two arrows coming out of it.

2. Press the mouse button and drag:
   ▲ To make a column narrower, drag to the left.
   ▲ To make a column wider, drag to the right.
   ▲ To make a row taller, drag down.
   ▲ To make a row shorter, drag up.

   As you drag, a dotted line moves along with the mouse pointer and the width or height of the column or row appears in a yellow box (**Figure 67**).

3. Release the mouse button. The column width or row height changes.

✔ Tips

■ When you change column width or row height, you change the width or height for the entire column or row, not just selected cells.

■ To change column width or row height for more than one column or row at a time, select multiple columns or rows and drag the border of one of them.

■ If you drag a column or row border all the way to the left or all the way up, you set the column width or row height to 0, hiding the column or row from view. I tell you more about hiding columns and rows next.

■ To quickly set the width or height of a column or row to fit its contents, double-click the column or row heading border. I tell you more about this AutoFit feature later in this chapter.

Figure 65 Position the mouse pointer on the right border of a column heading...

Figure 66 ...or on the bottom border of a row heading.

Figure 67 Drag to reposition the border.

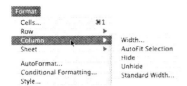

Figure 68 The Format menu's Column submenu.

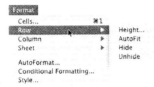

Figure 69 The Format menu's Row submenu.

Figures 70 & 71 The Column Width (left) and Row Height (right) dialogs.

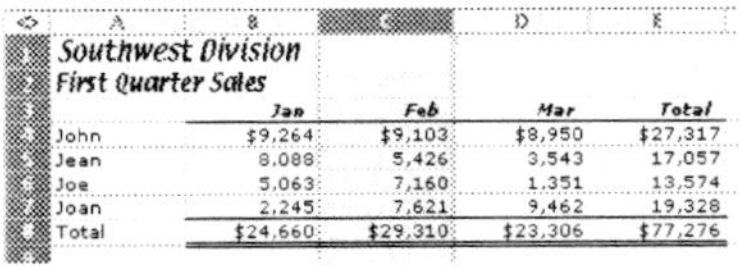

Figure 72 Select the column that you want to hide.

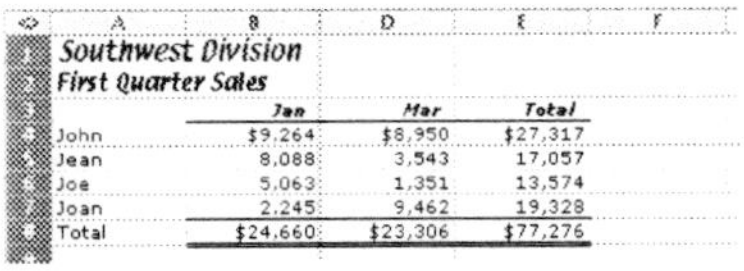

Figure 73 When you choose the Hide command, the column disappears.

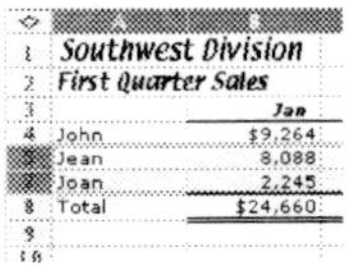

Figure 74
Select the rows above and below the hidden row.

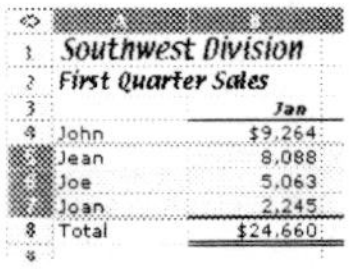

Figure 75
When you choose the Unhide command, the hidden row reappears.

To change column width or row height with menu commands

1. Select the column(s) or row(s) whose width or height you want to change.

2. Choose Format > Column > Width (**Figure 68**) or choose Format > Row > Height (**Figure 69**).

3. In the Column Width dialog (**Figure 70**) or Row Height dialog (**Figure 71**), enter a new value. Column width is expressed in standard font characters while row height is expressed in points.

4. Click OK to change the selected columns' width or rows' height.

To hide columns or rows

1. Select the column(s) (**Figure 72**) or row(s) you want to hide.

2. Choose Format > Column > Hide (**Figure 69**) or Format > Row > Hide (**Figure 70**). The selected column(s) or row(s) disappear (**Figure 73**).

✔ Tips

- Hiding a column or row is not the same as deleting it. Data in a hidden column or row still exists in the worksheet and can be referenced by formulas.

- Column numbers or row letters on either side of a hidden column or row appear in blue. This draws your attention to the fact that not all columns or rows are shown.

To unhide columns or rows

1. Select the columns or rows on both sides of the hidden column(s) or row(s) (**Figure 74**).

2. Choose Format > Column > Unhide (**Figure 68**) or Format > Row > Unhide (**Figure 69**).

   The hidden columns(s) or rows(s) reappear (**Figure 75**).

CHANGING COLUMN WIDTH & ROW HEIGHT

AutoFit

Excel's AutoFit feature automatically adjusts a column's width or a row's height so it's only as wide or as high as it needs to be to display the information within it. This is a great way to adjust columns and rows to use worksheet space more efficiently.

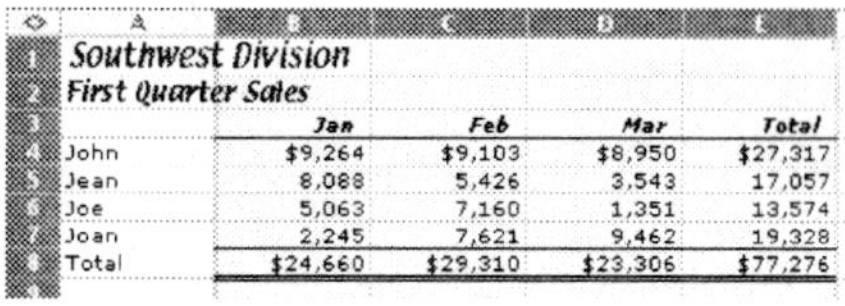

Southwest Division				
First Quarter Sales				
	Jan	Feb	Mar	Total
John	$9,264	$9,103	$8,950	$27,317
Jean	8,088	5,426	3,543	17,057
Joe	5,063	7,160	1,351	13,574
Joan	2,245	7,621	9,462	19,328
Total	$24,660	$29,310	$23,306	$77,276

Figure 76 Select the columns for which you want to change the width.

To use AutoFit

1. Select the column(s) or row(s) for which you want to change the width or height (**Figure 76**).
2. Choose Format > Column > AutoFit Selection (**Figure 68**) or Format > Column > AutoFit (**Figure 69**).

   or

   Double-click on the border to the right of the column heading (**Figure 65**) or below the row heading (**Figure 66**).

   The column width or row height changes to fit cell contents (**Figure 77**).

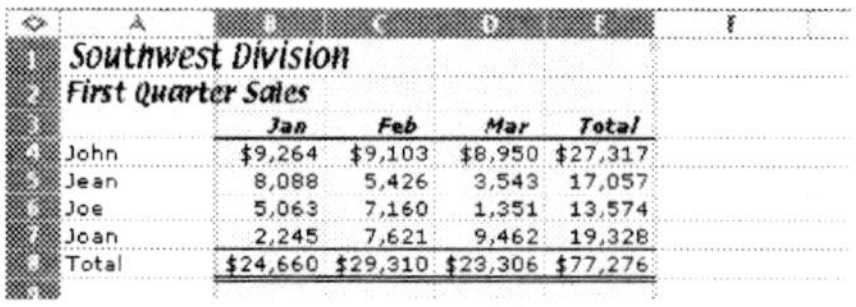

Southwest Division				
First Quarter Sales				
	Jan	Feb	Mar	Total
John	$9,264	$9,103	$8,950	$27,317
Jean	8,088	5,426	3,543	17,057
Joe	5,063	7,160	1,351	13,574
Joan	2,245	7,621	9,462	19,328
Total	$24,660	$29,310	$23,306	$77,276

Figure 77 When you choose the AutoFit Selection command, the width of the columns changes so they're only as wide as they need to be to fit cell contents.

✔ Tips

- To adjust a column's width without taking every cell into consideration—for example, to exclude a cell containing a lot of text—select only the cells for which you want to adjust the column (**Figure 78**). When you choose Format > Column > AutoFit Selection (**Figure 68**), only the cells you selected are measured for the AutoFit adjustment (**Figure 79**).
- Use the Wrap text and AutoFit features to keep your columns narrow. I tell you about Wrap text earlier in this chapter.

Southwest Division	
First Quarter Sales	
	Jan
John	$9,264
Jean	8,088
Joe	5,063
Joan	2,245
Total	$24,660

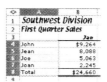

Figure 78 Select the cells that you want Excel to measure for the AutoFit feature.

Southwest Division		
First Quarter Sales		
	Jan	
John	$9,264	$9
Jean	8,088	5
Joe	5,063	7
Joan	2,245	7
Total	$24,660	$29

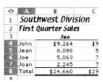

Figure 79 When you choose the AutoFit Selection command, Excel resizes the entire column based on the width of the contents in the selected cells.

Southwest Division				
First Quarter Sales				
	Jan	Feb	Mar	Total
John	9264	9103	8950	27317
Jean	8088	5426	3543	17057
Joe	5063	7160	1351	13574
Joan	2245	7621	9462	19328
Total	24660	29310	23306	77276

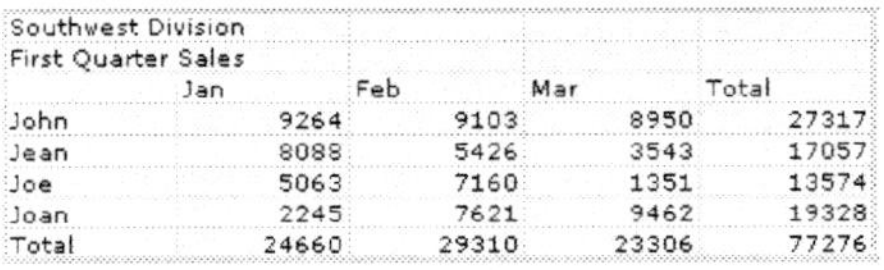

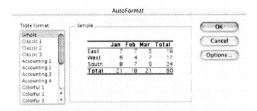

Figure 80 Select the part of the worksheet you want to format.

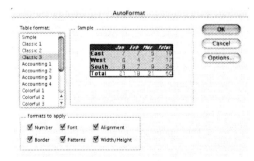

Figure 81 The AutoFormat dialog.

Southwest Division				
First Quarter Sales				
	Jan	Feb	Mar	Total
John	9264	9103	8950	27317
Jean	8088	5426	3543	17057
Joe	5063	7160	1351	13574
Joan	2245	7621	9462	19328
Total	24660	29310	23306	77276

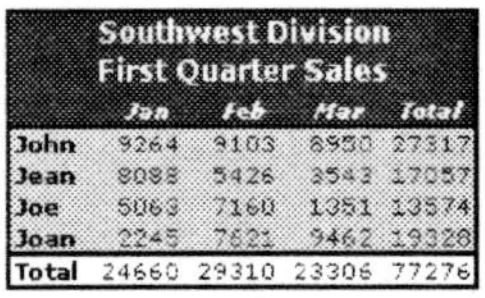

Figure 82 The worksheet in Figure 80 with the Classic 3 AutoFormat applied.

Figure 83 Clicking the Options button expands the AutoFormat dialog so you can select which parts of the format should be applied.

AutoFormat

Excel's AutoFormat feature offers a quick way to dress up tabular data in worksheets by applying predefined formats. If you're like me and like to leave design for designers, you'll welcome this feature.

To use AutoFormat

1. Select the portion of the worksheet you want to format (**Figure 80**).
2. Choose Format > AutoFormat (**Figure 8**) to display the AutoFormat dialog (**Figure 81**).
3. Choose a format from the Table format scrolling list. A preview of the format appears in the Sample area so you can decide whether you like it before you apply it.
4. When you're satisfied with your selection, click OK or press Return or Enter. Your worksheet is formatted instantly (**Figure 82**).

✔ Tip

- To pick and choose among the different kinds of formatting automatically applied, click the Options button in the AutoFormat dialog. The box expands to display check boxes for each type of formatting (**Figure 83**). To exclude a type of change from the AutoFormat process, turn off its check box.

Removing Formatting from Cells

You can use the Formats command on the Clear submenu under the Edit menu (**Figure 85**) to remove formatting from cells, leaving cell contents—such as values and formulas—intact.

✔ Tips

■ When you remove formats from a cell, you return font formatting to the normal font and number formatting to the General format. You also remove borders or shading added to the cell.

■ Removing formatting does not affect column width or row height.

To remove formatting from cells

1. Select the cell(s) you want to remove formatting from (**Figure 84**).

2. Choose Edit > Clear > Formats (**Figure 85**). The formatting is removed but cell contents remain (**Figure 86**).

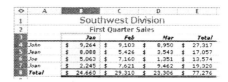

Figure 84 Select the cells you want to remove formatting from.

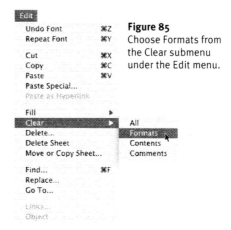

Figure 85 Choose Formats from the Clear submenu under the Edit menu.

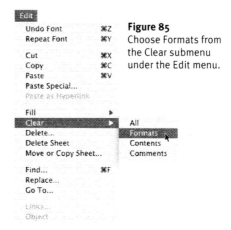

Figure 86 The formatting is removed but the cell contents remain.

REMOVING FORMATTING FROM CELLS

WORKING WITH GRAPHIC OBJECTS

Graphic Objects

Microsoft Excel makes it easy to add a variety of graphic objects to your worksheets and charts:

◆ **Drawn objects**, such as lines, arrows, and shapes, can draw attention to important information on a document.

◆ **AutoShapes** enable you to draw a variety of interesting and useful shapes quickly and easily.

◆ **Text boxes** offer a flexible way to add annotations to a document.

◆ **Clip art** can make a worksheet or chart more visually appealing with professionally created graphic images.

◆ **Pictures from files** on disk make it possible to add your own images, such as a company logo or product illustration.

◆ **Organization charts** can provide additional information about your company's organization.

◆ **WordArt** enables you to add highly stylized text to your documents.

◆ **Pictures from a scanner or camera** enable you to import images directly from your scanner or a digital camera into Excel documents.

This chapter explains how you can include all of these types of graphic objects in your Excel documents and format them so they look the way you want them to.

The Drawing Toolbar

Excel's Drawing toolbar (**Figure 1**) includes a wide range of tools you can use to add lines, arrows, shapes, and text boxes to your worksheets and charts. Through creative use of these tools, you can add impact and improve appearance for all of your Excel documents.

To display the Drawing toolbar

Click the Drawing button  on the Standard toolbar. The button turns gray (**Figure 2**) when the Drawing toolbar is displayed.

or

Choose View > Toolbars > Drawing (**Figure 3**).

To hide the Drawing toolbar

Click the Drawing button  on the Standard toolbar.

or

Choose View > Toolbars > Drawing (**Figure 3**).

Figure 1
The Drawing toolbar.

Figure 2 When you click the Drawing button, it turns gray.

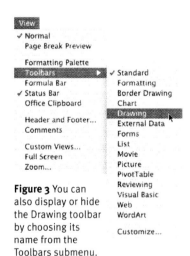

Figure 3 You can also display or hide the Drawing toolbar by choosing its name from the Toolbars submenu.

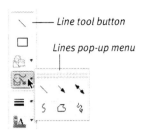

Figure 4 Although the Drawing toolbar includes a Line tool button, the Lines pop-up menu offers additional tools for drawing lines.

Drawing Objects

Many of the tools on the Drawing toolbar let you draw *objects*—lines or shapes—in worksheet or chart windows. Excel lets you draw lines, rectangles, squares, ovals, circles, shapes (including complex AutoShapes), and text boxes. Objects you draw can be selected, resized, moved, or copied at any time.

To draw a line or arrow

1. Click the appropriate button on the Drawing toolbar's Lines pop-up menu (**Figure 4**) to select it:

   ▲ **Line** \ draws straight lines. (The Line tool also has a button on the Drawing toolbar.)

   ▲ **Arrow** ＼ draws straight lines with an arrowhead on one end.

   ▲ **Double Arrow** ＼ draws straight lines with arrowheads on both ends.

   ▲ **Curve** 〜 draws smoothly curved lines.

   ▲ **Freeform** ⌒ draws lines combining straight and freeform segments.

   ▲ **Scribble** ✎ draws lines wherever you drag the mouse.

   When you click the tool's button the mouse pointer turns into a crosshairs pointer (**Figure 5**) or, in the case of the Scribble tool, a pencil (**Figure 6**).

2. Position the mouse pointer where you want to begin drawing.

3. To draw a line, arrow, or double arrow, press the mouse button down and drag. As you move the mouse, a line is drawn (**Figure 7**). Release the mouse button to stop drawing (**Figures 8** and **9**).

   or

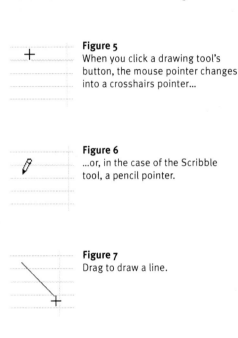

Figure 5
When you click a drawing tool's button, the mouse pointer changes into a crosshairs pointer...

Figure 6
...or, in the case of the Scribble tool, a pencil pointer.

Figure 7
Drag to draw a line.

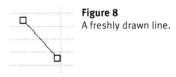

Figure 8
A freshly drawn line.

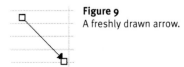

Figure 9
A freshly drawn arrow.

Continued on next page...

DRAWING LINES & ARROWS

Continued from previous page.

To draw a curve, move the mouse to stretch a line (**Figure 7**) and click where you want the curve to appear (**Figure 10**). Repeat this process to draw as many curves as desired. Then either click the starting point or double-click the ending point to stop drawing (**Figure 11**).

or

To draw a freeform shape, combine clicking and dragging to draw straight lines and freeform lines: click from point to point to draw straight lines and drag (with a pencil tool that appears automatically) to draw freeform lines (**Figure 12**). Either click the starting point or double-click the ending point to stop drawing (**Figure 13**).

or

To draw a scribble, press the mouse button down and drag the pencil pointer to get the desired line shape (**Figure 14**). Release the mouse button to stop drawing (**Figure 15**).

✔ Tips

- To draw a line or arrow that's perfectly vertical, horizontal, or at a 45° angle, hold down ⌜Shift⌟ in step 3.

- To force the line's end to snap to the worksheet grid, hold down ⌜⌥ ⌘⌟ in step 3.

- To draw multiple lines with the same tool, double-click the tool's button to select it. The tool remains active until you either click the button again, click another button, or press ⌜Esc⌟.

- The small white boxes in **Figures 8**, **9**, **11**, **13**, and **15** are selection handles. I tell you more about selection handles later in this chapter.

Figure 10 Using the Curve tool, click to indicate where the curve should appear.

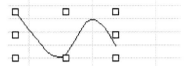

Figure 11 A curved line with two curves.

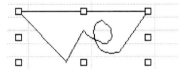

Figure 12 Using the Freeform tool, click to draw straight lines and drag to draw freeform lines.

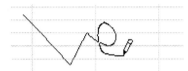

Figure 13 In this example, the line has been turned into a closed-off shape by clicking the starting point to complete the drawing.

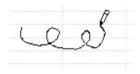

Figure 14 To use the Scribble tool, hold the mouse button down and drag the pencil pointer.

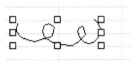

Figure 15 Releasing the mouse button completes the scribble.

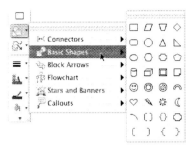

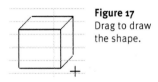

Figure 16 Choose a shape from one of the submenus on the AutoShapes pop-up menu.

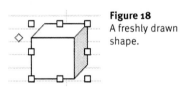

Figure 17
Drag to draw
the shape.

Figure 18
A freshly drawn
shape.

Figures 19 & 20
When you drag the AutoShapes menu (above) or one of its submenus (left) away from the toolbar, it turns into a floating toolbar.

To draw an AutoShape

1. Click a shape or line tool button on one of the submenus on the Drawing toolbar's AutoShapes pop-up menu (**Figure 16**). The mouse pointer turns into a crosshairs pointer (**Figure 5**).

2. Position the crosshairs where you want to begin drawing the shape or line.

3. Press the mouse button and drag. As you move the mouse, the shape or line begins to take form (**Figure 17**).

4. Release the mouse button to complete the shape (**Figure 18**).

✔ Tips

- The AutoShapes feature makes it easy to draw complex lines and shapes.

- The Connectors submenu offers options for creating lines that connect two shapes.

- The AutoShapes menu and its submenus (**Figure 16**) can be dragged off the toolbar to create a separate floating toolbar (**Figures 19** and **20**).

- You can also display the AutoShapes toolbar (**Figure 19**) by choosing Insert > Picture > AutoShapes (**Figure 25**). The other Picture submenu options are discussed later in this chapter.

- To draw multiple shapes with the same tool, double-click the tool's button to select it. The tool remains active until you either click the button again, click another button, or press (Esc).

To add a text box

1. Click the Text Box button on the Drawing toolbar (**Figure 1**). The mouse pointer turns into the letter *A* with a special crosshairs pointer (**Figure 21**).

2. Position the crosshairs where you want to begin drawing the text box.

3. Press the mouse button and drag. As you move the mouse, the text box begins to take form (**Figure 22**).

4. Release the mouse button to complete the text box. An insertion point appears within it (**Figure 23**).

5. Enter the text you want in the text box (**Figure 24**).

✔ Tips

- A text box is like a little word processing document within an Excel sheet. Once created, you can enter and format text within it.

- Text boxes offer more flexibility than worksheet cells when entering long passages of text.

- To edit text in a text box, double-click inside it to select one or more characters. Then use the arrow keys to move the insertion point. Use standard editing techniques to modify text.

Figure 21
The mouse pointer turns into a special crosshairs pointer when you click the Text Box button.

Figure 22
Drag to draw a text box.

Figure 23
When you release the mouse button, the text box appears with a blinking insertion point inside it.

Figure 24
You can type whatever text you like in the text box.

ADDING A TEXT BOX

Figure 25
The Insert menu's Picture submenu offers options for inserting all kinds of pictures.

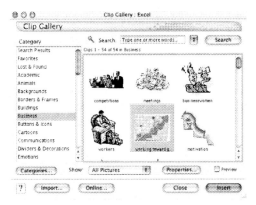

Figure 26 The Clip Gallery window offers thumbnail views of dozens of categorized pieces of clip art.

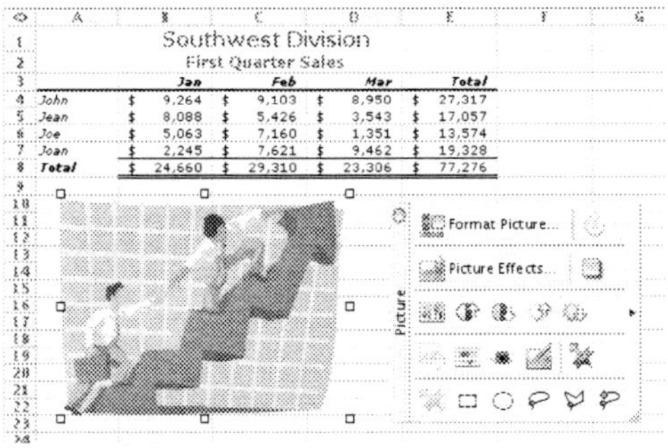

Figure 27 The clip art image is inserted in the document and the Picture toolbar appears.

Inserting Pictures

In addition to drawing graphic objects, you can also insert existing pictures into your documents. This enables you to include more complex graphic elements in your Excel worksheets and charts.

Although you can use buttons on the Drawing toolbar (**Figure 1**) to insert some types of pictures, the Picture submenu on the Insert menu (**Figure 25**) offers far more options.

To insert clip art

1. Choose Insert > Picture > Clip Art (**Figure 25**) or click the Insert Clip Art button on the Drawing toolbar (**Figure 1**) to display the Clip Gallery window (**Figure 26**).

2. Click a category name in the list on the left side of the window to display the clips within that category.

3. Click to select the clip that you want to insert.

4. Click the Insert button. The clip is inserted and the Picture toolbar appears (**Figure 27**).

✔ Tips

- To change a clip art image, double-click it to reopen the Clip Gallery window (**Figure 26**). Then follow steps 2 through 4.

- You can add your own clips to the Clip Gallery. Click the Import button and use the Import dialog that appears to locate, select, and import a picture file on disk.

- More clip art is available online. If you have an Internet connection, you can click the Online button to launch your Web browser and visit the Microsoft Web site where you can download additional clips.

- The Picture toolbar includes advanced tools for working with a selected picture.

INSERTING CLIP ART

To insert a picture from a file

1. Choose Insert > Picture > From File (**Figure 25**) or click the Insert Picture From File button ⊞ on the Drawing toolbar (**Figure 1**) to display the Choose a Picture dialog (**Figure 28**).

2. Locate and select the file you want to insert.

3. Click Insert. The picture file is inserted and the Picture toolbar appears (**Figure 29**).

✔ Tips

- As shown in **Figure 28**, if a preview exists for the image, it appears in the right side of the Choose a Picture dialog.

- The Picture toolbar includes advanced tools for working with a selected picture.

To insert an organization chart

1. Choose Insert > Picture > Organization Chart (**Figure 25**). The Organization Chart application launches (**Figure 30**).

2. Modify the contents of the default organization chart's boxes to add names, titles, and comments. To edit the contents of a box, click it and type in the new information.

3. Modify the chart's structure as follows:

   ▲ To add a box, click the button at the top of the screen for the type of box you want to add, then click the box in the chart that you want to attach it to.

   ▲ To remove a box, click the box to select it and press ⌈Delete⌋.

   ▲ To move a box, drag it to a new position on the chart.

4. When you are finished, choose Organization Chart > Quit Organization Chart.

5. A dialog like the one in **Figure 31** appears. Click Update. The organization chart is inserted in the document (**Figure 32**).

Figure 28 Use the Choose a Picture dialog to select an image file on disk, like a company logo.

Figure 29 Here's the logo inserted in a tall row at the top of a worksheet.

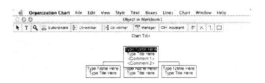

Figure 30 MS Organization Chart offers an easy way to create organization charts.

Figure 31 Click Update in this dialog to save the chart.

Figure 32 Here's the organization chart, inserted at the bottom of a worksheet.

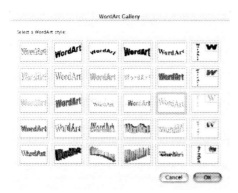

Figure 33 The WordArt Gallery dialog has many styles to choose from.

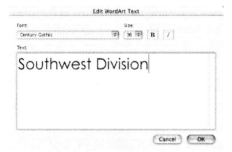

Figure 34 Enter and apply some text formatting to the text you want to appear.

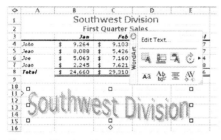

Figure 35 The WordArt image appears in the document, along with the WordArt toolbar.

To insert WordArt

1. Choose Insert > Picture > WordArt (**Figure 25**) or click the Insert WordArt button 🅰 on the Drawing toolbar (**Figure 1**).

2. In the WordArt Gallery dialog that appears (**Figure 33**), click to select a WordArt style.

3. Click OK.

4. In the Edit WordArt Text dialog that appears next (**Figure 34**), change the sample text to the text that you want to display. You can also select a different font and font size and turn on bold and/or italic formatting.

5. Click OK. The WordArt image is inserted in the document and the WordArt toolbar appears (**Figure 35**).

✔ Tip

- Once you have created a WordArt image, you can use buttons on the WordArt toolbar to modify it. The toolbar only appears when the WordArt image is selected.

To insert a picture from a scanner or a digital camera

1. Make sure the scanner software is properly installed and that the scanner is connected to your computer and turned on. Then place the image you wish to scan on the scanning surface.

   or

   Make sure the digital camera software is properly installed and that the camera is connected to your computer and turned on.

2. Choose Insert > Picture > From Scanner or Camera (**Figure 25**).

3. The Insert Picture from Scanner or Camera dialog appears (**Figure 36**). If necessary, use the menu to choose the device you wish to access, then click Acquire.

4. Excel launches the software for your device to access the picture(s) (**Figure 37**). Use that software to either scan or select the image you want to use.

   When you are finished, the image appears in the Excel document and the Picture toolbar appears (**Figure 38**).

✑ Important Note

- The Instructions on this page are based on the steps to complete the task in Excel 2001. Although I could not obtain a compatible scanner or digital camera to test and illustrate these steps (and believe me, I tried!), I am confident that the steps are virtually identical for Excel X.

✔ Tip

- If the Insert Picture from Scanner or Camera dialog (**Figure 36**) does not appear after step 3, your scanner or camera is either not installed or connected correctly or is incompatible with Mac OS X.

Figure 36 Use this dialog to select the scanner or camera you want to access.

Figure 37 Excel launches your scanner or camera software. In this example, it has launched the software for my new HP ScanJet 4470cse. (My old ScanJet IIcx finally died after eight years of service.)

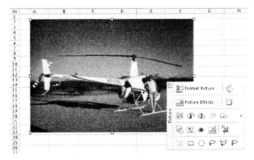

Figure 38 The scanned picture is inserted in the Excel document and the Picture toolbar appears.

Figure 39
When you position the mouse pointer on an object, the mouse pointer turns into a hand.

Figure 40
Selection handles appear around selected objects.

Working with Graphic Objects

Once you have drawn or inserted a graphic object into your Excel document, you can select, move, resize, modify, or delete it.

To select an object

1. Position the mouse pointer on the object. The mouse pointer turns into a hand (**Figure 39**).

2. Click. Selection handles appear around the object (**Figure 40**).

✔ Tips

- If a shape does not have any fill, you must click on its border to select it. I tell you about fill color later in this chapter.

- To change the mouse pointer into a selection pointer so the standard worksheet pointer (the fat plus sign) doesn't appear while you're working with drawing objects, click the Select Objects button ▸ on the Drawing toolbar (**Figure 1**). The button turns light gray and the mouse pointer changes to an arrow. To get the regular pointer back, click the Drawing Selection button again, double-click any worksheet cell, or press Esc once or twice.

To deselect an object

Click on any other object or anywhere else in the window. The selection handles disappear.

To select multiple objects

1. Follow the instructions on the previous page to select the first object (**Figure 41**).

2. Hold down ⟨Shift⟩ and continue to select objects until all have been selected (**Figure 42**).

or

1. Click the Select Objects button ▲ on the Drawing toolbar to activate the selection pointer.

2. Use the pointer to drag a rectangle that completely surrounds all the objects you want to select (**Figure 43**).

3. Release the mouse button. Selection handles appear around each object (**Figure 44**).

✔ Tips

■ To select all the objects on a worksheet, click the Select Objects button ▲ on the Drawing toolbar and press ⟨⌘ A⟩.

■ To deselect objects from a multiple selection, hold down ⟨Shift⟩ while clicking on the objects you want to deselect.

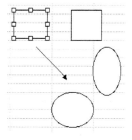

Figure 41
Select the first object.

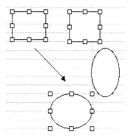

Figure 42
Then hold down ⟨Shift⟩ and click to select other objects.

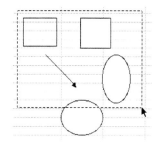

Figure 43
You can use the selection pointer to draw a boundary box that completely surrounds the objects you want to select.

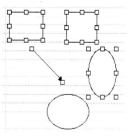

Figure 44
When you release the mouse button, the objects within the boundary are selected.

Figure 45
The Drawing
toolbar's Draw
pop-up menu.

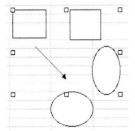

Figure 46
The objects selected
in **Figure 44** after
grouping them.

To group objects

1. Select all the objects you want to include in the group (**Figure 44**).

2. Choose Group from the Drawing toolbar's Draw menu (**Figure 45**).

   The objects are grouped together, with only one set of selection handles (**Figure 46**).

✔ Tips

■ Grouping multiple objects enables you to select, move, and modify all of the objects in the group by clicking any one of them.

■ In addition to grouping individual objects, you can also group groups of objects.

To ungroup objects

1. Select the grouped objects you want to ungroup (**Figure 46**).

2. Choose Ungroup from the Drawing toolbar's Draw menu (**Figure 45**).

   Separate selection handles appear for each object (**Figure 44**).

To move an object by dragging

1. Position the mouse pointer on the object so that the hand appears (**Figure 47**).

2. Press the mouse button and drag. An outline of the object moves along with the mouse pointer (**Figure 48**).

3. When the object's outline is in the desired position, release the mouse button. The object moves.

✔ Tips

■ To restrict an object's movement so that it moves only horizontally or vertically, hold down ⟨Shift⟩ while dragging.

■ To restrict an object's movement so that it snaps to the worksheet gridlines, hold down ⟨⌘⟩ while dragging.

To move an object with the Cut & Paste commands

1. Select the object you want to move.

2. Choose Edit > Cut (**Figure 49**), press ⟨⌘X⟩, or click the Cut button ✂ on the Standard toolbar. The object disappears.

3. To paste the object into a different sheet, switch to that sheet.

4. Choose Edit > Paste (**Figure 49**), press ⟨⌘V⟩, or click the Paste button 📋 on the Standard toolbar. The object appears.

5. If necessary, drag the object into the desired position on the sheet.

✔ Tip

■ This technique is most useful when moving an object to another sheet.

Figure 47
Position the mouse pointer on the object.

Figure 48
Drag to move the object.

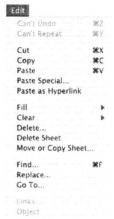

Figure 49
The Edit menu.

MOVING OBJECTS

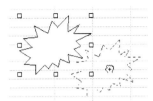

Figure 50
Hold down [Option] while dragging...

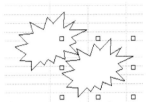

Figure 51
...to copy an object.

Figure 52
The Clear submenu under the Edit menu when an object is selected.

To copy an object by dragging

1. Position the mouse pointer on the object so that the hand appears (**Figure 47**).

2. While holding down [Option], press the mouse button and drag. An outline of the object moves along with the mouse pointer, which displays a plus sign inside it (**Figure 50**).

3. When you release the mouse button a copy of the object appears at the outline (**Figure 51**).

To copy an object with the Copy & Paste commands

1. Select the object you want to copy.

2. Choose Copy from the Edit menu (**Figure 49**), press ⌃⌘C, or click the Copy button on the Standard toolbar.

3. To paste the object into a different sheet, switch to that sheet.

4. Choose Paste from the Edit menu (**Figure 49**), press ⌃⌘V, or click the Paste button on the Standard toolbar.

To delete an object

1. Select the object(s) or group of objects you want to delete.

2. Press [Delete] or [Del].

   or

   Choose Edit > Clear > All (**Figure 52**) or press [Control] [B].

   The object(s) disappear.

COPYING & DELETING OBJECTS

143

To resize an object

1. Select the object you want to resize.

2. Position the mouse pointer on a selection handle. The mouse pointer turns into a box with triangles (**Figure 53**).

3. Press the mouse button and drag to stretch or shrink the object. The mouse pointer turns into a crosshairs and an outline of the object moves with your mouse pointer as you drag (**Figure 54**).

4. When the outline of the object reflects the size you want, release the mouse button. The object is resized (**Figure 55**).

✔ Tips

- To resize an object or group proportionally, hold down (Shift) while dragging a corner selection handle.

- To resize the object so that the handle you drag snaps to the worksheet gridlines, hold down (⌃ ⌘) while dragging.

- To resize multiple objects at the same time, select the objects, then resize one of them. All selected objects will stretch or shrink.

To customize an AutoShape

1. Select the AutoShape you want to customize.

2. Position the mouse pointer on the yellow diamond handle. The mouse pointer turns into a hollow white arrowhead pointer.

3. Drag the yellow diamond. As you drag, the outline of the customized shape moves with the mouse pointer (**Figures 56** and **58**).

4. Release the mouse button.The shape changes (**Figures 57** and **59**).

✔ Tip

- This technique can only be used on Auto-Shape lines or shapes that display a yellow diamond when selected.

Figure 53 Position the mouse pointer on a selection handle and it turns into a resizing pointer.

Figure 54 Drag to shrink (or stretch) the object.

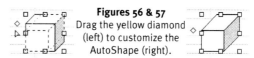

Figure 55 When you release the mouse button, the object resizes.

Figures 56 & 57 Drag the yellow diamond (left) to customize the AutoShape (right).

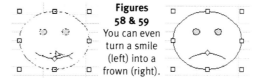

Figures 58 & 59 You can even turn a smile (left) into a frown (right).

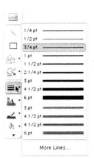

Figure 60 The Line Style button's menu.

Figure 61 The Font Color button's menu.

Figure 62 The Line Color button's menu.

Figure 63 The Fill Color button's menu.

Figure 64 The Arrow Style submenu under the Draw button's menu.

Figures 65, 66, & 67 Also under the Draw button's menu: the Dash Style submenu (left), the Shadow submenu (middle), and the 3-D submenu (right).

To format lines & shapes with the Drawing toolbar

1. Select the line or shape you want to format.

2. Use menus and submenus on the Drawing toolbar (**Figure 1**) to format the object:

   ▲ To change the line thickness of a line or shape border, choose an option from the Line Style button's menu (**Figure 60**).

   ▲ To change the color of text within an object, choose an option from the Font Color button's menu (**Figure 61**).

   ▲ To change the line color of a line or shape border, choose an option from the Line Color button's menu (**Figure 62**).

   ▲ To change the fill color of a shape, choose an option from the Fill Color button's menu (**Figure 63**).

   ▲ To add, change, or remove arrow components for a line or arrow, choose an option from the Arrow Style submenu under the Draw button's menu (**Figure 64**).

   ▲ To change the style of a dashed line or dashed shape border, choose an option from the Dash Style submenu under the Draw button's menu (**Figure 65**).

   ▲ To add, remove, or change the shadow of a line or shape, choose an option from the Shadow submenu under the Draw button's menu (**Figure 66**).

   ▲ To add, change, or remove three dimensional effects for a simple shape, choose an option from the 3-D submenu under the Draw button's menu (**Figure 67**).

✔ Tips

- The formatting options that are available depend on the line or shape that is selected.

- You can combine as many formatting options as you like.

To format objects with the Format dialog

1. Select the graphic object you want to format and choose the first option on the Format menu or press ⌃ ⌘ 1. As shown in **Figures 68**, **69**, and **70**, the option that appears varies depending on the type of object you selected.

   or

   Double-click the object you want to format.

   A Format dialog appears (**Figures 71**, **72**, and **73**). (The full name of the dialog varies depending on the type of object you selected or double-clicked.

2. Click the tab for the type of formatting you want to apply. The tabs that appear vary depending on what you are formatting. Here are the possibilities:

   ▲ **Font** (**Figure 73**) enables you to change font formatting for the object.

   ▲ **Alignment** enables you to change text alignment options for the object.

   ▲ **Colors and Lines** (**Figures 71** and **72**) enables you to change fill, line, and arrow formatting for the object.

   ▲ **Size** enables you to resize, rotate, and scale the object.

   ▲ **Picture** enables you to crop and adjust the image.

   ▲ **Protection** enables you to lock the image to prevent changes when protection is turned on.

   ▲ **Properties** enables you to set object positioning and printing options.

   ▲ **Margins** enables you to set margin options for the object.

3. Make changes as desired in the tab.

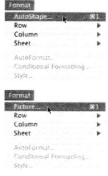

Figures 68, 69, & 70
The first option on the Format menu enables you to format whatever type of object is selected. As you can see, the wording of the command changes based on what is selected when you display the menu.

Figure 71 The Format AutoShape dialog, ...

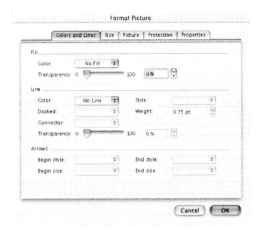

Figure 72 ...the Format Picture dialog, ...

Figure 73 ...and the Format Text Box dialog are just three examples of the Format dialog that appears for objects.

4. Repeat steps 2 and 3 for each type of formatting you want to change.

5. When you're finished setting options in the dialog, click OK.

✔ Tips

■ You can combine as many formatting options as you like to customize the appearance of lines and shapes.

■ As you can imagine, with many different types of objects, there are literally dozens of combinations of dialog tabs and available settings. It's impossible to illustrate them all here. Explore these dialogs on your own to see what kind of formatting you can do with them.

To format objects with the Formatting Palette

1. Select the graphic object you want to format.

2. If necessary, choose View > Formatting Palette or click the Formatting Palette button  on the Standard toolbar to display the Formatting Palette. As you can see in **Figures 74**, **75**, and **76**, the appearance of the Formatting Palette changes depending on the type of object you selected.

3. Set options as desired in the Formatting Palette. The settings you make are applied immediately to the object.

✔ Tips

- You can combine as many formatting options as you like to customize the appearance of lines and shapes.

- With many different types of objects, there are many ways the Formatting Palette can appear. It's impossible to illustrate all possibilities here. Explore the Formatting Palette's options on your own to see what kind of formatting you can do with them.

Figure 74
The Formatting Palette only shows options that can apply to whatever is selected. For example, here's how it looks when an AutoShape, …

Figure 75
…Picture, …

Figure 76
…or Text Box is selected.

Figure 77
Because each object is drawn in a separate layer, objects can be obscured by other objects "on top" of them.

Figure 78
To change an object's layer, start by selecting it.

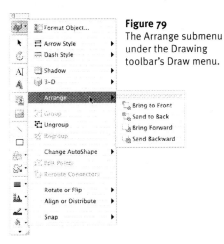

Figure 79
The Arrange submenu under the Drawing toolbar's Draw menu.

Figure 80
A selected object can be brought to the top layer...

Figure 81
...or sent to the bottom layer.

Stacking Order

Each time you draw a shape, Excel puts it on a new drawing layer. When you draw a shape that overlaps another shape, the first shape may be partially obscured by the one "on top" of it (**Figure 77**).

To change stacking order

1. Select the object(s) you want to move to another layer (**Figure 78**).

2. Choose an option from the Arrange submenu on the Drawing toolbar's Draw menu (**Figure 79**):

   ▲ **Bring to Front** moves the object(s) to the top layer (**Figure 80**).

   ▲ **Send to Back** moves the object(s) to the bottom layer (**Figure 81**).

   ▲ **Bring Forward** moves the object(s) up one layer.

   ▲ **Send Backward** moves the object(s) down one layer.

✔ Tips

■ Once you've arranged objects in the order you want, consider grouping them so they stay just the way you want them to. I tell you how to group objects earlier in this chapter.

■ You cannot move graphic objects behind the worksheet layer.

CHANGING STACKING ORDER

CREATING CHARTS

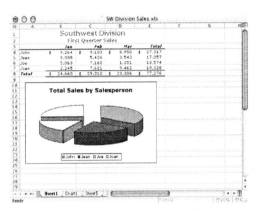

Figure 1 Here's a 3-D pie chart embedded in a worksheet file.

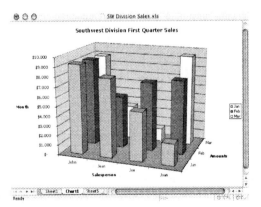

Figure 2 Here's a 3-D column chart on a chart sheet of its own.

Charts

A chart is a graphic representation of data. A chart can be embedded in a worksheet (**Figure 1**) or can be a chart sheet of its own (**Figure 2**).

With Microsoft Excel, you can create many different types of charts. The 3-D pie chart and 3-D column chart shown here (**Figures 1** and **2**) are only two examples. Since each type of chart has at least one variation and you can customize any chart you create, there's no limit to the number of ways you can present data graphically with Excel.

✔ Tips

- Include charts with worksheets whenever you want to emphasize worksheet results. Charts can often communicate information like trends and comparative results better than numbers alone.

- A skilled chartmaker can, through choice of data, chart format, and scale, get a chart to say almost anything about the data it represents!

The Chart Wizard

Excel's Chart Wizard walks you through the creation of a chart. It uses illustrated dialogs to prompt you for information. In each step of the Chart Wizard, you get to see what your chart looks like. At any point, you can go back and make changes to selections. When you're finished, your chart appears. You can then use a variety of chart formatting commands and buttons to change the look of your chart.

151

To use the Chart Wizard

1. Select the data you want to include in the chart (**Figure 3**).

2. Choose Insert > Chart (**Figure 4**) or click the Chart Wizard button  on the Standard toolbar.

3. In the Chart Wizard – Chart Type dialog (**Figure 5**), click to select one of the chart types in the scrolling list. Then click to select one of the chart sub-types on the right side of the dialog. Click Next.

4. In the Chart Wizard – Chart Source Data dialog (**Figure 6**), check the contents of the Data range text box to assure that it indicates the data you want to chart. You can see which data range will be charted by clicking the Collapse Dialog button so you can see the sheet behind the dialog (**Figure 7**). If incorrect, select the correct range. If necessary, click the Expand Dialog button to display the entire dialog again. You can also select a different Series in radio button to change the way data is charted. Then click Next.

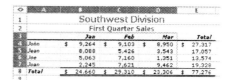

Figure 3 Select the data you want to chart.

Figure 4
Choose Chart from the Insert menu.

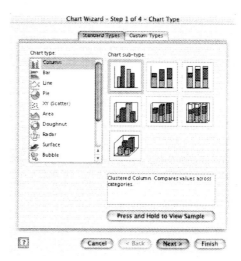

Figure 5 The first step of the Chart Wizard enables you to select a chart type.

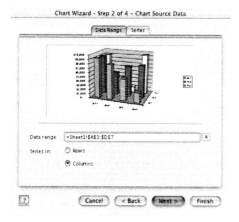

Figure 6 The second step of the Chart Wizard enables you to check and, if necessary, change the range to be charted.

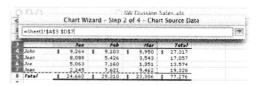

Figure 7 You can collapse the Chart Wizard dialog to see what range is selected.

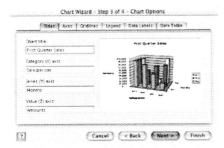

Figure 8 Chart Wizard Title options.

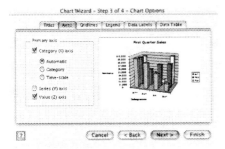

Figure 9 Chart Wizard Axes options.

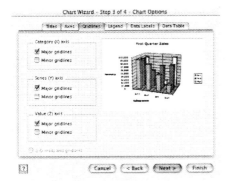

Figure 10 Chart Wizard Gridlines options.

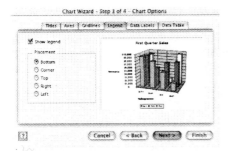

Figure 11 Chart Wizard Legend options.

5. In the Chart Wizard – Chart Options dialog, use the tabs at the top of the dialog to set a variety of formatting options:

▲ **Titles (Figure 8)** enables you to set a chart title and axes titles.

▲ **Axes (Figure 9)** enables you to select which axes you want to display.

▲ **Gridlines (Figure 10)** enables you to select which gridlines to display.

▲ **Legend (Figure 11)** enables you to show and position or hide the legend.

▲ **Data Labels (Figure 12)** enables you to set the type of data labels that should be displayed.

▲ **Data Table (Figure 13)** enables you to include a data table with the chart.

Set options as desired. When you change a setting, the sample chart changes accordingly. When you are finished, click Next.

Continued on next page...

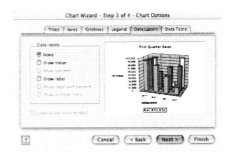

Figure 12 Chart Wizard Data Labels options.

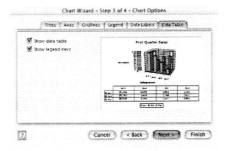

Figure 13 Chart Wizard Data Table options.

USING THE CHART WIZARD

153

Continued from previous page.

6. In the Chart Wizard — Chart Location dialog (**Figure 14**), select the radio button to set the location for the chart:

▲ **As new sheet** puts the chart on a new chart sheet. You can enter a name in the text box to name the new sheet when you create it.

▲ **As object in** puts the chart on another sheet in the workbook. You can use the pop-up menu to select the sheet.

7. Click Finish.

Excel creates and inserts the chart with the settings and in the location you specified.

✔ Tips

■ At any time while using the Chart Wizard, you can click the Back button to move to a previous step. Any changes you make in a previous step are carried forward when you continue.

■ In step 3, to see what your data would look like when charted with the chart type and sub-type you select, click and hold down the Press and Hold to View Sample button (**Figure 15**).

■ In step 3, you can select one of the custom chart types by clicking the Custom Types tab (**Figure 16**). Then follow the instructions in step 3 for that tab.

■ In step 4, you can add, modify, or delete data series for the chart in the Series tab (**Figure 17**). I tell you about working with data series later in this chapter.

■ I explain all the options in step 5 throughout this book.

Figure 14 The final step of the Chart Wizard.

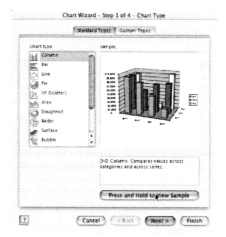

Figure 15 You can preview what your chart will look like with the chart type and sub-type you selected by clicking a button in the first window of the Chart Wizard.

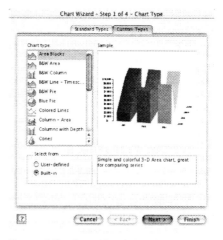

Figure 16 The Chart Wizard also allows you to select some custom chart types.

USING THE CHART WIZARD

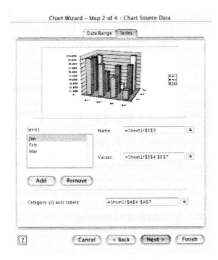

Figure 17 You can also add, modify, or remove data series from a chart within the Chart Wizard.

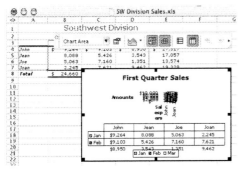

Figure 18 When you create an embedded chart, Excel just plops it on the worksheet.

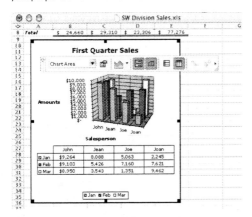

Figure 19 You can move and resize a chart to improve its appearance.

■ In step 5, axes and gridlines options are only available for charts that have axes or gridlines. Pie charts, for example, have neither axes nor gridlines.

■ A chart embedded in a worksheet or a chart sheet is a special kind of graphic. You can move, copy, resize, or delete it just like any other graphic object. I tell you how to work with graphics in **Chapter 7**.

■ If an embedded chart is too small to properly display data (**Figure 18**), resize it. The larger the chart, the better it will display (**Figure 19**).

■ You can also improve the appearance of an embedded chart by resizing or removing chart elements such as legends, axes labels, and data tables.

■ You're not stuck with the formatting you select in the Chart Wizard. I tell you about chart formatting options throughout this chapter.

■ Don't be afraid to experiment with the Chart Wizard. Try different options to see what effects you can achieve. You can always delete the chart and start fresh. Deleting a chart does not change data.

To reuse the Chart Wizard

1. Activate the chart by switching to its chart sheet or, if it's an embedded chart, by clicking within it.

2. Click the Chart Wizard button ![button] on the Standard toolbar.

3. Follow the steps on the previous pages to set or change Chart Wizard options for the chart.

Worksheet & Chart Links

When you create a chart based on worksheet data, the worksheet and chart are linked. Excel knows exactly which worksheet and cells it should look at to plot the chart. If the contents of one of those cells changes, the chart changes accordingly (**Figures 20** and **21**).

✔ Tips

- The link works both ways. With some chart types, you can drag a data point to change the data in the source worksheet (**Figure 22**). This makes a good planning tool for businesses interested in maintaining trends.

- Excel's Range Finder feature places a color-coded box around ranges in a selected chart (**Figure 23**), making them easy to spot.

- You can see (and edit) the links between a chart and a worksheet by activating the chart, selecting one of the data series, and looking at the formula bar. You should see a formula with a SERIES function that specifies the sheet name and absolute cell references for the range making up that series. **Figure 23** shows an example.

- If you delete worksheet data or an entire worksheet that is linked to a chart, Excel warns you with a dialog like the one in **Figure 24**. If you removed the data by mistake, choose Undo Delete from the Edit menu, click the Undo button  on the Standard toolbar, or press ⌘ Z to get the deleted data back.

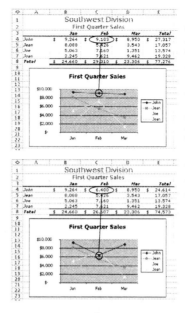

Figures 20 & 21 A linked worksheet and chart before (top) and after (bottom) a change to a cell's contents. When you change one, the other changes automatically.

Figure 22 Dragging a data point changes the data in the linked cell.

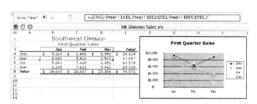

Figure 23 This illustration shows both the Range Finder feature and the SERIES formula.

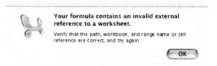

Your formula contains an invalid external reference to a worksheet.

Verify that the path, workbook, and range name or cell reference are correct, and try again.

OK

Figure 24 If you delete cells linked to a chart, you may see a dialog like this.

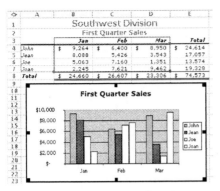

Figure 25 When you activate a chart, Range Finder frames appear around each data series.

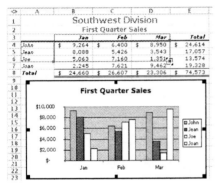

Figure 26 Drag a Range Finder handle to change the size of the series.

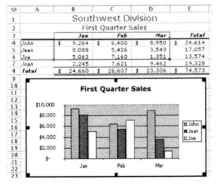

Figure 27 When you release the mouse button, the series—and the chart—change.

Data Series & Points

A *data series* is a group of related data in a chart. A data series normally corresponds to the values in a linked range of cells in a single column or row of a single worksheet. When plotted on a chart, each data series is assigned its own color or pattern.

Each cell within a data series is called a *data point*. Data points are individually plotted on a chart.

You can change data series included in a chart at any time using four different methods:

◆ Use Range Finder handles to modify a series in an embedded chart.

◆ Use the Source Data dialog to add, modify, or remove a series.

◆ Use the Copy and Paste commands to paste in a new series.

◆ Use drag-and-drop editing to add a new series.

I tell you about all these techniques next.

To modify a data series with Range Finder handles

1. Click the chart to activate it. Range Finder frames with handles appear around each data series (**Figure 25**).

2. Position the mouse pointer on the handle for the series you want to change. The mouse pointer turns into a box with triangles in two corners.

3. Press the mouse button, and drag to stretch or shrink the series (**Figure 26**).

4. When you release the mouse button, the series (and any related series) changes, thus changing the information plotted in the chart (**Figure 27**).

✔ Tip

■ You can only use this method with an embedded chart.

USING RANGE FINDER HANDLES

To modify data series with the Source Data dialog

1. Activate the chart by switching to its chart sheet or, if it's an embedded chart, by clicking within it.

2. Choose Chart > Source Data (**Figure 28**) to display the Source Data dialog (**Figures 29** and **30**).

3. Click the Data Range tab (**Figure 29**):

   ▲ To change the range of data plotted in the chart, select a new data range. As you select the range, it is automatically entered in the Data range text box.

   ▲ To switch the series from column to row or row to column, select the appropriate Series in radio button.

   or

   Click the Series tab (**Figure 30**):

   ▲ To add a data series, click the Add button, then drag in the worksheet to enter a range in the Name and Values text boxes.

   ▲ To modify a data series, select the name of the series you want to change, then drag in the worksheet to modify the range in the Name and/or Values text boxes.

   ▲ To remove a data series, select the name of the series you want to remove and click the Remove button.

4. Consult the sample chart in the dialog to see the effect of your changes. When the chart reflects the correct data ranges, click OK.

✔ Tips

■ The Source Data dialog looks (and works) just like the second step of the Chart Wizard (**Figures 6** and **17**). In fact, you can use the Chart Wizard to make any of the changes discussed on this page.

Figure 28
The Chart menu appears only when a chart is active.

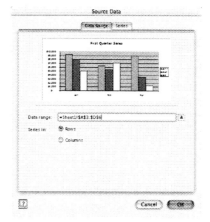

Figure 29 The Data Range tab of the Source Data dialog.

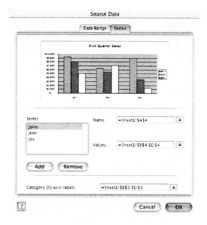

Figure 30 The Series tab of the Source Data dialog.

■ You can click the Collapse Dialog ⬆ or Expand Dialog ⬇ buttons to change the size of the Source Data dialog.

■ Removing a data series does not delete data from the source worksheet.

USING THE SOURCE DATA DIALOG

Figure 31 Select the data that you want to add to the chart.

Figure 32 The Edit menu includes the Copy, Paste, and Paste Special commands, which you can use to add data to a chart.

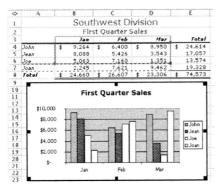

Figure 33 When you paste in the data, the chart changes accordingly.

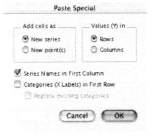

Figure 34 The Paste Special dialog offers additional options for pasting data into charts.

To add a data series with the Copy & Paste commands

1. In the worksheet, select the data you want to add to the chart (**Figure 31**). Be sure to include column or row headings if they should be included as labels.

2. Choose Edit > Copy (**Figure 32**), press ⌃ ⌘ C or click the Copy button on the Standard toolbar. A marquee appears around the selected cells.

3. Activate the chart to which you want to add the data by switching to its chart sheet or, if it's an embedded chart, by clicking within it.

4. Choose Edit > Paste (**Figure 32**), press ⌃ ⌘ V, or click the Paste button on the Standard toolbar. The chart changes to include the additional data (**Figure 33**).

✔ Tips

■ In order for this technique to work properly, the data you add must be the same kind of data originally charted. For example, if you originally plotted totals to create a pie chart, you can't successfully add a series of numbers that aren't totals to the chart.

■ For additional control over how data is pasted into a chart, choose Edit > Paste Special (**Figure 32**) in step 4 above. The Paste Special dialog (**Figure 34**) will sometimes appear on its own when you paste a range into a chart.

To add a data series with drag & drop

1. In the worksheet, select the data you want to add to the chart (**Figure 35**). Be sure to include column or row headings if they should be included as labels.

2. Position the mouse pointer on the border of the selection. The mouse pointer turns into a hand.

3. Press the mouse button and drag the selection on top of the chart. The mouse pointer hand gets a little plus sign inside it and the chart border changes (**Figure 36**).

4. Release the mouse button. The chart changes to include the additional data (**Figure 37**).

✔ Tips

- In order for this technique to work properly, the data you add must be the same kind of data originally charted. For example, if you originally plotted totals to create a pie chart, you can't successfully add a series of numbers that aren't totals to the chart.

- This technique only works for charts that are embedded in the worksheet containing the original data.

- To add data contained in noncontiguous ranges, use one of the other methods discussed in this section.

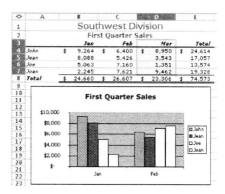

Figure 35 Select the data you want to add to the chart.

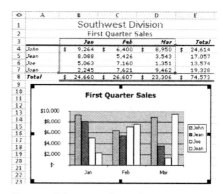

Figure 36 Drag the selection onto the chart.

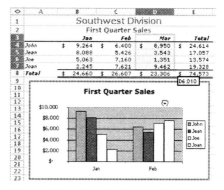

Figure 37 When you release the mouse button, the data is added to the chart.

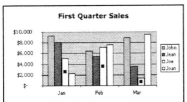

Figure 38
Select the series you want to remove.

To remove a data series

1. Click to select the series you want to remove. Selection handles appear at each data point in the series (**Figure 38**).

2. Choose Edit > Clear > Series (**Figure 39**), press ⌃⌘B, or press Delete.

    The series disappears (**Figure 40**). If the chart included a legend, it is revised to exclude the deleted data.

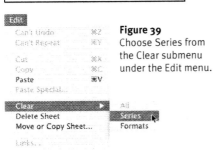

Figure 39
Choose Series from the Clear submenu under the Edit menu.

✔ Tips

- Removing a series from a chart does not delete data from the source worksheet.

- You can also remove a data series with the Source Data dialog (**Figure 30**). I tell you how earlier in this chapter.

Figure 40
All trace of the series is removed from the chart.

Chart Elements

Each chart is made up of multiple elements, each of which can be selected, then modified or formatted to fine-tune the appearance of a chart.

To identify a chart element

Point to the element you want to identify. Excel displays the name (and values, if appropriate) for the element in a yellow Chart Tip box (**Figure 41**).

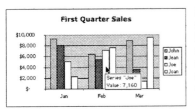

Figure 41
Chart tips identify the chart elements and values you point to.

To select a chart element

Click the element you want to select. Selection handles or a selection box (or both) appear around it (**Figure 42**).

✔ Tips

- To select a single data point, first click to select the data series, then click the point to select it.

- Excel displays the name of a selected chart element in the Name Box on the formula bar (**Figure 42**).

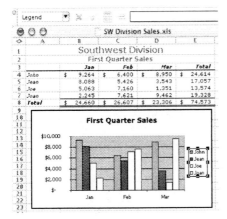

Figure 42 The name of a selected element appears in the Name Box on the formula bar.

Chart Type

Excel includes dozens of standard and custom chart types. You select the chart type when you create a chart with the Chart Wizard, but you can change the type at any time. You can also add your formatted charts to the Chart Gallery so you can use them to create future charts.

To change the chart type

1. Activate the chart by switching to its chart sheet or, if it's an embedded chart, by clicking within it.

2. Choose Chart > Chart Type (**Figure 28**) to display the Chart Type dialog.

3. Click the Standard Types tab (**Figure 43**):

   ▲ To select a standard chart type, select a Chart type, then select a Chart sub-type.

   ▲ To apply a chart type to a selected data series, turn on the Apply to selection check box.

   ▲ To remove formatting you have applied to the chart, turn on the Default formatting check box.

   or

   Click the Custom Types tab:

   ▲ To select a built-in chart type, select the Built-in radio button (**Figure 44**), then select a Chart type.

   ▲ To select a user-defined chart type, select the User-defined radio button (**Figure 45**), then select a Chart type.

4. Click OK to apply the chart type.

✔ Tip

■ The Chart Type dialog looks (and works) just like the first step of the Chart Wizard (**Figures 5** and **15**). In fact, you can use the Chart Wizard to make any of the changes discussed on this page.

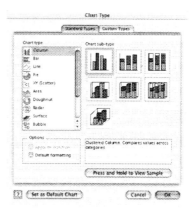

Figure 43 The Standard Types tab of the Chart Types dialog.

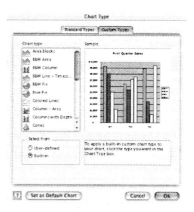

Figure 44 The Custom Types tab of the Chart Types dialog with Built-in selected.

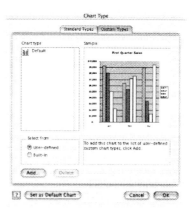

Figure 45 The Custom Types tab of the Chart Types dialog with User-defined selected.

CHANGING THE CHART TYPE

Figure 46 Use the Add Custom Chart Type dialog to enter a name and description for a chart type.

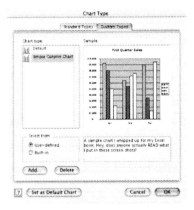

Figure 47 The chart type you added appears in the User-defined Chart type list.

To set the default chart type

1. Choose Chart > Chart Type (**Figure 28**) to display the Chart Type dialog.

2. Click the Standard Types tab (**Figure 43**).

3. Select the Chart type and sub-type you want to set as the default chart type.

4. Click the Set as Default Chart button.

5. Click OK.

✔ Tip

■ The default chart type is the one automatically selected for creating a new chart.

To add a user-defined chart to the Chart Type dialog

1. Activate the formatted chart you want to add by switching to its chart sheet or, if it's an embedded chart, by clicking within it.

2. Choose Chart > Chart Type (**Figure 28**) to display the Chart Type dialog.

3. Click the Custom Types tab.

4. Select the User-defined radio button (**Figure 45**).

5. Click the Add button.

6. In the Add Custom Chart Type dialog that appears (**Figure 46**), enter a name and description for the chart in the appropriate text boxes.

7. Click OK. The chart appears in the User-defined Chart type list (**Figure 47**).

8. Click OK.

✔ Tip

■ This feature makes it easy to create the same basic charts over and over again with different data—like you might have to do for a monthly report.

Chart Options

Chart options refer to the inclusion and basic formatting of chart elements such as titles, axes, gridlines, legends, data labels, and data tables. You set chart options with the Chart Options dialog.

To use the Chart Options dialog

1. Activate the chart by switching to its chart sheet or, if it's an embedded chart, by clicking within it.

2. Choose Chart > Chart Options (**Figure 28**) to display the Chart Options dialog (**Figures 48** through **53**).

3. Click the tab for the type of option you want to set.

4. Set options as desired.

5. Repeat steps 3 and 4 for each type of option you want to set.

6. Click OK to apply your settings.

✔ Tips

- I provide details on all options on the following pages.

- The Chart Options dialog looks (and works) just like the third step of the Chart Wizard (**Figures 8** through **13**). In fact, you can use the Chart Wizard to make any of the changes discussed on this page.

- Each time you make a change in the Chart Options dialog, the effect of your change is reflected in the chart preview within the dialog. Use this feature to check your changes before clicking OK to apply them to the chart.

- The options available in the Chart Options dialog vary based on the type of chart that is selected. If a specific option is not available, either it will not appear or it will appear in gray within the dialog.

USING THE CHART OPTIONS DIALOG

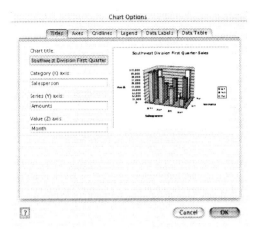

Figure 48 The Titles tab of the Chart Options dialog for a 3-D column chart. The sample illustration shows all titles set.

Titles

Titles are textual labels that appear in specific locations on the chart.

To set chart titles

1. In the Chart Options dialog, click the Titles tab to display its options (**Figure 48**).

2. Enter titles in the desired text boxes:

   ▲ **Chart title** is the chart's main title. It appears at the top of the chart.

   ▲ **Category (X) axis** is the category axis title. Available for most 2-D and 3-D chart types, it appears along the bottom (front) axis.

   ▲ **Series (Y) axis** is the series axis title. Available for most chart types, it appears down the left side of a 2-D chart and along the bottom (back) axis of 3-D chart.

   ▲ **Value (Z) axis** is the value axis title. Available only for 3-D chart types, it appears down the left side of the chart.

To remove a chart title

1. In the Chart Options dialog, click the Titles tab to display its options (**Figure 48**).

2. Clear the text box(es) for the titles you want to remove.

Axes

Axes are the bounding lines of a chart. 2-D charts have two axes: X and Y. 3-D charts have three axes: X, Y, and Z. Pie and doughnut charts do not have axes at all.

✔ Tip

■ In case you're wondering, *axes* (pronounced *ax-eez*) is the plural of *axis*. While axes are also tools for chopping wood, you can't chop wood with Excel.

To set axes options

1. In the Chart Options dialog, click the Axes tab to display its options (**Figure 49**).

2. Turn on the check boxes for the axes you want to display:

   ▲ **Category (X) axis** appears along the bottom (front) axis.

   ▲ **Series (Y) axis** appears down the left side of a 2-D chart and along the bottom (back) axis of 3-D chart.

   ▲ **Value (Z) axis**, which is available only for 3-D chart types, appears down the left side of the chart.

3. If you turned on the Category (X) axis option in step 2, select one of the formatting option radio buttons:

   ▲ **Automatic** instructs Excel to check the formatting of the category data to determine whether it should use time-scale or category formatting.

   ▲ **Category** instructs Excel to use the category data for the X axis.

   ▲ **Time-scale** instructs Excel to create a time scale for the X axis.

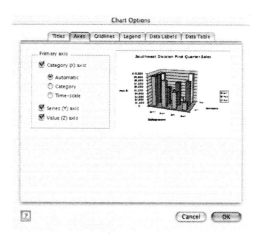

Figure 49 The Axes tab of the Chart Options dialog for a 3-D column chart. The sample illustration shows all axes displayed.

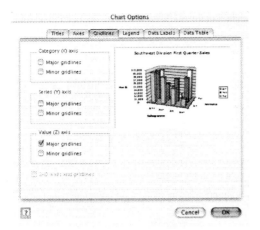

Figure 50 The Gridlines tab of the Chart Options dialog for a 3-D column chart. The sample illustration shows only the major gridlines for the Value (Z) axis turned on.

Gridlines

Gridlines are lines indicating major and minor scale points along a chart's walls. They can make it easier to follow chart points to corresponding values on a chart axis. Pie and doughnut charts do not have gridlines.

✔ Tip

- Although gridlines can make a chart's data easier to read, too many gridlines can clutter a chart's walls, making data impossible to read.

To set gridlines

1. In the Chart Options dialog, click the Gridlines tab to display its options (**Figure 50**).

2. Turn on the check boxes for the gridlines you want to display on each axis:

   ▲ **Major gridlines** correspond to major tickmark units for the axis scale.

   ▲ **Minor gridlines** correspond to minor tickmark units for the axis scale.

3. To apply a 2-D appearance to 3-D chart walls and gridlines, turn on the 2-D walls and gridlines check box. This option is only available for certain types of charts.

✔ Tips

- I explain how to set the scale for an axis later in this chapter.

- I define the three axes on the previous page.

Legend

A legend is a box with color-coded labels identifying a chart's data series. You can turn a legend on or off and set its position within the chart area.

✔ Tip

■ Excel creates the legend based on cells selected as part of the data source. That's why it's a good idea to include headings in the selected range when you create a chart.

To add a legend

1. In the Chart Options dialog, click the Legend tab to display its options (**Figure 51**).

2. Turn on the Show legend check box.

3. Select one of the radio buttons for a legend position:

   ▲ **Bottom** displays the legend at the bottom-center of the chart.

   ▲ **Corner** displays the legend at the top-right corner of the chart.

   ▲ **Top** displays the legend at the top-center of the chart.

   ▲ **Right** displays the legend at the right-middle of the chart.

   ▲ **Left** displays the legend at the left-middle of the chart.

✔ Tips

■ You can also move a legend by dragging it to a new position within the chart.

■ The legend position can affect the size of a chart's plot area.

To remove the legend

1. In the Chart Options dialog, click the Legend tab to display its options (**Figure 51**).

2. Turn off the Show legend check box.

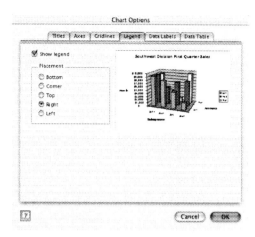

Figure 51 The Legend tab of the Chart Options dialog for a 3-D column chart. The sample illustration shows a legend placed on the right side of the chart.

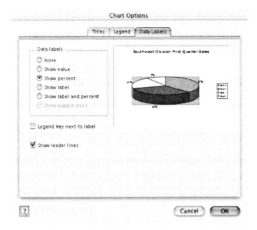

Figure 52 The Data Labels tab of the Chart Options dialog for a 3-D pie chart. The sample illustration shows percent data labels.

Data Labels

Data labels provide additional information about specific data points.

✔ Tip

- The Chart Options dialog enables you to set data labels for all chart points. To set data labels for just a single data series or data point, select the series or point, then use the Format dialog, which I tell you about later in this chapter.

To set data labels

1. In the Chart Options dialog, click the Data Labels tab to display its options (**Figure 52**).

2. Select one of the Data labels radio buttons:

   ▲ **None** removes all data labels.

   ▲ **Show value** displays the value for each data point.

   ▲ **Show percent** displays the percentage of the whole for each data point. This option is only available for pie and doughnut charts.

   ▲ **Show label** displays the legend label for each data point.

   ▲ **Show label and percent** displays both the legend label and percentage of the whole for each data point. This option is only available for pie and doughnut charts.

   ▲ **Show bubble sizes** displays the size of bubbles in a bubble chart.

3. To show the legend color key beside a data label, turn on the Legend key next to label check box.

4. For a pie or doughnut chart, to display a line from the data point to the data label, turn on the Show leader lines check box.

Data Table

A data table is the data plotted on the chart, in tabular format.

✔ Tips

- Data tables are more useful on chart sheets than on embedded charts, since embedded charts can include the worksheet on which the chart is based.

- Data tables are not available for pie and doughnut charts.

To add a data table

1. In the Chart Options dialog, click the Data Table tab to display its options (**Figure 53**).

2. Turn on the Show data table check box.

3. To show the legend color key in the data table, turn on Show legend keys check box.

To remove a data table

1. In the Chart Options dialog, click the Data Table tab to display its options (**Figure 53**).

2. Turn off the Show data table check box.

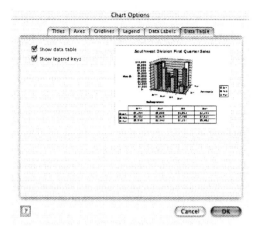

Figure 53 The Data Table tab of the Chart Options dialog for a 3-D column chart. The sample illustration shows a data table with legend keys turned on.

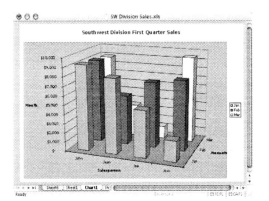

Figure 54 Formatting can make this boring, default chart...

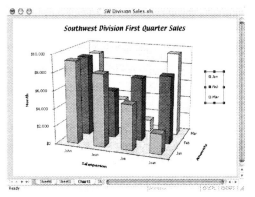

Figure 55 ...look interesting!

Formatting Chart Elements

You can use the Format dialog to apply a variety of formatting to chart elements:

◆ **Font** enables you to change the appearance of an element's font characters.

◆ **Number** enables you to change the number formatting of values.

◆ **Alignment** enables you to change the alignment and orientation of text.

◆ **Patterns** enables you to change an element's color and pattern. It also enables you to set styles for axis *tick marks*—the tiny lines that mark values and labels on a chart's axes.

◆ **Placement** enables you to set the position for a chart legend.

◆ **Scale** enables you to change the values that appear on an axis.

◆ **Shape** enables you to change the shape of data points.

◆ **Data Labels** enables you to set data labels for a single data series or data point. I discuss these options earlier in this chapter.

◆ **Series Order** enables you to change the order in which data series appear.

◆ **Options** enables you to set data series spacing options.

Figures 54 and **55** may give you an idea of what you can do with chart formatting.

In this section, I tell you how chart formatting works and discuss some of the formatting options available just for charts.

✔ Tip

■ I discuss pattern, font, number, and alignment formatting in **Chapter 6**. I discuss legend position and data labels earlier in this chapter.

To use the Format dialog

1. Select the chart element that you want to format and choose the first command under the Format menu (**Figures 56, 57,** and **58**), press ⌘ ⌘ 1, or click the Format button 🔛 on the Chart toolbar.

or

Double-click the element that you want to format.

2. In the Format dialog that appears, click the tab for the type of option you want to set.

3. Set options as desired.

4. Repeat steps 2 and 3 for each type of option you want to set.

5. Click OK to apply the formatting.

✔ Tips

- The exact name of the menu command in step 1 varies depending on the chart element that is selected. You can see this in **Figures 56, 57,** and **58**.

- The exact name of the Format dialog in step 2 varies depending on the chart element that is selected. You can see this in **Figures 59** and **61**.

To set the data point shape

1. Open the Format Data Series dialog for a selected data series.

2. Click the Shape tab to display its options (**Figure 59**).

3. Click to select the desired shape.

4. Click OK. The shape is applied to the selected data series (**Figure 60**).

✔ Tip

- This option is only available for certain 3-D charts.

Figures 56, 57, & 58
The first command under the Format menu enables you to format the selected chart element.

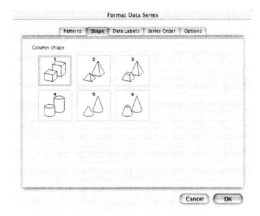

Figure 59 The Shape tab of the Format Data Series dialog enables you to select a shape to apply to the selected series in a 3-D chart.

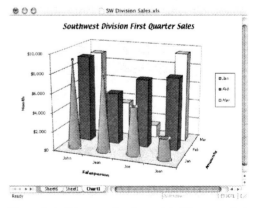

Figure 60 In this example, shape style #6 was applied to one data series.

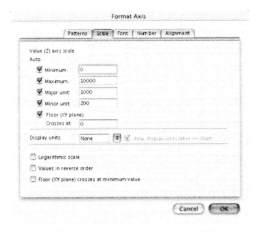

Figure 61 The Scale tab of the Format Axis dialog.

To set the scale

1. Open the Format Gridlines or Format Axis dialog for the gridline or axis for which you want to set the scale.

2. Click the Scale tab to display its options (**Figure 61**).

3. Enter the scale values you want to use in the text boxes:

    ▲ **Minimum** is the minimum value on the scale. It is normally set to 0.

    ▲ **Maximum** is the maximum value on the scale. It is normally set to a round number larger than the highest value plotted.

    ▲ **Major unit** is the unit corresponding to major gridlines and tick marks.

    ▲ **Minor unit** is the unit corresponding to minor gridlines and tick marks.

    ▲ **Floor (XY plane) Crosses at** is the value at which the X and Y axes cross each other. It is normally set to 0.

4. Turn on check boxes for special scale options as desired:

    ▲ **Logarithmic scale** recalculates the values in the text boxes as powers of 10.

    ▲ **Values in reverse order** reverses the order in which the scale appears, putting the largest values at the bottom or left side of the axis.

    ▲ **Floor (XY plane) crosses at minimum value** overrides the Floor (XY plane) Crosses at value and sets it to the minimum value.

5. Click OK.

✔ Tip

■ When you enter a value in a text box, its corresponding check box should turn itself off automatically; you can turn it back on to use the default setting.

To set tick marks

1. Open the Format Axis dialog for the axis for which you want to set the tick marks.

2. Click the Patterns tab to display its options (**Figure 62**).

3. Select the radio button for the desired Tick mark labels option:

   ▲ **None** omits tick mark labels.

   ▲ **Low** displays tick mark labels at the bottom or to the right of the plot area.

   ▲ **High** displays tick mark labels at the top or to the left of the plot area.

   ▲ **Next to axis** displays tick mark labels next to the selected axis. This is the default option.

4. Select the radio buttons for the desired Major tick mark type and Minor tick mark type:

   ▲ **None** omits tick marks.

   ▲ **Inside** displays tick marks inside the plot area.

   ▲ **Outside** displays tick marks outside the plot area.

   ▲ **Cross** displays tick marks that cross the axis line.

5. If desired, use options in the Lines area to modify the appearance of the Axis.

6. Click OK.

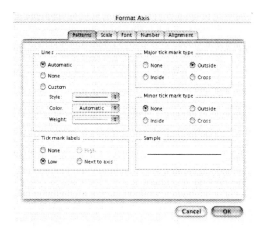

Figure 62 The Patterns tab of the Format Axis dialog.

Figures 63, 64, & 65
The Formatting Palette offers different options depending on what chart element is selected. These examples show the Formatting Palette for a Data Series (left), Axis (bottom-left), and Chart Title (bottom-right).

Figure 66
Use the Change formatting for pop-up menu to select the chart element you want to format.

Category Axis
Category Axis Title
Chart Area
✓ Chart Title
Corners
Floor
Legend
Plot Area
Series Axis
Series Axis Title
Value Axis
Value Axis Major Gridlines
Value Axis Title
Walls
Series "Jan"
Series "Feb"
Series "Mar"

To format chart elements with the Formatting Palette

1. If necessary, choose View > Formatting Palette to display the Formatting Palette.

Then:

2. Select the chart element that you want to format. The appearance of the Formatting Palette changes to offer options for the item you selected (**Figures 63**, **64**, and **65**).

3. Make changes in the Formatting Palette as desired.

Or then:

2. Choose the chart element you want to format from the Change formatting for pop-up menu near the bottom of the Formatting Palette (**Figure 66**).

3. Click the Format button 🖼 beside the pop-up menu to display the Format dialog.

4. Make changes as desired in the Format dialog.

5. Click OK to save your changes.

✔ Tips

■ You can make many—but not all—formatting changes to chart elements using the Formatting Palette.

■ The Format dialog for chart elements is discussed on the previous few pages.

Other Formatting Options

In addition to formatting individual chart elements, you can make other modifications to a chart to change the way it appears. Here are a few additional options you may find handy.

To move a chart element

1. Click the element to select it.

2. Position the mouse pointer on the element, press the mouse button, and drag. As you drag, an outline of the element moves with the mouse pointer (**Figure 67**).

3. Release the mouse button. The element moves (**Figure 68**).

✔ Tip

■ You can use this technique with most chart elements.

To "explode" a pie chart

1. Select the data point for the pie piece you want to move.

2. Drag the pie piece away from the pie (**Figure 69**).

3. Release the mouse button. The piece moves away from the pie (**Figure 70**).

✔ Tip

■ If desired, you can drag more than one piece away from the pie.

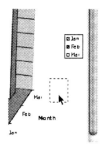 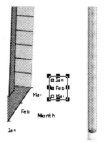

Figure 67 To move a chart element, drag it to its new position.

Figure 68 When you release the mouse button, it moves.

Figure 69 When you move a piece of a pie chart away from the rest of the pie...

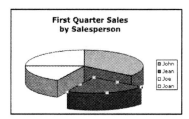

Figure 70 ...you get an "exploded" effect.

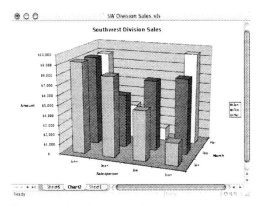

Figure 71 A chart before rotation.

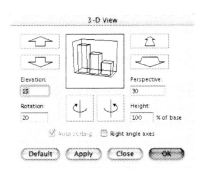

Figure 72 The 3-D View dialog.

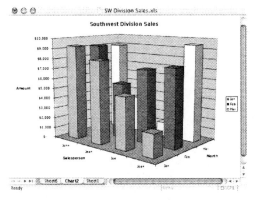

Figure 73 The chart from **Figure 71** after rotation.

To rotate a 3-D chart

1. Activate the chart you want to rotate (**Figure 71**).

2. Choose Chart > 3-D View (**Figure 28**).

3. In the 3-D View dialog (**Figure 72**), click the Elevation, Rotation, and Perspective buttons to change the view of the chart.

4. When you're finished making changes, click OK. The chart rotates (**Figure 73**).

✔ Tips

- You can click the Apply button in the 3-D View dialog (**Figure 72**) to get a first-hand look at the modified chart without closing the dialog. You may have to drag the Format 3-D View dialog out of the way to see your chart.

- You can click the Default button in the 3-D View dialog to return the chart to its default rotation.

- Some changes in the 3-D View dialog may change the size of the chart.

To resize a chart element

1. Click the element to select it.

2. Position the mouse pointer on one of the resizing handles for the element, press the mouse button, and drag. As you drag, the border of the element moves with the mouse pointer (**Figure 74**).

3. Release the mouse button. The element resizes (**Figure 75**).

✔ Tip

■ You can use this technique with most chart elements.

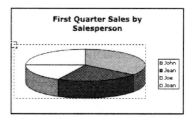

Figure 74 Drag a selection handle...

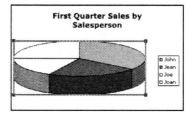

Figure 75 ...to resize almost any chart element.

Printing

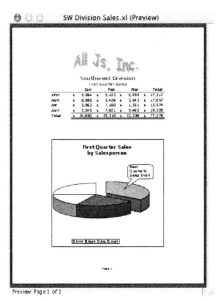

Preview: Page 1 of 1

Figure 1 Print Preview lets you see reports before you commit them to paper.

Printing

In most cases, when you create a worksheet or chart, you'll want to print it. With Microsoft Excel, you can print all or part of a sheet, multiple sheets, or an entire workbook—all at once. Excel gives you control over page size, margins, headers, footers, page breaks, orientation, scaling, page order, and content. Its Print Preview feature (**Figure 1**) shows you what your report will look like when printed, so you can avoid wasteful, time-consuming reprints.

Printing is basically a three-step process:

1. Use the Page Setup dialog to set up your report for printing. You can skip this step if you set the report up the last time you printed it and don't need to change the setup.

2. Use the Print Preview feature to take a look at your report before committing it to paper. You can skip this step if you already know what the report will look like.

3. Use the Print command to send the desired number of copies to the printer for printing.

In this chapter, I explain each of these steps.

✔ Tip

- When you save a document, Excel saves many Page Setup and Print options with it.

Print Center

Mac OS X introduced Print Center, a utility that enables you to identify printers and work with print jobs.

When you configure Mac OS X for printing, you add each of your printers to Print Center's Printer List (**Figure 2**). This list can include printers that are directly connected to your computer or those accessible via network. The printers on this list appear in pop-up menus in the Page Setup (**Figure 5**) and Print (**Figures 30** through **39**) dialogs.

Mac OS X includes *printer driver* software that enables your computer to communicate with printers. If you have a printer that is not recognized by Mac OS X, you will have to install the printer driver that came with the printer or that can be downloaded from the printer manufacturer's Web site.

✔ Tips

■ The options in the Print dialog will vary depending on the printer you choose. It is impossible to show all possibilities in this book. Instead, I provide specific information for two printers: a Hewlett-Packard LaserJet 2100TN PostScript laser printer (connected via Ethernet network) and an Epson Stylus Color 740 inkjet printer (directly connected via USB). The options supported by your printer will be similar to one of these.

■ To learn more about Print Center and the printing options supported by your printer, consult the documentation that came with Mac OS or your printer. Or track down a copy of the Peachpit Press book, *Mac OS X: Visual QuickStart Guide.*

Figure 2 Print Center's Printer List on my computer. The Printer List window on your computer will list your printers.

Figure 3 The Page tab of Excel's Page Setup dialog.

Figure 4
The File menu offers a number of printing-related commands.

Page Setup

The Page Setup dialog (**Figure 3**) lets you set up a document for printing. Setup options are organized under the following tabs:

- **Page** (**Figure 3**) lets you set the orientation, scaling, first page number, and print quality.

- **Margins** (**Figures 7** and **8**) lets you set the page margins, the distance the header and footer should be from the edge of the paper, and the positioning of the document on the paper.

- **Header/Footer** (**Figure 9**) lets you select a standard header and footer or create custom ones.

- **Sheet** (**Figure 15**) lets you specify the print area, print titles, items to print, and page order. If a chart sheet is active when you choose Page Setup, you'll see a Chart tab (**Figure 22**) rather than a Sheet tab. Use it to specify the printed chart size and print quality.

✔ Tip

- You may have noticed that this Page Setup dialog looks very different from the Apple standard. If you want to see the standard Apple Page Setup dialog (**Figure 5**) for your printer, click the Options button in the Excel Page Setup dialog.

To open Excel's Page Setup dialog

Choose File > Page Setup (**Figure 4**).

or

Click the Setup button in the Print Preview toolbar (**Figure 23**).

To set the paper size

1. Click the Options button on any tab in Excel's Page Setup dialog (**Figure 3**).

2. In the Apple Page Setup dialog that appears (**Figure 5**), choose a paper size from the pop-up menu.

3. Click OK to save your settings and dismiss the dialog.

To set page options

1. In Excel's Page Setup dialog, click the Page tab to display its options (**Figure 3**).

2. In the Orientation area, select the desired orientation radio button:

   ▲ **Portrait**, the default option for worksheets, prints vertically down the page.

   ▲ **Landscape**, the default option for chart sheets, prints horizontally across the page.

3. For a worksheet only, in the Scaling area, select the desired scaling radio button:

   ▲ **Adjust to** enables you to specify a percentage of the normal size for printing. Be sure to enter a value in the text box. This option is selected by default with 100 in the text box.

   ▲ **Fit to** instructs Excel to shrink the report so it fits on the number of pages you specify. Be sure to enter values in the two text boxes.

4. If desired, in the First page number text box, enter a value that should be used as the page number on the first page of the report. This enables you to start page numbering at a value other than 1.

5. Choose an option from the Print quality pop-up menu (**Figure 6**). The default value is High.

6. Click OK to save your settings.

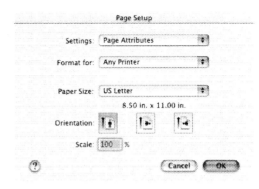

Figure 5 The Apple Page Setup dialog.

Figure 6
The Print quality pop-up menu.

Normal
• High
300 dpi

✔ Tips

■ You can also change the page orientation in the Apple Page Setup dialog (**Figure 5**).

■ Neither scaling option is available for chart sheets. You can change the scaling for a chart sheet on the Chart tab of the Page Setup dialog, which I discuss later in this chapter.

SETTING PAPER SIZE & PAGE OPTIONS

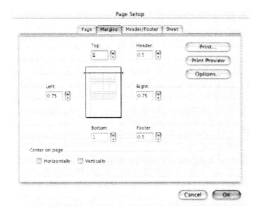

Figure 7 The Margins tab of the Page Setup dialog for a worksheet...

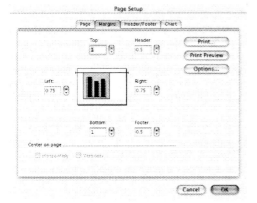

Figure 8 ...and for a chart sheet.

To set margins & centering options

1. In Excel's Page Setup dialog, click the Margins tab to display its options (**Figure 7** or **8**).

2. Enter values in the Top, Left, Right, and Bottom text boxes to set the amount of space between the edge of the paper and the report content.

3. Enter values in the Header and Footer text boxes to set the amount of space between the edge of the paper and the header and footer content.

4. For a worksheet only, turn on the desired Center on page check boxes:

   ▲ **Horizontally** centers the report content between the left and right margins.

   ▲ **Vertically** centers the report content between the top and bottom margins.

5. Click OK to save your settings.

✔ Tips

■ As you make changes in this window, the preview area changes accordingly. This helps you get an idea of what the document will look like when previewed or printed.

■ You can also set margins in the Print Preview window. I tell you how later in this chapter.

■ Do not set margins to smaller values than the Header and Footer values or Excel will print your report over the header or footer.

■ Some printers cannot print close to the edge of the paper. If part of your report is cut off when printed, increase the margin, header, and footer values.

To add built-in headers & footers

1. In Excel's Page Setup dialog, click the Header/Footer tab to display its options (**Figure 9**).

2. Choose options from the Header and Footer pop-up menus (**Figure 10**).

   The option(s) you selected appear in the sample area(s) in the dialog (**Figure 11**).

3. Click OK to save your settings.

✔ Tips

- The pop-up menu for Footer is identical to the one for Header.

- Excel gets your name and company name from entries you made when you installed Excel. You can change the name by choosing Preferences from the Tools menu, entering a new User name in the General tab, and clicking OK. You cannot change the company name without reinstalling Excel.

- To change the formatting of text in the header or footer, you need to use the Custom Header or Custom Footer button in the Header/Footer tab of the Page Setup dialog. I tell you about that next.

To add custom headers & footers

1. In Excel's Page Setup dialog, click the Header/Footer tab to display its options (**Figure 9**).

2. To add a header, click the Custom Header button to display the Header dialog (**Figure 12**).

3. Enter the text or codes that you want to appear in the header in the Left section, Center section, and Right section text boxes. You can use the buttons in **Table 1** to format selected text or insert codes for dynamic information. **Figure 13** shows an example.

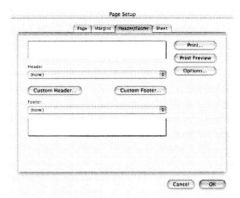

Figure 9 The Header/Footer tab of the Page Setup dialog.

Figure 10 The Header and Footer pop-up menus offer a number of predefined headers and footers.

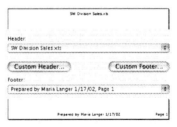

Figure 11 The header and footer you select appear in the sample areas in the dialog.

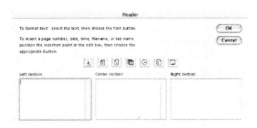

Figure 12 The Header dialog.

Table 1

Buttons for Inserting Dynamic Information into Headers or Footers	
BUTTON	**USE**
	Use the Font button to format selected text. I tell you about the Font dialog in **Chapter 6**.
	Use the Page Number button to insert the *&[Page]* code. This inserts the page number.
	Use the Total Pages button to insert the *&[Pages]* code. This inserts the total pages number.
	Use the Date button to insert the *&[Date]* code. This inserts the print date.
	Use the Time button to insert the *&[Time]* code. This inserts the print time.
	Use the Filename button to insert the *&[File]* code. This inserts the workbook name.
	Use the Sheet Name button to insert the *&[Tab]* code. This inserts the sheet name.

Figure 13 An example of a custom header entered into the Header dialog.

Figure 14 Here's the header from **Figure 13** in the Page Setup dialog.

4. Click OK to save your settings.

The settings appear in the Page Setup dialog (**Figure 14**).

5. To add a footer, click the Custom Footer button. This displays the Footer dialog, which looks and works just like the Header dialog.

6. Repeat steps 3 and 4 for the footer.

7. Click OK in the Page Setup dialog to save your settings.

✔ Tips

- In step 3, to enter an ampersand (&) character in a header or footer, type *&&* where you want it to appear.

- To specify the starting page number to be printed in the header or footer, enter a value in the First page number text box of the Page tab of the Page Setup dialog (**Figure 3**).

- Dynamic information is information that changes automatically. For example the page number changes automatically for each page and the print date changes automatically each day you print the file. Using the buttons or codes for dynamic information (**Table 1**) ensures header and footer contents are accurate.

To remove headers & footers

1. In Excel's Page Setup dialog, click the Header/Footer tab to display its options (**Figure 9**).

2. Choose (none) from the Header and Footer pop-up menus (**Figure 10**).

The header and footer disappear from the dialog.

3. Click OK to save your settings.

To set sheet options

1. In Excel's Page Setup dialog, click the Sheet tab to display its options (**Figure 15**).
2. To print less than the entire worksheet, enter a range in the Print area text box (**Figure 16**).
3. To display column or row titles on all pages of a lengthy report, enter row or column (or both) ranges in the Rows to repeat at top or Columns to repeat at left text boxes (**Figure 16**). **Figures 17** through **19** show how this affects the printout.
4. Turn on check boxes in the center of the dialog to set additional print options as desired:
   - ▲ **Gridlines** prints the worksheet gridlines.
   - ▲ **Black and white** prints the worksheet in black and white. This can save time if you print on a color printer.
   - ▲ **Draft quality** reduces printing time by omitting gridlines and most graphics.
   - ▲ **Row and column headings** prints the column letters and row numbers with the worksheet.
5. To print worksheet comments, choose an option other than (None) from the Comments pop-up menu (**Figure 20**).
6. Select a Page order option for a long or wide worksheet:
   - ▲ **Down, then over** prints all rows of the first few columns first, then prints rows from subsequent columns.
   - ▲ **Over, then down** prints all columns of the first bunch of rows first, then prints columns from subsequent rows.
7. Click OK to save your settings.

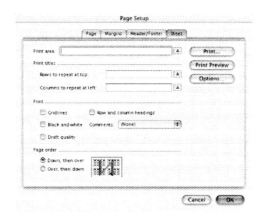

Figure 15 The Sheet tab of the Page Setup dialog.

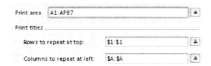

Figure 16 This example shows the proper way to enter ranges for the Print area and Print titles.

Payments Table

	5.00%	5.25%	5.50%	5.75%	6.00%	6.25%
10,000	53.68	55.22	56.78	58.36	59.96	61.57
15,000	80.52	82.83	85.17	87.54	89.93	92.36
20,000	107.36	110.44	113.56	116.71	119.91	123.14
25,000	134.21	138.05	141.95	145.89	149.89	153.93
30,000	161.05	165.66	170.34	175.07	179.87	184.72
35,000	187.89	193.27	198.73	204.25	209.84	215.50

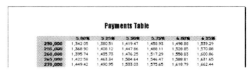

Figure 17 Here's the first page of a lengthy report.

Payments Table

250,000	1,342.05	1,380.51	1,419.47	1,458.93	1,498.88	1,539.29
255,000	1,368.90	1,408.12	1,447.86	1,488.11	1,528.85	1,570.08
260,000	1,395.74	1,435.73	1,476.25	1,517.29	1,558.83	1,600.86
265,000	1,422.58	1,463.34	1,504.64	1,546.47	1,588.81	1,631.65
270,000	1,449.42	1,490.95	1,533.03	1,575.65	1,618.79	1,662.44

Figure 18 Without page titles, the headings don't appear on subsequent pages.

Payments Table

	5.00%	5.25%	5.50%	5.75%	6.00%	6.25%
250,000	1,342.05	1,380.51	1,419.47	1,458.93	1,498.88	1,539.29
255,000	1,368.90	1,408.12	1,447.86	1,488.11	1,528.85	1,570.08
260,000	1,395.74	1,435.73	1,476.25	1,517.29	1,558.83	1,600.86
265,000	1,422.58	1,463.34	1,504.64	1,546.47	1,588.81	1,631.65
270,000	1,449.42	1,490.95	1,533.03	1,575.65	1,618.79	1,662.44

Figure 19 But with page titles set as they are in **Figure 16**, headings appear on every page.

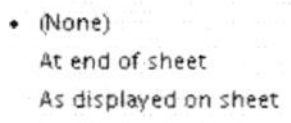

- (None)
  At end of sheet
  As displayed on sheet

Figure 20
The Comments
pop-up menu.

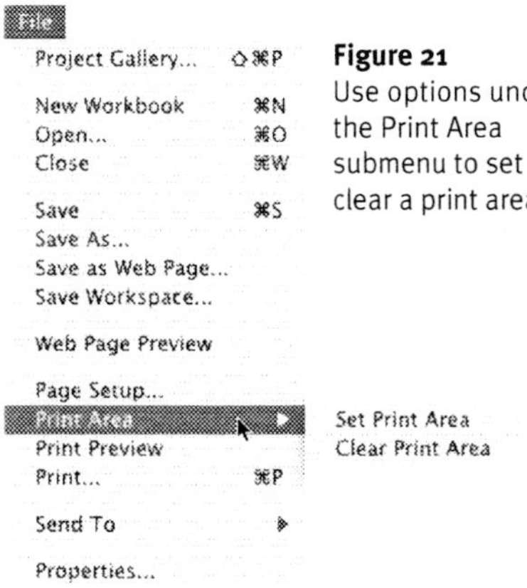

File

Project Gallery...   ⇧⌘P
New Workbook   ⌘N
Open...   ⌘O
Close   ⌘W
Save   ⌘S
Save As...
Save as Web Page...
Save Workspace...
Web Page Preview
Page Setup...
Print Area   ▶   Set Print Area
Print Preview   Clear Print Area
Print...   ⌘P
Send To   ▶
Properties...

Figure 21
Use options under
the Print Area
submenu to set or
clear a print area.

✔ Tips

- In steps 2 and 3, you can enter each range manually by typing it into the text box or have Excel enter it automatically for you by clicking in the text box, then selecting the range in the worksheet window.

- You can use the Collapse Dialog button ▲ to collapse the dialog so you can see the worksheet behind it. You can then use the Expand Dialog button ▼ to restore the dialog so you can finish working with it.

- You can also specify the range of cells to print by selecting the range in the worksheet, then choosing File > Print Area > Set Print Area (**Figure 21**). The Clear Print Area command clears any previously set print area.

- I tell you about worksheet comments in **Chapter 11**.

SETTING SHEET OPTIONS

To set chart options

1. In Excel's Page Setup dialog, click the Chart tab to display its options (**Figure 22**).

2. Select one of the Printed chart size radio buttons:

    ▲ **Use full page** expands the chart so it fills the page. The size of chart objects may change, relative to each other.

    ▲ **Scale to fit page** expands the chart proportionally until it fills the space between one set of opposite margins.

    ▲ **Custom** uses the custom scale set in the Apple Page Setup dialog (**Figure 5**).

3. To print the chart in black and white with patterns replacing colors, turn on the Print in black and white check box.

4. Click OK to save your settings.

✔ Tip

■ For the largest possible image, make sure Landscape is the selected orientation in the Page tab of the Page Setup dialog (**Figure 3**). I tell you about orientation earlier in this chapter.

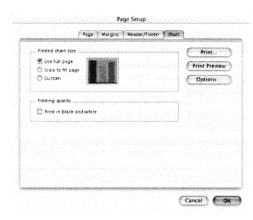

Figure 22 The Chart tab of the Page Setup dialog.

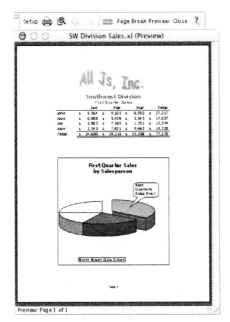

Figure 23 A worksheet with embedded chart in Print Preview.

Print Preview

Excel's Print Preview feature lets you see what a report will look like before you print it. If a report doesn't look perfect, you can use Setup, Margins, and Page Break Preview buttons right inside the Print Preview dialog to make adjustments. When you're ready to print, click the Print button.

To preview a report

Choose File > Print Preview (**Figure 4**).

or

Click the Print Preview button 🔍 on the Standard toolbar.

or

Click the Print Preview button in the Page Setup or Print dialog.

A preview of the current sheet appears (**Figure 23**). It reflects all Page Setup dialog settings. The Print Preview toolbar appears above the window.

✔ Tip

- You can use buttons on the Print Preview toolbar to work with the document:
  - ▲ To view the other pages of the report, click the Next ⇨ or Prev ⇦ button.
  - ▲ To zoom in to see report detail, click the Zoom button 🔍. (You can also click the mouse pointer, which looks like a magnifying glass, on the area you want to magnify.)
  - ▲ To open the Print dialog and print, click the Print button 🖨. I tell you about the Print dialog later in this chapter.
  - ▲ To change Page Setup dialog options, click the Setup button.
  - ▲ To close the Print Preview dialog, click the Close button.

To change margin options & column widths

1. On the Print Preview toolbar, click the Margins button . Handles for margins, header and footer locations, and column widths appear around the report preview (**Figure 24**).

2. Position the mouse pointer over the handle or guideline for the margin, header, footer, or column you want to change. The mouse pointer turns into a line with two arrows coming out of it (**Figure 25**).

3. Press the mouse button and drag to make the change. A measurement for your change appears in the status bar as you drag.

4. Release the mouse button to complete the change. The report reformats automatically.

✔ Tips

■ The changes you make by dragging handles in the Print Preview dialog will be reflected in the appropriate text boxes of the Page Setup dialog.

■ I tell how to change margins and header and footer locations with the Page Setup dialog earlier in this chapter. I tell you how to change column widths in the worksheet window or with the Column Width dialog in **Chapter 6**.

Figure 24 When you click the Margins button, handles for margins, header, footer, and columns appear.

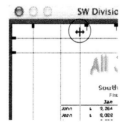

Figure 25
Position the mouse pointer on a handle and drag to change the measurement.

Figure 26
The View menu.

To set page breaks

1. In normal view, choose View > Page Break Preview (**Figure 26**).

or

In the Print Preview window (**Figure 23**), click the Page Break Preview button.

The sheet appears in Page Break Preview view (**Figure 27**).

2. Position the mouse pointer over one of the dashed, blue page break lines. The mouse pointer turns into a box with triangles on its sides.

3. Press the mouse button and drag to make the change. A dark line moves with the mouse pointer (**Figure 28**).

4. Release the mouse button. The page break shifts to the new position and turns into a solid blue line. Any automatic page break to its right or below it also shifts (**Figure 29**).

5. To return to Normal view, choose View > Normal (**Figure 26**).

or

To return to Print Preview, choose File > Print Preview (**Figure 4**) or click the Print Preview button on the Standard toolbar.

✔ Tips

■ The first time you use the Page Break Preview feature, a dialog with instructions appears (**Figure 27**). You must click OK to dismiss the dialog before you can drag page breaks. Turn on the check box within the dialog if you don't want to see it again.

■ You may need to scroll within the window to see all the page breaks for a very large worksheet.

■ You can use this feature to change both vertical and horizontal page breaks.

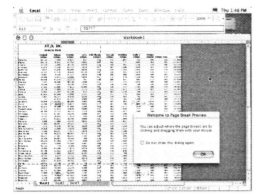

Figure 27 Page Break Preview view, with its instruction dialog.

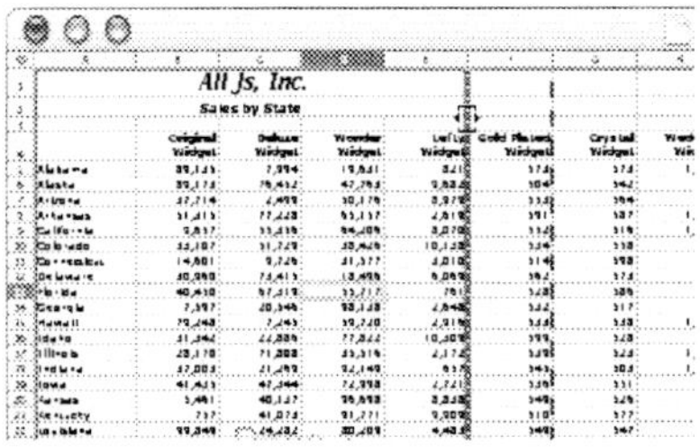

Figure 28 Drag a page break to change it.

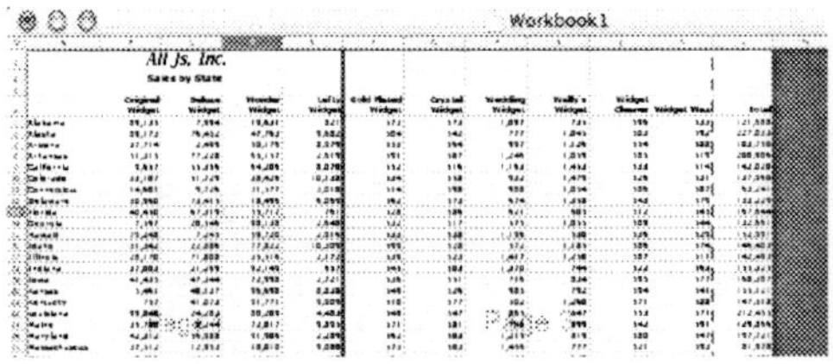

Figure 29 When you move one page break, the ones beyond it also move. In this example, a new page break was inserted.

SETTING PAGE BREAKS

Printing

The Print dialog enables you to set print options and send a document to the printer.

Print dialog options are broken down into a number of settings panes, which vary depending on the type of printer. For example, here are the panes available for my two printers:

◆ **Copies & Pages** (**Figure 30**) enables you to set the number of document copies and the range of document pages to print.

◆ **Layout** (**Figure 31**) enables you to specify the number of pages per sheet of paper, a layout direction, and border.

◆ **Output Options** (**Figure 32**) enables you to save a document as a PDF or PostScript file.

◆ **Paper Feed** (**Figure 33**) enables you to select paper feed methods or trays.

◆ **Error Handling** (**Figure 34**) enables you to specify how PostScript and other errors should be handled.

◆ **Printer Features** (**Figure 35**) enables you to set options for features specific to your printer.

◆ **Print Settings** (**Figure 36**) and **Advanced Settings** (**Figure 37**) enable you to set options for the type of paper, ink cartridge, print quality, and other print options.

◆ **Color Management** (**Figure 38**) enables you to set color options.

◆ **Summary** (**Figure 39**) summarizes all Print dialog settings.

After setting options, click the Print button to send the document to the selected printer.

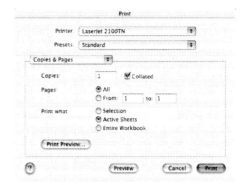

Figure 30 The Copies & Pages pane of the Print dialog.

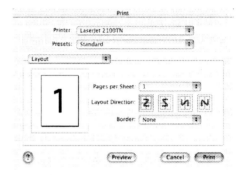

Figure 31 The Layout pane of the Print dialog.

Figure 32 The Output Options pane of the Print dialog.

Figure 33 The Paper Feed pane of the Print dialog. This pane is specific to the LaserJet 2100TN, which has several paper feed trays.

Figure 34 The Error Handling pane of the Print dialog. This pane appears for PostScript printers; the bottom half is specific to a LaserJet 2100TN.

Figure 37 ...and this Advanced Settings pane for the same printer offers some more advanced options.

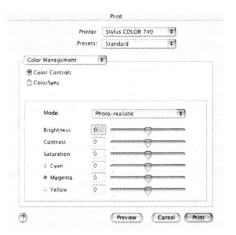

Figure 35 The Printer Features pane of the Print dialog. This tab only appears for some printers—in this example, the LaserJet 2100TN.

Figure 38 The Color Management pane of the Print dialog offers color options for color printers.

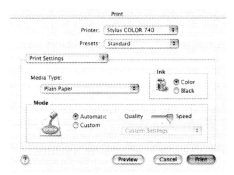

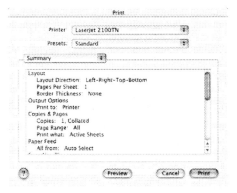

Figure 36 This Print Settings pane for a Stylus Color 740 offers some basic paper, ink, and mode options, ...

Figure 39 The Summary pane of the Print dialog summarizes all Print dialog settings.

✔ Tips

- Remember, Print dialog panes and their options vary greatly depending on the selected printer.

- This part of the chapter explains how to set options in the most commonly used Print dialog pane, Copies & Pages (**Figure 30**). It also explains how to use the Output Options pane (**Figure 32**) to save a document as a PDF or PostScript file.

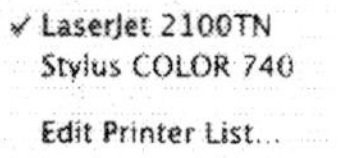

To open the Print dialog

Choose File > Print (**Figure 4**) or press ⌃ ⌘ P.

or

Click the Print button 🖶 on the Print Preview toolbar (**Figure 23**).

The Copies & Pages pane of the Print dialog appears (**Figure 30**).

✔ Tip

- Clicking the Print button 🖶 on the Standard or Print Preview toolbar sends the document directly to the printer, without opening the Print dialog.

To choose a destination printer

In the Print dialog (**Figure 30**), choose the printer you want to print on from the Printer pop-up menu (**Figure 40**).

✔ Tip

- Choosing Edit Printer List from the Printer pop-up menu (**Figure 40**) displays Print Center's Printer List (**Figure 2**) so you can add or remove printers.

✔ LaserJet 2100TN
Stylus COLOR 740

Edit Printer List…

Figure 40 The Printer pop-up menu lists all printers in Print Center's Printer List.

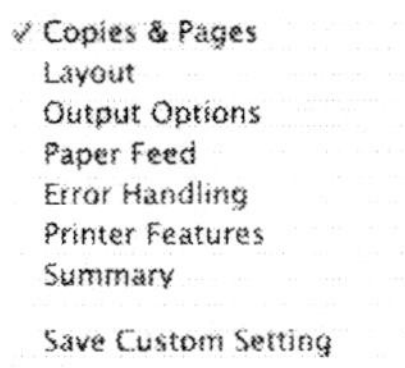

Figure 41
Use this pop-up menu to switch from one type of option to another. This is how the menu looks when a PostScript printer is selected.

To specify the number of copies & pages to print

1. In the Print dialog, if necessary, choose Copies & Pages from the third pop-up menu (**Figure 41**) to display Copies & Pages options (**Figure 30**).

2. Enter the number of copies you want to print in the Copies text box.

3. If you want to print more than one copy and want the copies collated, turn on the Collated check box.

4. Select one of the Pages options:

   ▲ **All** sets the page range to all pages.

   ▲ **From/to** enables you to enter the beginning and ending page numbers for a page range.

5. Select one of the Print what options:

   ▲ **Selection** prints only selected cells, charts, or other objects.

   ▲ **Active Sheets** prints only the sheets with selected sheet tabs. (Normally, only one sheet is selected; I tell you how to select multiple sheets in **Chapter 1**.)

   ▲ **Entire Workbook** prints all of the sheets in the workbook.

SETTING COPIES & PAGE OPTIONS

To set other Print dialog options

1. In the Print dialog, choose the category of option you want to set from the third pop-up menu (**Figure 41**). The pane for the option you selected appears (**Figures 30** through **39**).

2. Set options as desired.

3. Repeat steps 1 and 2 for each category of options you want to set.

✔ Tips

■ These other options are specific to your printer, not to Microsoft Excel.

■ I tell you about Output Options on the next page.

To save Print options

In the Print dialog , choose Save Custom Setting from the third pop-up menu (**Figure 41**).

After a moment, the settings are saved as Custom.

To use Custom Print options

In the Print dialog, choose Custom from the Presets pop-up menu (**Figure 42**).

All Print dialog settings are restored to the last settings you saved.

To print

Click the Print button in the Print dialog (**Figures 30** through **39**).

The document is sent to the printer.

✔ Tip

■ To monitor a document's print status, open Print Center and double-click the name of the printer in the Printer List window (**Figure 2**).

✔ Standard
　Custom

Figure 42 The Presets pop-up menu after saving Print dialog settings.

Figure 43 When you turn on the Save as File check box, you can choose a file format and click a Save button to save the file.

Figure 44 The Format pop-up menu.

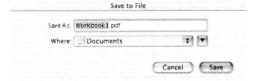

Figure 45 Use a standard Save As dialog to enter a name and specify a disk location for the file.

Saving a Document as a PDF or PostScript File

In Excel X, you can use the Print dialog to save a document as a PDF or PostScript file. PDF (which stands for *Portable Document Format*) files can be opened and read with the Preview application that comes with Mac OS X or with Adobe Acrobat Reader on virtually any computer or operating system. PostScript files contains complex printing instructions written in the PostScript language and are often used to output documents to high-resolution printing devices such as imagesetters.

✔ Tip

- PDF files offer a great way to share Excel worksheets and charts with computer users who don't have Excel.

To save a document as a PDF or PostScript file

1. In the Print dialog, choose Output Options from the third pop-up menu (**Figure 41**) to display the Output Options pane (**Figure 32**).

2. Turn on the Save as File check box (**Figure 43**).

3. Choose an option from the Format pop-up menu (**Figure 44**).

4. Click Save.

5. Use the Save to File dialog that appears (**Figure 45**) to enter a name and specify a disk location for the file.

6. Click Save to save the file to disk.

✔ Tip

- The PostScript option is only available on the Format pop-up menu (**Figure 44**) if a PostScript printer is chosen from the Printer pop-up menu (**Figure 40**).

Working with Lists

List Basics

Microsoft Excel's list or database features and functions help make it a flexible tool for creating, maintaining, and reporting data. With Excel, you can use a form to enter data into a list, filter information, sort records, and automatically generate subtotals. You can use Excel's calculating, formatting, charting, and printing features on your list, too.

In Excel, a *list* is any group of worksheet data with unique labels in the first row. You don't need to do anything special to identify a list—Excel is smart enough to know one when it sees it. **Figure 1**, for example, shows the first few rows of a list that Excel can recognize as a database.

A list is organized into fields and records. A *field* is a category of information. In **Figure 1**, *Product Code*, *Department*, and *Cost* are the first three fields. A *record* is a collection of fields for one thing. In **Figure 1**, *row 2* shows the record for the item with product code *AXN1812P* and *row 3* shows the record for *QRI817L*.

✔ Tips

- Fields are always in columns while records are always in rows.

- In Excel, you can use the words *list* and *database* interchangeably—they refer to basically the same thing.

Inventory.xls

	Product Code	Department	Cost	Sale Price	Reorder Point	Qty on Hand	Time to Order?	Resale Value	Markup
2	AXN1812P	Men's Clothes	14.63	61.99	120	362		22,440	424%
3	QRI817L	Bed & Bath	10.86	18.99	50	16	Reorder Now!	304	175%
4	BJB526U	Women's Clothes	13.69	33.99	100	257		8,735	248%
5	OZW228W	Automotive	12.01	59.99	40	189		11,338	500%
6	ZET21W	Pets	7.85	9.99	60	467		4,665	127%
7	WRT188W	Computers	7.72	31.99	140	288		9,213	414%
8	VNE134Y	Electronics	5.81	11.99	180	34	Reorder Now!	408	206%

Figure 1 The first few rows of a worksheet that Excel can automatically recognize as a list.

To create a list

1. In a worksheet window, enter unique column titles for each of the fields in your list (**Figure 2**). These will be the field names.

2. Beginning with the row immediately below the one containing the column titles, enter the data for each record (**Figure 3**). Be sure to put the proper information in each column.

✔ Tips

- Use only one cell for each column title. If the field name is too long to fit in the cell, use the Wrap text (**Figure 4**) or Shrink to fit alignment option for the cell. I tell you about alignment options in **Chapter 6**.

- Do not skip rows when entering information. A blank row indicates the end of the database above it.

- You can format your list any way you like (**Figure 4**). Formatting does not affect the way Excel works with the list data.

- Your list can include formulas. Excel treats the results of the formulas like any other field.

- As you create a list, a dialog like the one in **Figure 5** may appear. Clicking Yes enables you to work on the list with the List Manager, which I cover later in this chapter.

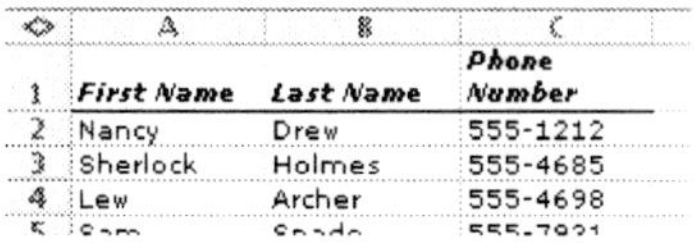

To enter data with AutoComplete

1. Enter list data as instructed above. As you type characters into a cell, Excel displays an AutoComplete pop-up menu that shows all entries that begin with the characters you typed (**Figure 6**).

2. To choose one of the entries on the Auto-Complete menu, click it (**Figure 7**) or use the arrow keys to highlight it and press Return.

   or

   To enter something different, continue typing to complete the entry.

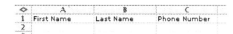

Figure 2 Enter unique field names in the first row of the list.

Figure 3 Enter the data, one record per row.

Figure 4 Formatting a list doesn't affect the way Excel works with data.

Figure 5 When Excel realizes that you're working with a list, it asks if you want to use the list manager.

Figure 6 When the first characters you type match an existing entry in the column, Excel displays the AutoComplete pop-up menu.

Figure 7 You can then use your mouse to click the existing entry that you want to enter in the cell.

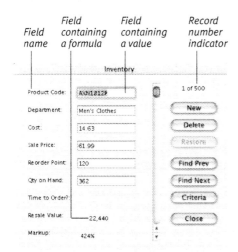

Field name

Field containing a formula

Field containing a value

Record number indicator

Figure 8 The data form offers another way to enter, edit, delete, and find records.

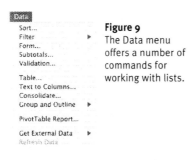

Figure 9 The Data menu offers a number of commands for working with lists.

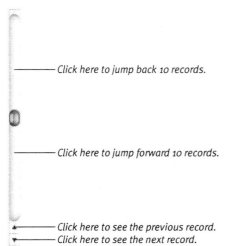

———— Click here to jump back 10 records.

———— Click here to jump forward 10 records.

———— Click here to see the previous record.
———— Click here to see the next record.

Figure 10 Use the scroll bar in the data form to browse records.

Using the Data Form

Excel's data form feature creates a dialog with custom text boxes for fields (**Figure 8**). You can use this dialog to enter, edit, delete, and find records in a database.

To open the data form

1. Select any cell in the list.

2. Choose Data > Form (**Figure 9**).

To browse records

Use the scroll bar (**Figure 10**) as follows:

◆ To see the next record, click the down arrow on the scroll bar.

◆ To see the previous record, click the up arrow on the scroll bar.

◆ To jump ahead 10 records, click the scroll bar beneath the scroll box.

◆ To jump back 10 records, click the scroll bar above the scroll box.

To enter, edit, and delete data

To create a new record, click the New button and enter the information into the empty text boxes for each field.

or

To edit a record, locate the record you want to edit and make changes in the appropriate text boxes.

or

To delete a record, locate the record you want to delete and click the Delete button.

✔ Tips

■ Excel records your changes when you move to another record or click the Close button to close the form.

■ If a field contains a formula, Excel carries the formula forward from the previous record and performs the calculation.

To find records

1. In the data form, click the Criteria button. A criteria form appears (**Figure 11**).

2. Enter search criteria in the field(s) in which you expect to find a match (**Figure 12**).

3. Click the Find Next button to move forward through the list for records that match the criteria.

   or

   Click the Find Prev button to move backward through the list for records that match the criteria.

   Excel beeps when it reaches the end or beginning of the matches.

✔ Tips

- You can enter criteria in any combination of fields. If you enter criteria into multiple fields, Excel looks for records that match all criteria.

- The more fields you enter data into, the more specific you make the search and the fewer matches you'll find.

- You can use comparison operators (**Table 1**) and wildcard characters (**Table 2**) in conjunction with criteria. For example, *>100* finds records with values greater than 100 in the field in which the criteria is entered.

- You can also use Excel's AutoFilter feature to quickly locate and display all records that match search criteria. I tell you how later in this chapter.

Figure 11 The data form turns into a criteria form when you click the Criteria button.

Department: Computers

Figure 12 Enter the search criteria in the field in which you expect to find a match.

Table 1

Comparison Operators	
OPERATOR	**MEANING**
=	Equal To
<>	Not Equal To
>	Greater Than
>=	Greater Than or Equal To
<	Less Than
<=	Less Than or Equal To

Table 2

Wildcard Characters	
CHARACTER	**MEANING**
?	Any single character
*	Any group of characters

The List Manager

Excel's List Manager (**Figure 13**) offers a number of features that make it easier to work with lists.

- ◆ A *list frame* surrounds the list so you can see exactly what is included in the list.

- ◆ A new record row appears at the bottom of the list, so it's easy to add more data and carry formulas forward to new records.

- ◆ Column headings are kept separate from list contents, so they can never be accidentally sorted into the list's data.

- ◆ Column headings include a Sort and Filter menu that you can use to rearrange or locate records based on column contents.

- ◆ The List toolbar offers buttons and menus specifically for working with lists.

There are two ways you can use the List Manager with a list:

- ◆ Create a list from scratch with the List Wizard.

- ◆ Convert an existing worksheet list to a list object.

✔ Tips

- ■ A list frame only appears around list objects in worksheets when the List Manager is active (**Figure 13**). When the List Manager is not active, a blue border appears around the list instead.

- ■ A worksheet that is dedicated to a single list which is maintained by the List Manager is called a *list sheet*.

New record row | List toolbar | List frame | Column headings | Sort and Filter button

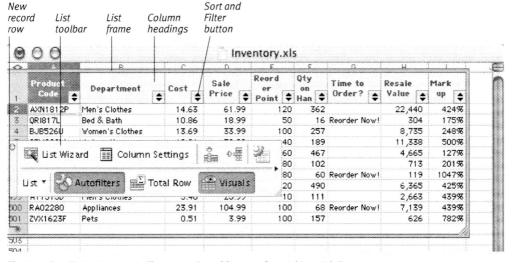

Figure 13 Excel's List Manager offers a number of features for working with lists.

To create a list with the List Wizard

1. Choose File > Project Gallery or press [Shift][⌃][⌘][P] to open the Project Gallery dialog (**Figure 14**).

2. Select Blank Documents from the Category list and the List Wizard icon from the Catalog list. Then click OK.

3. The List Wizard – Step 1 of 3 dialog appears (**Figure 15**). Set options as follows to create a brand new list:

   ▲ Select the None option under "Where is the data for your list?"

   ▲ Select the New worksheet option under "Where do you want to put this list?"

   Click Next.

4. The List Wizard Step – 2 of 3 dialog appears (**Figure 16**). In the Column name text box, enter the name for the first column (or field) you want to include in your list. Choose an option from the Data type pop-up menu (**Figure 17**). Then click the Add button. Repeat this process for each column you want to include in the database. **Figure 18** shows an example of what the column list might look like with columns added. Click Next.

5. The List Wizard Step – 3 of 3 dialog appears next (**Figure 19**). Set options as desired:

   ▲ **List name** is the name of the list.

   ▲ **Autoformat list after editing** uses the AutoFormat feature to format the list. If you enable this option, click the AutoFormat button to display the AutoFormat dialog (**Figure 20**) and set options. (I tell you about Excel's Auto-Format feature in **Chapter 6**.)

   ▲ **Repeat column headers on each printed page** automatically sets up column headings as titles that will print on each page. (I tell you about setting print titles in **Chapter 9**.)

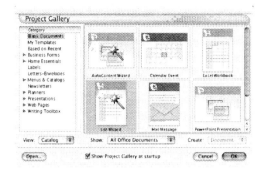

Figure 14 You can create a new document with the List Wizard from within the Project Gallery dialog.

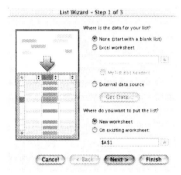

Figure 15 The first step of the List Wizard asks you where the data is and where it should go.

Figure 16 Next, the List Wizard prompts you to enter column headings for the list's fields.

Figure 17 When creating columns, you can specify the type of data each column should contain.

Figure 18
Here's what a list of columns might look like.

Figure 19
The third step of the List Wizard offers options for naming and formatting the list.

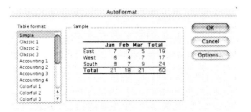

Figure 20 You can set formatting options with the AutoFormat dialog.

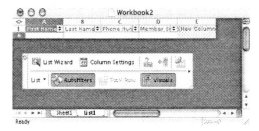

Figure 21 The List Wizard creates a list sheet with List Manager features built in.

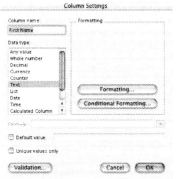

Figure 22
You can specify additional formatting and content options for any column in the list.

▲ **Show totals row** adds a totals row to the bottom of the list and automatically calculates a sum for each column containing number values.

▲ **Show list visuals** lets you specify whether Excel should display visual elements such as the Sort and Filter menu in column headings. The options are Off (don't show elements), On (show elements), or Auto (show elements when appropriate).

6. Click Finish. Excel creates a list sheet to your specifications, all ready to accept data entry (**Figure 21**).

✔ Tips

■ In step 4, if you choose Calculated Column from the Data Type pop-up menu, you can use the Column Settings dialog (**Figure 22**) to enter a formula for the column. Clicking the Settings button in step 4 also displays this dialog for the currently selected field, enabling you to specify formatting and validation options for the field.

■ Another way to start the List Wizard is to choose Insert > List (**Figure 23**). This makes it easy to insert a list in the active worksheet.

To convert a worksheet list to a list object with the List Wizard

1. Click to select any cell in the list.

2. Choose Insert > List (**Figure 23**).

3. The List Wizard – Step 1 of 3 dialog appears. As shown in **Figure 24**, it should already have options set that recognize the list, but if it doesn't, set options as follows:

   ▲ Select the Excel worksheet radio button beneath "Where is the data for your list?" Then, if necessary, enter the range of cells containing the list and specify whether the list has column headings (headers).

   ▲ Select the On existing worksheet radio button beneath "Where do you want to put this list?" Then select the first cell of the database's range to specify where the list will appear.

4. Follow steps 4 through 6 on the previous two pages to fine-tune the list using List Wizard options.

   or

   Click Finish.

   The existing list is converted into a list object in the worksheet, with a list frame around it and other List Manager features visible (**Figure 13**).

✔ Tip

■ You can also convert a list into a list object by clicking Yes in the dialog that may appear when you are working with a list object (**Figure 5**).

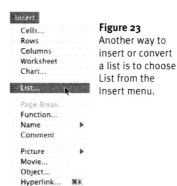

Figure 23
Another way to insert or convert a list is to choose List from the Insert menu.

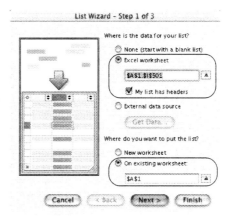

Figure 24 If a list is selected when you open the List Wizard dialog, settings for that list should automatically appear.

Figure 25 The new record row is marked with an asterisk (*).

	ATTSTSD	Men's Clothes	5.46	25.99	10	11
300	RA02280	Appliances	23.91	104.99	100	6
501	ZVX1623F	Pets	0.51	3.99	100	15

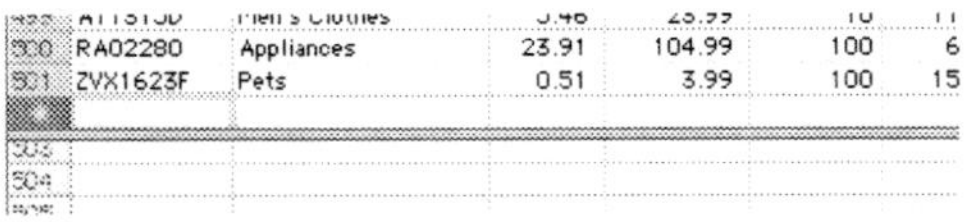

Figure 26 To add a record, click in the first cell of the row to activate it.

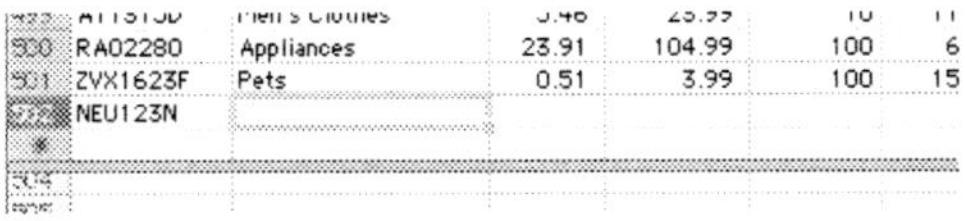

	ATTSTSD	Men's Clothes	5.46	25.99	10	11
300	RA02280	Appliances	23.91	104.99	100	6
501	ZVX1623F	Pets	0.51	3.99	100	15
	NEU123N					

Figure 27 A new row appears beneath it when you begin to enter data.

To add new records with the List Manager

1. If necessary, click anywhere in the list to activate the List Manager.

2. Scroll down to the bottom of the list. The row after the last one containing data should display an asterisk (*) in its row heading (**Figure 25**). This is the new record row.

3. Click in the first cell of the new record row (**Figure 26**).

4. Enter the record's data in the row just as you'd enter data into any other worksheet cells or list.

✔ Tips

- In step 4, when you enter data into the first cell of the record's row, the list expands to add a new row. This new row is marked with an asterisk (**Figure 27**) and is the new record row.

- You can delete a record by deleting its row.

AutoFilter

The AutoFilter feature puts Sort and Filter pop-up menus in the list headers (**Figures 28** and **29**). You can use these menus to choose criteria in the column and display only those records that match the criteria.

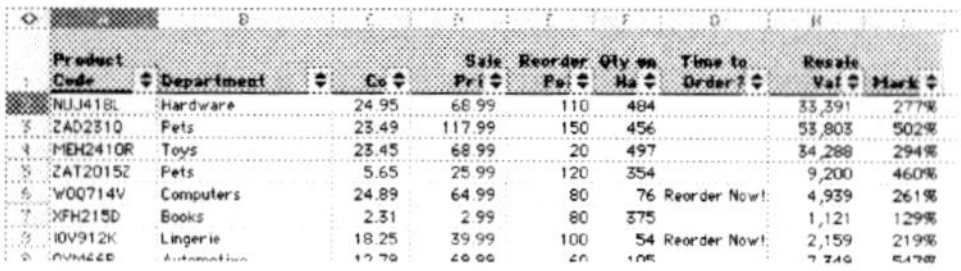

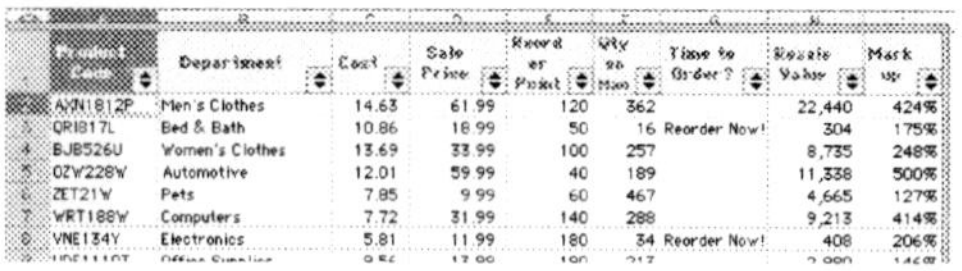

To display Sort and Filter menus in worksheet lists

1. Select any cell in the list.

2. Choose Data > Filter > AutoFilter (**Figure 30**). Excel scans the data and creates pop-up menus for each field (**Figure 28**).

To display Sort and Filter menus in List Manager lists

1. If necessary, scroll to the top of the list and select any cell in the list to activate the List Manager.

2. Sort and Filter buttons should appear for each header in the list. If they do not, click the Autofilters button on the List toolbar to display them (**Figure 25**).

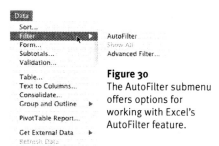

Figures 28 & 29 The AutoFilter feature works with pop-up menus on each column header. This feature is available for worksheet lists (above) or List Manager lists (below).

Figure 30
The AutoFilter submenu offers options for working with Excel's AutoFilter feature.

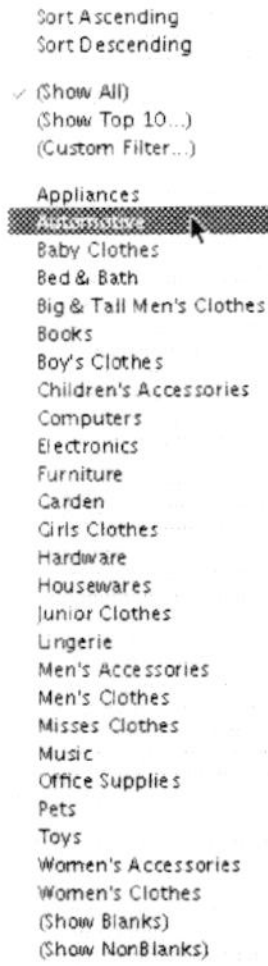

FINDING RECORDS WITH AUTOFILTER

Sort Ascending
Sort Descending

✓ (Show All)
(Show Top 10...)
(Custom Filter...)

Appliances
Automotive
Baby Clothes
Bed & Bath
Big & Tall Men's Clothes
Books
Boy's Clothes
Children's Accessories
Computers
Electronics
Furniture
Garden
Girls Clothes
Hardware
Housewares
Junior Clothes
Lingerie
Men's Accessories
Men's Clothes
Misses Clothes
Music
Office Supplies
Pets
Toys
Women's Accessories
Women's Clothes
(Show Blanks)
(Show NonBlanks)

Figure 31
Choose search criteria from the Sort and Filter pop-up menu. This menu is for the Department column.

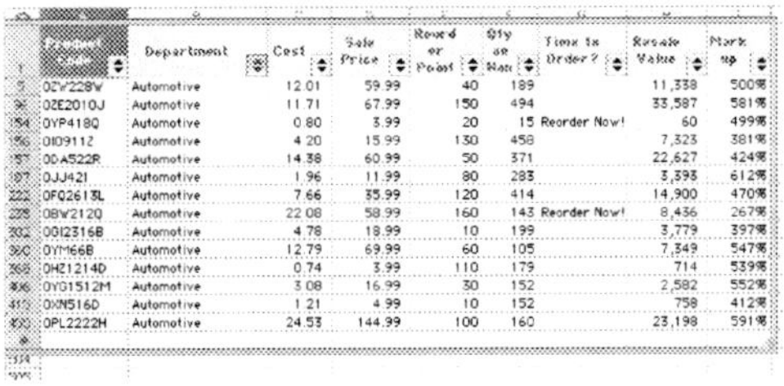

Figure 32 Excel displays only the records that match the criteria you chose.

Top 10 AutoFilter

Show

Top ⬍ 10 ⬍ Items ⬍

Cancel   OK

Figure 33 Use the Top 10 AutoFilter to find the top or bottom number or percent of items.

To find records with AutoFilter

Use the Sort and Filter pop-up menu for a column (**Figure 31**) to choose the criteria you want to match in that column.

Only the records matching the criteria you selected are displayed (**Figure 32**).

✔ Tips

■ To display all of the records again, choose Data > Filter > Show All (**Figure 30**) or choose (Show All) from the Sort and Filter pop-up menu you used to filter the data (**Figure 31**).

■ You can filter data by more than one column. Just choose the criteria you want from each column. The records that are displayed will match all criteria.

To use the Top 10 AutoFilter

1. Choose (Show Top 10...) from the Sort and Filter pop-up menu for the field by which you want to filter information (**Figure 31**).

2. In the Top 10 AutoFilter dialog (**Figure 33**), set options to display the top or bottom items or percent based on the field you selected. Click OK.

   Excel filters the database and displays only the records that match the settings you entered.

✔ Tip

■ You can only display the Top 10 AutoFilter dialog for a field that contains values.

To set a custom AutoFilter

1. Choose (Custom Filter…) from the Sort and Filter pop-up menu for the field for which you want to set criteria (**Figure 31**). The Custom AutoFilter dialog (**Figure 34**) appears.
2. Use the pop-up menus (**Figure 35**) to choose one or two comparison operators.
3. Use the pop-up menus or text boxes to enter one or two criteria.
4. Select the And or Or radio button to tell Excel whether it should match both criteria (And) or either criteria (Or).
5. Click OK. Excel filters the records to show only those matching the criteria you entered (**Figure 36**).

✔ Tip

- Criteria can include wildcard characters (**Table 2**).

To use multiple AutoFilters

Choose filters from the pop-up menus for each of the fields for which you want to set criteria. Excel will display only the records that match all of the filters (**Figure 37**).

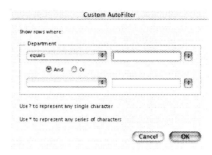

Figure 34 The Custom AutoFilter dialog.

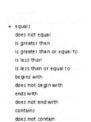

Figure 35 Use this pop-up menu to select a comparison operator.

Product Code	Department	Cost	Sale Price	Reorder Point	Qty on Hand	Time to Order?	Resale Value	Mark up
GNA141H	Junior Clothes	6.42	8.99	50	113		1,016	140%
FZX1916K	Misses Clothes	8.58	46.99	100	280		13,157	548%
FCV423R	Misses Clothes	4.69	13.99	130	233		3,260	298%
FEU2113N	Misses Clothes	11.60	13.99	100	286		4,001	121%
GBV921Z	Junior Clothes	12.70	16.99	130	308		5,233	134%
GRC2213T	Junior Clothes	20.07	59.99	190	394		23,636	299%
GXE1419E	Junior Clothes	4.76	11.99	30	68		815	252%
FLC611M	Misses Clothes	24.63	68.99	20	61		4,208	280%
GZG126P	Junior Clothes	23.90	88.99	110	286		25,451	372%
GYM29L	Junior Clothes	15.46	64.99	160	77	Reorder Now!	5,004	420%
FOP1615H	Misses Clothes	2.39	12.99	140	157		2,039	544%
GKS255F	Junior Clothes	0.98	1.99	160	455		905	203%
GRZ2010Y	Junior Clothes	24.89	53.99	70	338		18,249	217%
GJY125H	Junior Clothes	6.75	25.99	60	370		9,616	385%
FOX112Y	Misses Clothes	4.48	12.99	120	143		1,858	290%
GII1423R	Junior Clothes	5.32	18.99	60	94		1,785	357%
GTL103G	Junior Clothes	0.63	1.99	190	329		655	316%
FFW1919R	Misses Clothes	3.41	9.99	40	437		4,366	293%
GZA157Z	Junior Clothes	3.22	7.99	60	370		2,956	248%
GHY173K	Junior Clothes	17.88	31.99	40	31	Reorder Now!	992	179%
GIJ1117G	Junior Clothes	9.70	46.99	150	268		12,593	484%
GPF1125N	Junior Clothes	4.99	20.99	10	419		8,795	421%
FPK8130	Misses Clothes	0.85	1.99	40	356		708	234%
FUZ1426A	Misses Clothes	2.88	5.99	190	18	Reorder Now!	108	208%
FTQ914Y	Misses Clothes	22.00	93.99	50	50		4,700	427%
GUA1619W	Junior Clothes	10.17	12.99	0	266		3,455	128%
GHP710T	Junior Clothes	9.99	42.99	80	113		4,858	430%
GWV227Z	Junior Clothes	3.06	12.99	20	490		6,365	425%

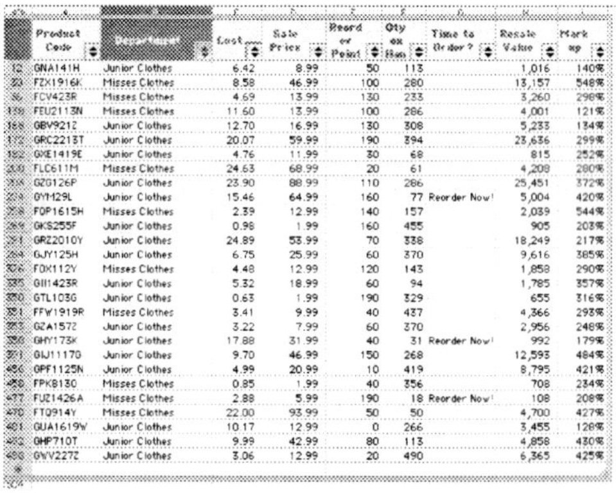

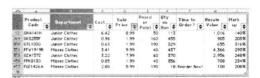

Figure 36 In this example, the Custom AutoFilter was used to find all inventory items in the Junior Clothes or Misses Clothes department.

Product Code	Department	Cost	Sale Price	Reorder Point	Qty on Hand	Time to Order?	Resale Value	Mark up
GNA141H	Junior Clothes	6.42	8.99	50	113		1,016	140%
GKS255F	Junior Clothes	0.98	1.99	160	455		905	203%
GTL103G	Junior Clothes	0.63	1.99	190	329		655	316%
FFW1919R	Misses Clothes	3.41	9.99	40	437		4,366	293%
GZA157Z	Junior Clothes	3.22	7.99	60	370		2,956	248%
FPK8130	Misses Clothes	0.85	1.99	40	356		708	234%
FUZ1426A	Misses Clothes	2.88	5.99	190	18	Reorder Now!	108	208%

Figure 37 This example adds another filter to **Figure 36**: Sale Price is less than 10.

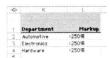

	Department	Markup
1		
2	Automotive	>250%
3	Electronics	>250%
4	Hardware	>250%
5		

Figure 38
Create a criteria range with field names and values that you want to match.

Figure 39
The Advanced Filter dialog, all set up to filter a list.

Figure 40 The criteria in **Figure 38** yielded these records.

Advanced Filters

Advanced filters enable you to specify even more criteria than you can with AutoFilters. First set up a criteria range, then use the Advanced Filter dialog to perform the search.

To use advanced filters

1. Create a criteria range by copying the data labels in the list to a blank area of the worksheet and then entering the criteria in the cells beneath it (**Figure 38**).

2. Choose Data > Filter > Advanced Filter (**Figure 30**).

3. In the Advanced Filter dialog (**Figure 39**), select a radio button to specify whether the matches should replace the original list (Filter the list, in-place) or be created elsewhere (Copy to another location).

4. In the List range text box, confirm that the correct cell references for your list have been entered.

5. In the Criteria range text box, enter the cell references for the range containing your criteria (including the field labels).

6. If you selected the Copy radio button in step 3 above, enter a cell reference for the first cell of the new list in the Copy to text box.

7. To omit duplicate records from the results list, turn on the Unique records only check box.

8. Click OK. Excel searches for records that match the criteria and either replaces the original list or creates a new list with the matches (**Figure 40**).

✔ Tip

■ You can enter a range into any of the text boxes in the Advanced Filter dialog by selecting the range you want to enter.

Sorting

You can sort lists by any column(s). Excel will quickly put database information in the order you specify.

To sort a list

1. Select any cell in the list.

2. Choose Data > Sort (**Figure 9**) to display the Sort dialog (**Figure 41**).

3. Choose a primary sort field from the Sort by pop-up menu (**Figure 42**).

4. Select a sort order radio button:

   ▲ **Ascending** is lowest to highest.

   ▲ **Descending** is highest to lowest.

5. If desired, repeat steps 3 and 4 for a secondary and tertiary sort field using options in the Then by areas.

6. If the list has column titles, select the Header row radio button; otherwise, select the No header row radio button.

7. Click OK. Excel sorts the list as you specified (**Figure 43**).

or

1. Select a cell in the column for the field by which you want to sort.

2. Click the Sort Ascending button 🔽 to sort from lowest to highest value or the Sort Descending button 🔽 to sort from highest to lowest value. (Both buttons are on the Standard toolbar.)

or

Choose Sort Ascending or Sort Descending from the Sort and Filter pop-up menu for the column you want to sort by (**Figure 31**).

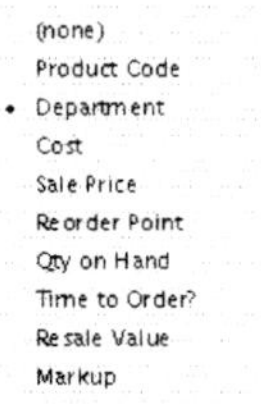

Figure 41
The Sort dialog, with a primary and secondary sort set up.

Figure 42
The Sort by (or Then by) pop-up menu lists all database fields.

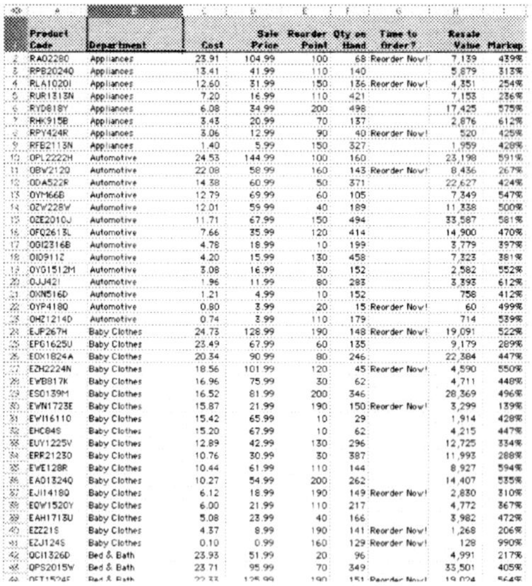

Figure 43 The beginning of a list sorted as shown in Figure 41.

SORTING LISTS

✔ Tips

- You can sort an entire list, a filtered list, or a list created with the Advanced Filter dialog.

- The two Then by fields in the Sort dialog are "tie-breakers" and are only used if the primary sort field has more than one record with the same value. **Figures 41** and **43** show how they can be used.

- If the results of a sort are not what you expected, choose Edit > Undo, press ⌃ ⌘ Z, or click the Undo button ↺ ▾ on the Standard toolbar to restore the original sort order.

- If you make the wrong selection in the My list has area at the bottom of the dialog, you could sort column titles along with the rest of the list. Undo the sort and try again.

- If you select a cell in the column by which you want to sort, that column is automatically referenced in the Sort dialog when you open it.

- To sort by more than three columns, sort by the least important columns first, then by the most important ones. For example, to sort a list by columns A, B, C, D, and E, you'd sort first by columns D and E, then by columns A, B, and C.

- In order to use Excel's Subtotal feature, you must first sort the data by the column for which you want subtotals. I tell you about the Subtotal feature next.

SORTING TIPS

Subtotals

Excel's Subtotal feature enters formulas with the SUBTOTAL function in sorted database lists. The SUBTOTAL function (**Figure 44**) returns a subtotal for a sorted list. It uses the following syntax:

SUBTOTAL(*function_num,ref***)**

The function_num argument is a number that specifies which function to use. **Table 3** shows the valid values. (I tell you about most of these functions in **Chapter 5**.) The ref argument is the range of cells to subtotal.

To subtotal a list

1. Sort the list by the field(s) for which you want subtotals (**Figure 43**) and select any cell in the list.

2. Choose Data > Subtotals (**Figure 9**) to display the Subtotal dialog (**Figure 44**).

3. Choose the name of the field to be grouped for subtotaling from the At each change in pop-up menu. The field you select will probably be one of the fields you sorted by.

4. Choose a function from the Use function pop-up menu (**Figure 45**).

5. In the Add subtotal to scrolling list, use the check boxes to choose the field(s) to subtotal.

6. If desired, use the check boxes at the bottom of the dialog to set other options.

7. Click OK. Excel turns the list into an outline and enters row titles and subtotals (**Figure 46**).

✔ Tips

- To remove subtotals, click the Remove All button in the Subtotal dialog (**Figure 44**).

- Excel's outline feature groups information into different levels. You can show or hide information based on its level.

Table 3

Valid *function_num* Values for the SUBTOTAL Function	
NUMBER	**FUNCTION NAME**
1	AVERAGE
2	COUNT
3	COUNTA
4	MAX
5	MIN
6	PRODUCT
7	STDEV
8	STDEVP
9	SUM
10	VAR
11	VARP

Figure 44 The Subtotal dialog.

Figure 45
Use this pop-up menu to choose a function for the Subtotal. In most cases, you'll choose Sum.

Outline buttons
& bars   =SUBTOTAL(9,C2:C9)

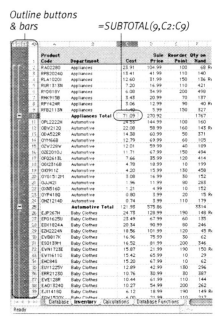

Figure 46 Here's part of the list in **Figure 43** with subtotals.

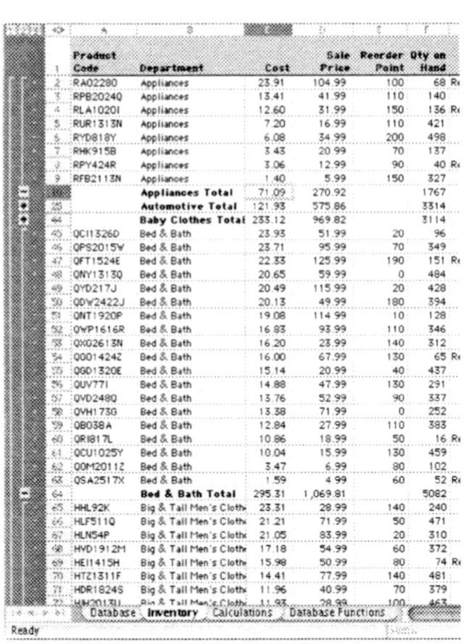

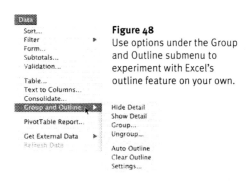

Figure 47 Here's the outline from **Figure 46** with some of the detail hidden.

To work with a subtotal outline

Click outline symbols on the left side of the window to display or hide detail:

◆ Click a minus sign button to collapse the outline for that section.

◆ Click a plus sign button to expand the outline for that section.

◆ Click one of the outline level numbers to collapse or expand the entire outline to that level.

Figure 47 shows an outline created by the Subtotal command partially collapsed. Note how the outline buttons and bars are set to the left of the data.

✔ Tip

■ You can create an outline for virtually any spreadsheet data. Although creating outlines is beyond the scope of this book, here's a hint to get you started if you decide to explore this feature: Use commands on the Group and Outline submenu under the Data menu (**Figure 48**) to create and clear groups and outlines.

Figure 48
Use options under the Group and Outline submenu to experiment with Excel's outline feature on your own.

Database Functions

Excel includes several database and list management functions. (SUBTOTAL, which I discuss earlier in this chapter, is one of them.) Here are a few of the most commonly used functions, along with their syntax:

DSUM(*database,field,criteria*)

DAVERAGE(*database,field,criteria*)

DCOUNT(*database,field,criteria*)

DCOUNTA(*database,field,criteria*)

DMAX(*database,field,criteria*)

DMIN(*database,field,criteria*)

The database argument is the cell references for a range containing the database or list. The field argument is the name of the field you want to summarize. The criteria argument is either the data you want to match or a range containing the data you want to match.

Figure 49 shows an example of these database functions in action, using the criteria range in **Figure 38**.

✔ Tips

- Each database function corresponds to a mathematical or statistical function and performs the same kind of calculation— but on records matching criteria only. I tell you about other functions in **Chapter 5**.

- You can enter database functions with the Formula Palette. I tell you how to use the Formula Palette in **Chapter 5**.

DSUM	595.05	=DSUM($A$1 :$I$501 ,"Cost" ,$K$1 :$L$4)
DAVERAGE	12.396875	=DAVERAGE($A$1 :$I$501 ,"Cost" ,$K$1 :$L$4)
DCOUNT	48	=DCOUNT($A$1 :$I$501 ,"Cost" ,$K$1 :$L$4)
DCOUNTA	48	=DCOUNTA($A$1 :$I$501 ,"Cost" ,$K$1 :$L$4)
DMAX	24.95	=DMAX($A$1 :$I$501 ,"Cost" ,$K$1 :$L$4)
DMIN	0.11	=DMIN($A$1 :$I$501 ,"Cost" ,$K$1 :$L$4)

Figure 49 These formulas use database functions to summarize information based on criteria. The database is the 500-record list used throughout this chapter. The field is the Cost field, which is found in column C of the database. The criteria range is the range illustrated in **Figure 38**.

WORKING WITH OTHERS

Collaboration Features

In office environments, a document is often the product of multiple people. In the old days, a draft worksheet or financial report would be printed and circulated among reviewers. Along the way, it would be marked up with colored ink and covered with sticky notes full of comments. Some poor soul would have to make sense of all the markups and notes to create a clean document. The process was time consuming and was sometimes repeated through several drafts to fine-tune the document for publication.

Microsoft Excel, which is widely used in office environments, includes many features that make the collaboration process quicker and easier:

◆ **Properties** stores information about the document's creator and contents.

◆ **Comments** enables reviewers to enter notes about the document. The notes don't print—unless you want them to.

◆ **Revision Tracking** enables reviewers to edit the document while keeping the original document intact. Changes can be accepted or rejected to finalize the document.

◆ **Document Protection** limits how a document can be changed.

◆ **Save options** protect documents from being opened or modified.

◆ **Workbook sharing** enables multiple users to access the same workbook file at the same time via a network.

Document Properties

The Properties dialog (**Figures 2** and **4**) enables you to store information about a document. This information can be viewed by anyone who opens the document.

✔ Tips

- The Properties dialog is organized into tabs for storing information. I cover the Summary and Statistics tabs here; explore the other tabs on your own.

- Information in the Properties dialog is also used by Find File, Excel's internal file searching feature. A discussion of Find File is beyond the scope of this book, however, you can explore it on your own by clicking the Find File button in Excel's Open dialog (**Figure 3**).

To open the Properties dialog

1. Open the document for which you want to view or edit properties.

2. Choose File > Properties (**Figure 1**).

To enter summary information

1. Open the Properties dialog.

2. If necessary, click the Summary tab to display its options (**Figure 2**).

3. Enter or edit information in each field as desired:

   - ▲ **Title** is the title of the document. This does not have to be the same as the file name.

   - ▲ **Subject** is the subject of the document.

   - ▲ **Author** is the person who created the document. This field may already be filled in based on information stored in the General tab of the Preferences dialog.

Figure 1
The File menu.

Figure 2 The Summary tab of the Properties dialog offers text boxes for entering information about the document.

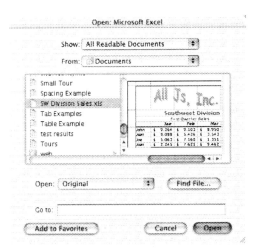

Figure 3 When you create a preview picture, it appears in the Open dialog.

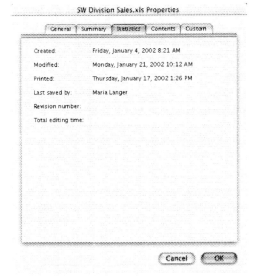

Figure 4 The Statistics tab of the Properties dialog provides additional information about the document.

▲ **Manager** is the person responsible for the document content.

▲ **Company** is the organization for which the author or manager works.

▲ **Category** is a category name assigned to the document. It can be anything you like.

▲ **Keywords** are important words related to the document.

▲ **Comments** are notes about the document.

▲ **Hyperlink base** is an Internet address or path to a folder on a hard disk or network volume. This option works in conjunction with hyperlinks inserted in the document.

4. To create a document preview image that will appear in the Preview area of the Open dialog (**Figure 3**), turn on the Save preview picture check box.

5. Click OK to save your entries.

✔ Tips

■ It is not necessary to enter information in any Summary tab text boxes (**Figure 2**).

■ I tell you more about the General tab of the Preferences dialog in **Chapter 15**.

To view document statistics

1. Open the Properties dialog.

2. If necessary, click the Statistics tab to display its information (**Figure 4**).

3. When you are finished viewing statistics, click OK to dismiss the dialog.

✔ Tip

■ Information in the Statistics tab (**Figure 4**) cannot be changed.

Comments

Comments are annotations that you and other document reviewers can add to a document. These notes can be viewed on screen but don't print unless you want them to.

To insert a comment

1. Select the cell for which you want to insert a comment (**Figure 5**).

2. Choose Insert > Comment (**Figure 6**).

   Two things happen: A comment marker (a tiny red triangle) appears in the upper-right corner of the cell and a yellow box with your name and a blinking insertion point appears (**Figure 7**).

3. Type your comment into the yellow box. It can be as long or as short as you like (**Figure 8**).

4. When you are finished, click anywhere else in the worksheet window. Your comment is saved and the yellow box disappears.

✔ Tip

- Excel gets your name from the General pane of the Preferences dialog. I tell you more about that in **Chapter 15**.

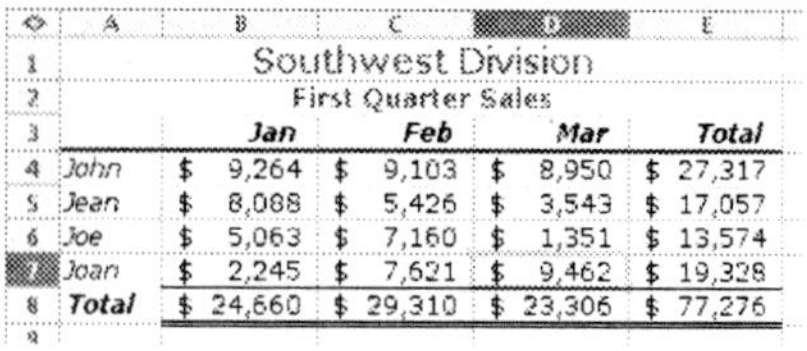

Figure 5 Start by selecting the cell you want to enter a comment for.

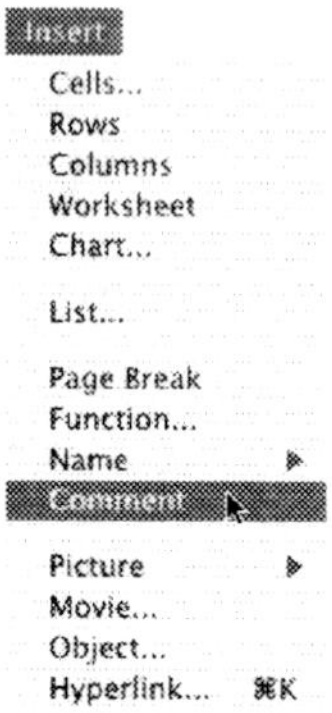

Figure 6 Choose Comment from the Insert menu.

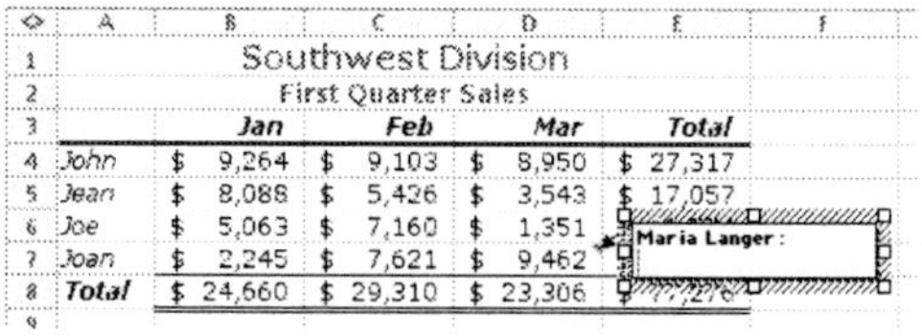

Figure 7 Excel prepares to accept your comment.

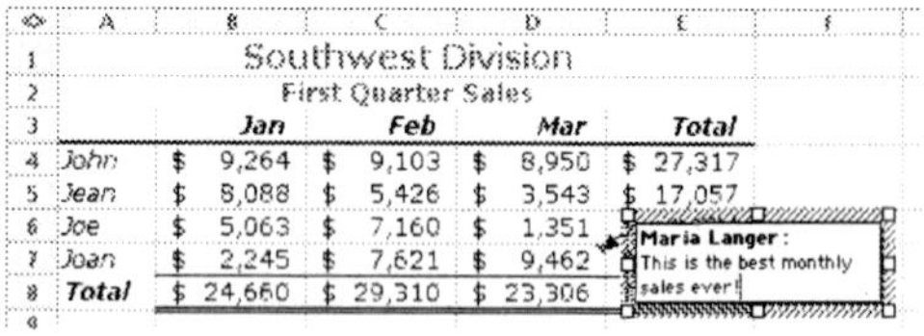

Figure 8 Enter your comment in the yellow box.

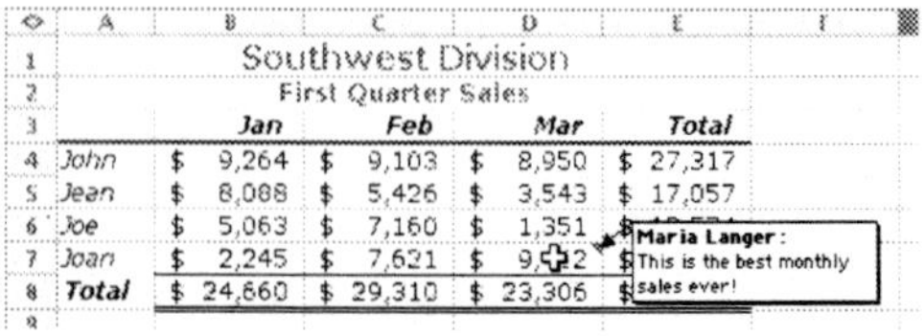

Figure 9 When you position the mouse pointer over a cell with a comment marker, the comment appears in a yellow box.

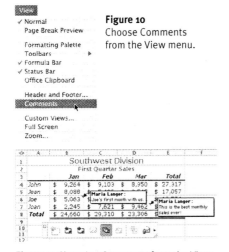

Figure 10
Choose Comments
from the View menu.

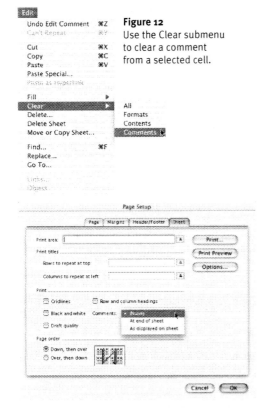

Figure 11 Choosing Comments from the View menu displays all comments for visible cells, along with the Reviewing toolbar.

Figure 12
Use the Clear submenu to clear a comment from a selected cell.

Figure 13 Use the Comments pop-up menu in the Page Setup dialog to set up comments for printing.

To view comments

Position the mouse pointer over a cell with a comment marker. A yellow box appears containing the name of the person who wrote the comment and the comment itself (**Figure 9**).

or

Choose View > Comments (**Figure 10**). All comments for visible cells appear in yellow boxes (**Figure 11**).

✔ Tip

■ When you display Comments instructed above, the Reviewing toolbar may appear (**Figure 11**). It includes buttons for Excel's Comments and Revisions features.

To delete a comment

1. Select the cell containing the comment you want to remove.

2. Choose Edit > Clear > Comments (**Figure 12**). The comment marker and comment are removed.

To print comments

1. Follow the instructions in **Chapter 9** to prepare the sheet for printing and open the Page Setup dialog.

2. Choose an option from the Comments pop-up menu in the Sheet tab (**Figure 13**).

3. Click Print.

4. In the Print dialog that appears, click Print to print the sheet and its comments.

VIEWING, DELETING, & PRINTING COMMENTS

Revision Tracking

Excel's revision tracking feature enables multiple reviewers to edit a document without actually changing it. Instead, each reviewer's markups are displayed in the document window. At the conclusion of the reviewing process, someone with final say over document content reviews all of the edits and either accepts or rejects each of them. The end result is a final document that incorporates the accepted changes.

To turn revision tracking on or off

1. Choose Tools > Track Changes > Highlight Changes (**Figure 14**).

2. In the Highlight Changes dialog that appears (**Figure 15**), toggle check boxes to set up the revision tracking feature:

   ▲ **Track changes while editing** enables the revision tracking feature. Turn on this check box to track changes. Turn off this check box to disable the revision tracking feature.

   ▲ **When** enables you to determine which changes should be tracked based on when the changes were made. If you turn on this check box, choose an option from the pop-up menu (**Figure 16**).

   ▲ **Who** enables you to specify which changes should be tracked based on who made them. If you turn on this check box, choose an option from the pop-up menu (**Figure 17**).

   ▲ **Where** enables you to specify which changes should be tracked based on which cells the changes were made in. If you turn on this check box, enter a range of cells in the text box beside it.

   ▲ **Highlight changes on screen** displays revision marks in the document window.

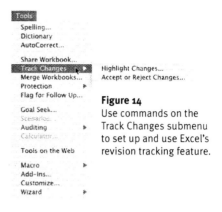

Figure 14
Use commands on the Track Changes submenu to set up and use Excel's revision tracking feature.

Figure 15 The Highlight Changes dialog lets you enable and configure the revision tracking feature.

Figures 16 & 17 Use these two pop-up menus to specify which changes to track based on when they were made (left) or who made them (right).

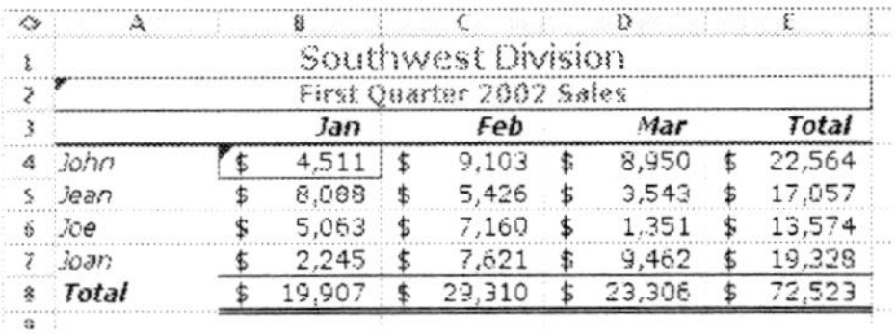

Southwest Division				
First Quarter 2002 Sales				
	Jan	Feb	Mar	Total
John	$ 4,511	$ 9,103	$ 8,950	$ 22,564
Jean	$ 8,088	$ 5,426	$ 3,543	$ 17,057
Joe	$ 5,063	$ 7,160	$ 1,351	$ 13,574
Joan	$ 2,245	$ 7,621	$ 9,462	$ 19,328
Total	$ 19,907	$ 29,310	$ 23,306	$ 72,523

Figure 18 When you edit the document, the cells you changed are marked.

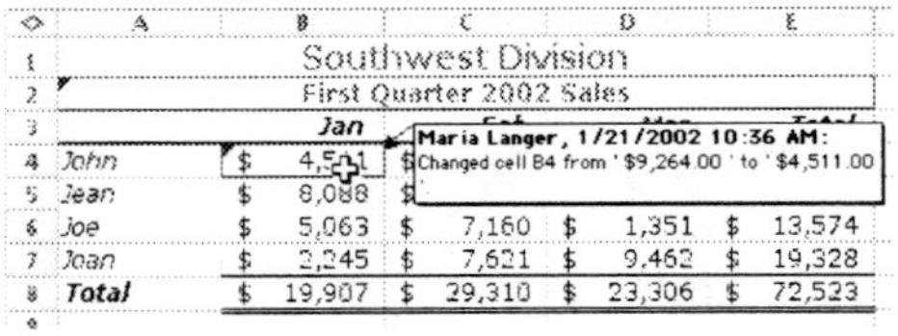

Figure 19 When you point to a revision mark, a box appears with information about it.

- ▲ **List changes on a new sheet** records changes in a separate History worksheet. This option is only available after you have saved the workbook file as a shared workbook.

3. Click OK.
4. If prompted, save the workbook file.

✔ Tip

- Turning on revision tracking also shares the workbook file. I tell you more about workbook sharing later in this chapter.

To track changes

1. Turn on revision tracking as instructed on the previous page.
2. Make changes to the document.

   The cells you changed get a colored border around them and a color-coordinated triangle appears in the upper-left corner (**Figure 18**).

✔ Tip

- If the document is edited by more than one person, each person's revision marks appear in a different color. This makes it easy to distinguish one editor's changes from another's.

To view revision information

Point to a revision mark. A yellow box with information about the change appears (**Figure 19**).

✔ Tip

- This is a handy way to see who made a change and when it was made.

To accept or reject revisions

1. Choose Tools > Track Changes > Accept or Reject Changes (**Figure 14**).

2. If prompted, save the workbook file.

3. The Select Changes to Accept or Reject dialog appears (**Figure 20**). Use options in the dialog to select which changes you want to review. The options work like those in the Highlight Changes dialog (**Figure 15**) discussed on the previous two pages.

4. Click OK.

5. Excel selects the first change and displays the Accept or Reject Changes dialog (**Figure 21**).

   ▲ To accept the selected change, click the Accept button. Excel selects the next change.

   ▲ To reject the selected change, click the Reject button. The cell reverts to its original contents and Excel selects the next change.

   ▲ To accept all changes, click the Accept All button. Skip the remaining steps.

   ▲ To reject all changes, click the Reject All button. All changed cells in the selection revert to their original contents. Skip the remaining steps.

6. Repeat step 5 for each change Excel selects.

   When Excel has reached the end of the document, the Accept or Reject Changes dialog disappears.

To remove revision marks

1. Choose Tools > Track Changes > Highlight Changes (**Figure 14**).

2. In the Highlight Changes dialog (**Figure 15**), turn off the Track Changes while editing check box and click OK.

3. Excel asks if you want to turn off sharing (**Figure 22**). Click Yes. The revision marks disappear.

Figure 20 The Accept or Reject Changes dialog.

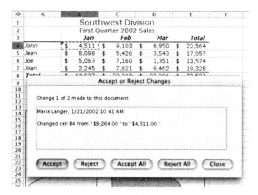

Figure 21 Excel selects the changed cell and displays information about the change in the Accept or Reject Changes dialog.

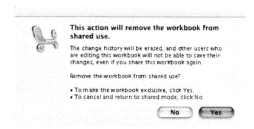

Figure 22 To hide revision marks, you must turn off workbook sharing.

Figure 23
The Protection submenu under the Tools menu.

Document Protection

Excel's Document Protection features enable you to limit the types of changes others can make to a document. There are three types of protection:

◆ **Protect Sheet** protects worksheet components:

  ▲ **Contents** protects cells from changes.

  ▲ **Objects** protects objects such as embedded charts and graphic objects from changes.

  ▲ **Scenarios** protects scenarios from changes. (Scenarios is an advanced feature of Excel not covered in this book.)

◆ **Protect Workbook** protects workbook components:

  ▲ **Structure** prevents workbook sheets from being inserted, deleted, moved, hidden, unhidden, or renamed.

  ▲ **Windows** protects workbook windows from being moved, resized, hidden, unhidden, or closed.

◆ **Protect and Share Workbook** enables you to share the workbook but only with change tracking enabled.

You set up all protection options using commands on the Protection submenu under the Tools menu (**Figure 23**).

✔ Tips

■ I explain how revision tracking works earlier in this chapter.

■ In addition to document protection, you can password protect a document to prevent it from being opened or changed. I explain how later in this chapter.

DOCUMENT PROTECTION

To protect a sheet

1. Choose Tools > Protection > Protect Sheet (**Figure 23**).

2. In the Protect Sheet dialog that appears (**Figure 24**), turn on check boxes for the type of protection you want.

3. If desired, enter a password in the Password text box.

4. Click OK.

5. If you entered a password, the Confirm Password dialog appears (**Figure 25**). Enter the password again and click OK.

✔ Tips

- Entering a password in the Protect Worksheet dialog (**Figure 25**) is optional. However, if you do not use a password with this feature, the document can be unprotected by anyone.

- If you enter a password in the Protect Document dialog (**Figure 25**), don't forget it! If you can't remember the password, you can't unprotect the document!

- If you try to change a protected item, Excel displays a dialog (**Figure 26**) or Office Assistant balloon reminding you that the item is protected.

- You can turn off protection for selected cells. Before protecting the sheet, select the cells for which you want to allow modification. Choose Format > Cells to display the Format Cells dialog and click the Protection tab (**Figure 27**). Turn off the Locked check box and click OK. Then, when you protect the sheet's contents, the unlocked cells can still be modified.

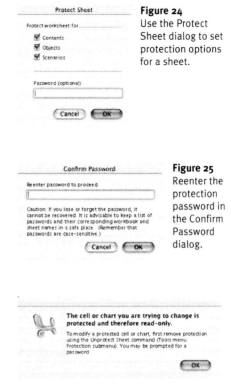

Figure 24
Use the Protect Sheet dialog to set protection options for a sheet.

Figure 25
Reenter the protection password in the Confirm Password dialog.

Figure 26 Excel tells you when you're trying to edit a protected item.

Figure 27 Turn off the Locked check box to allow modification to selected cells in a protected sheet.

PROTECTING A SHEET

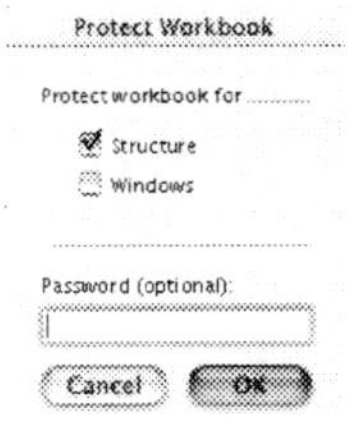

Figure 28
Use the Protect Workbook dialog to protect a workbook's structure and/or windows.

Figure 29 Use the Protect Shared Workbook dialog to allow others to share the workbook, but only with change tracking enabled.

To protect a workbook

1. Choose Tools > Protection > Protect Workbook (**Figure 23**).

2. In the Protect Workbook dialog that appears (**Figure 28**), turn on check boxes for the type of protection you want.

3. If desired, enter a password in the Password text box.

4. Click OK.

5. If you entered a password, the Confirm Password dialog appears (**Figure 25**). Enter the password again and click OK.

✔ Tip

- With workbook protection options enabled, Excel disables any menu commands or shortcut keys that you would use to make unallowed changes.

To protect a workbook for sharing & change tracking

1. Choose Tools > Protection > Protect and Share Workbook (**Figure 23**).

2. In the Protect Shared Workbook dialog that appears (**Figure 29**), turn on the Sharing with track changes check box.

3. If desired, enter a password in the Password text box.

4. Click OK.

5. If you entered a password, the Confirm Password dialog appears (**Figure 25**). Enter the password again and click OK.

6. When prompted to save the workbook, click OK. Excel turns on change tracking and workbook sharing.

PROTECTING WORKBOOKS

To unprotect a sheet or workbook

1. Choose the desired option from the Protection submenu under the Tools menu (**Figure 30**).

2. If protection is enforced with a password, a dialog like the one in **Figure 31** or **32** appears. Enter the password and click OK.

To turn off workbook sharing & change tracking protection

1. Choose Tools > Protection > Unprotect Shared Workbook (**Figure 33**).

2. If protection is enforced with a password, a dialog like the one in **Figure 34** appears. Enter the password and click OK.

3. Excel may ask if you want to remove the workbook from shared use (**Figure 22**). Click Yes.

✔ Tip

■ If protection is not enforced with a password, the dialog mentioned in step 3 may not appear. In that case, you must disable workbook sharing in the Share Workbook dialog, which is discussed later in this chapter.

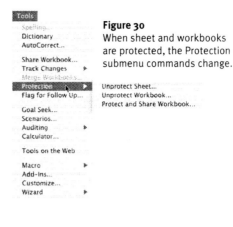

Figure 30
When sheet and workbooks are protected, the Protection submenu commands change.

Figures 31 & 32
Use dialogs like these to enter a password to unprotect a sheet (top) or workbook (bottom).

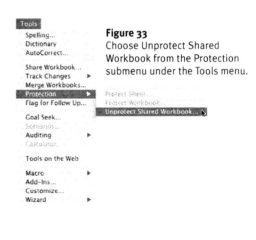

Figure 33
Choose Unprotect Shared Workbook from the Protection submenu under the Tools menu.

Figure 34
Use this dialog to enter a password to remove protection for workbook sharing and change tracking.

Figure 35 The Save As dialog.

Figure 36 Use the Save Options dialog to set all kinds of options for protecting a file.

Save Options & Password Protection

Excel's save options enable you to set up passwords to prevent a document from being opened or from being modified.

To set save options

1. Choose File > Save As (**Figure 1**).

2. In the Save As dialog that appears (**Figure 35**), click the Options button.

3. Set options in the Save Options dialog (**Figure 36**) as desired:

   ▲ **Always create backup** tells Excel to save the previous version of the file as a backup when saving the current version. (The old file is named "Backup of *filename*".)

   ▲ **Password to open** is the password that must be entered in order to open the file.

   ▲ **Password to modify** is the password that must be entered in order to save changes to the file.

   ▲ **Read-only recommended** tells Excel to recommend that the file be opened as a read-only file when the user tries to open it.

4. Click OK.

5. If you entered a password in step 3, a dialog like the one in **Figure 25** appears, asking you to confirm it. Reenter the password and click OK. (If you entered two passwords, this dialog appears twice.)

✔ Tip

■ I tell you more about saving files in **Chapter 4**.

To open a file with save options set

1. Choose File > Open (**Figure 1**).

2. Use the Open dialog that appears (**Figure 3**) to locate, select, and open the file.

3. If the file requires a password to open it, a dialog like the one in **Figure 37** appears. Enter the password and click OK.

4. If the file requires a password for modification, a dialog like the one in **Figure 38** appears. You have two choices:

   ▲ Enter the password and click OK.

   ▲ Click Read Only to open the file as a read-only file.

5. If the file was set up so read-only access is recommended, a dialog like the one in **Figure 39** appears, asking if you want to open the file as a read-only file. You have three choices:

   ▲ Click Cancel to not open the file at all.

   ▲ Click No to open the file as a regular file.

   ▲ Click Yes to open the file as a read-only file.

✔ Tip

■ If a file is opened for read-only access only, you cannot save changes to the file—a dialog like the one in **Figure 40** appears if you try. You can identify a file opened as a read-only file by the words "Read-Only" in the document window's title bar (**Figure 41**).

Figure 37 Use a dialog like this to enter a password to open a file.

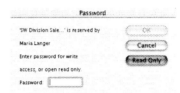

Figure 38 Use a dialog like this to enter a password to open a file for modification.

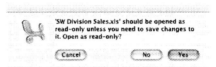

Figure 39 If read-only access is recommended for a file, Excel displays a dialog like this one when you open it.

Figure 40 Excel displays a dialog like this if you try to save a file that is opened for read-only access.

Figure 41 Not sure if a document is opened as a read-only file? Just look in the title bar.

OPENING FILES WITH SAVE OPTIONS SET

Figure 42
To enable or disable workbook sharing, choose Share Workbook from the Tools menu.

Figure 43 Sharing a workbook is as easy as turning on a check box.

Figure 44 You can identify a shared workbook by the word "Shared" in its title bar.

Workbook Sharing

Excel's workbook sharing feature enables multiple people to work on the same workbook at the same time. This feature is designed for work environments with networked computer systems.

To share a workbook

1. Choose Tools > Share Workbook (**Figure 42**).

2. In the Share Workbook dialog that appears, click the Editing tab to display its options (**Figure 43**).

3. Turn on the check box beside Allow changes by more than one user at the same time.

4. Click OK.

5. Excel may prompt you to save the workbook. If so, save it.

✔ Tip

- You can identify a workbook that has sharing enabled by the word "Shared" in its titled bar (**Figure 44**).

To open a shared workbook

1. Choose File > Open (**Figure 1**).

2. Use the Open dialog that appears (**Figure 3**) to open the network volume on which the workbook resides, then locate, select, and open the file.

To stop sharing a workbook

1. Choose Tools > Share Workbook (**Figure 42**).

2. In the Share Workbook dialog that appears, click the Editing tab to display its options (**Figure 45**).

3. To stop a specific user from sharing the workbook, select the user's name in the user list and click the Remove User button. Then click OK in the warning dialog that appears (**Figure 46**).

   or

   To stop all users from sharing the workbook, turn off the check box beside Allow changes by more than one user at the same time.

4. Click OK.

5. Excel may prompt you to save the workbook. If so, save it.

✔ Tips

- The Share Workbook dialog for a file lists all of the users who have the file open (**Figure 45**).

- If you remove a user from workbook sharing, when he tries to save the workbook, a dialog like the one in **Figure 47** appears, telling him that he is no longer sharing the workbook and offering instructions on how to save his changes.

Figure 45 The Share Workbook dialog lists all users who have the workbook file open.

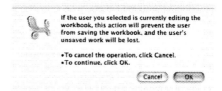

Figure 46 This warning appears when you remove a user from sharing a workbook file.

Figure 47 When a user is removed from sharing a workbook file, he sees this message when he attempts to save changes to the file.

DISABLING WORKBOOK SHARING

USING OTHER APPLICATIONS

Using Excel with Other Applications

Excel works well with a number of other applications. These programs can expand Excel's capabilities:

◆ OLE objects created with other Microsoft Office applications can be inserted into Excel documents.

◆ Excel documents can be inserted into documents created with other Microsoft Office applications.

◆ Excel documents can be e-mailed to others using Entourage.

◆ FileMaker Pro databases can be used as sources for Excel workbook files.

This chapter explains how you can use Excel with some of these other applications.

✔ Tip

■ This chapter provides information about applications other than Microsoft Excel. To follow instructions for a specific program, that program must be installed on your computer.

OLE Objects

An *object* is all or part of a file created with an OLE-aware application. *OLE* or *Object Linking and Embedding* is a Microsoft technology that enables you to insert a file as an object within a document (**Figure 1**)—even if the file was created with a different application. Double-clicking the inserted object launches the application that created it so you can modify its contents.

Excel's Object command enables you to insert OLE objects in two different ways:

◆ **Create and insert a new OLE object.** This method launches a specific OLE-aware application so you can create an object. When you are finished, you quit the application to insert the new object in your document.

◆ **Insert an existing OLE object.** This method displays the Insert as Object dialog (**Figure 6**) that you can use to locate, select, and insert an existing file as an object.

✔ Tips

■ All Microsoft applications are OLE-aware. Many software applications created by other developers are also OLE-aware; check the documentation that came with a specific software package for details.

■ Microsoft Excel comes with a number of OLE-aware applications that can be used to insert objects. The full Microsoft Office package includes even more of these applications.

■ **Chapter 7**, which covered inserting graphic objects, offered a glimpse of OLE objects in its discussion of Organization Chart, one of the OLE-aware applications that comes with Excel.

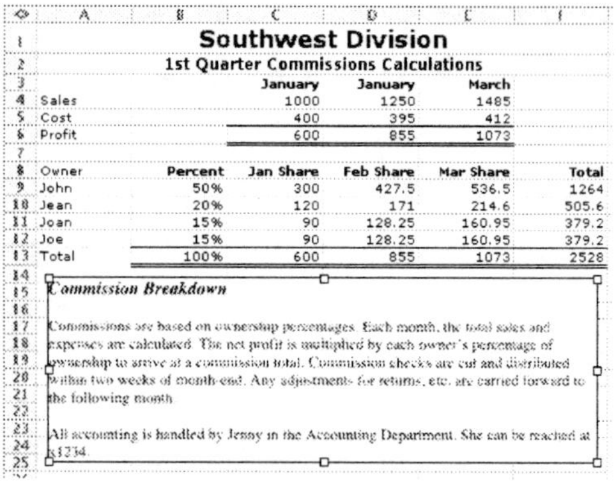

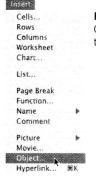

Figure 1 A Microsoft Word document object inserted in a Microsoft Excel worksheet.

Figure 2 Choose Object from the Insert menu.

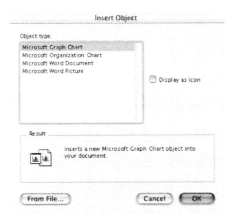

Figure 3 The Insert Object dialog. If you did not install Excel as part of a Microsoft Office installation, you may see fewer options in the Object type list than what is shown here.

Figure 4 A Microsoft Word X document window.

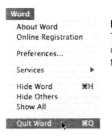

Figure 5
The Quit command on the Word menu.

To insert a new object

1. Select a cell near where you want the object to appear.

2. Choose Insert > Object (**Figure 2**) to display the Insert Object dialog (**Figure 3**).

3. Click to select the type of object that you want to insert.

4. Click OK.

   Excel launches the application that you selected. It may take a moment for it to appear. **Figure 4** shows a Microsoft Word document window and toolbar.

5. Use the application to create the object that you want.

6. When you are finished creating the object, choose the Quit command from the application menu (**Figure 5**). The application closes and the object is inserted in the document (**Figure 1**).

7. If necessary, drag the object into position in the Excel document.

✔ Tips

- The exact wording of the Quit command in step 6 varies depending on the application with which you are working. In some instances, you may be prompted to save changes before quitting the application.

- For more information about using one of the OLE-aware applications that comes with Excel or Office, use the application's Help menu or Office Assistant.

INSERTING OBJECTS

To insert an existing object

1. Position the insertion point where you want the object to appear.

2. Choose Insert > Object menu (**Figure 2**) to display the Insert Object dialog (**Figure 3**).

3. Click the From File button to display the Insert as Object dialog (**Figure 6**).

4. Locate and select the file that you want to insert.

5. Click OK. The file is inserted as an object in the document.

✔ Tip

- To insert a file as an object, the application that created the file must be properly installed on your computer or accessible through a network connection. Excel displays a dialog or Office Assistant balloon if the application is missing.

To customize an inserted object

Follow the instructions in the previous two sections to create and insert a new object or insert an existing object. In the Insert Object (**Figure 3**) or Insert as Object (**Figure 6**) dialog, turn on check boxes as desired:

- ◆ **Link to File** creates a link to the object's file so that when it changes, the object inserted within the Excel document can change. This option is only available when inserting an existing file as an object.

- ◆ **Display as Icon** (**Figure 7**) displays an icon that represents the object rather than the object itself.

Figure 6 Use this dialog to insert an existing file as an object.

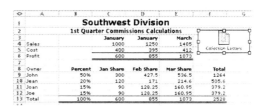

Figure 7 A Microsoft Word X document displayed as an icon.

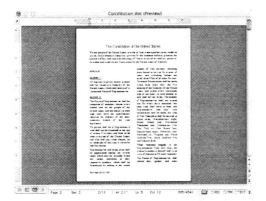

Figure 8 Word processing software like Word is most often used to create formatted documents.

Using Word with Excel

Word is the word processing component of Microsoft Office. A *word processor* is a program for creating formatted text-based documents (**Figure 8**). Word can also create mailing labels, merge static text with data (a data merge or mail merge), and create documents with pictures and other graphic elements.

You can use Word with Excel to:

◆ Include information from a Word document in an Excel document (**Figure 1**).

◆ Perform a Word data merge with an Excel list as a data source.

✔ Tips

■ Because performing a data merge is primarily a function of Word rather than Excel, it is not covered in detail in this book.

■ To learn more about using Word X, pick up a copy of *Word X for Mac OS X: Visual QuickStart Guide*, a Peachpit Press book by Maria Langer.

To include Word document content in an Excel document

To insert a Word document as an object in an Excel document, consult the section about OLE objects earlier in this chapter.

or

1. In the Word document, select the text that you want to include in the Excel document (**Figure 9**).

2. Choose Edit > Copy or press ⌃ ⌘ C (**Figure 10**).

3. Switch to Excel and either:

   ▲ Double-click in the cell where you want the content to appear to position the insertion point there (**Figure 11**).

   ▲ Create a text box to hold the content and position the insertion point inside the text box (**Figure 12**).

4. Choose Edit > Paste or press ⌃ ⌘ V (**Figure 13**). The selection appears in the Excel document within the selected cell (**Figure 14**) or in the text box (**Figure 15**).

✔ Tip

■ You can also use drag-and-drop editing techniques to drag a Word document selection into an Excel document. I tell you about drag-and-drop in **Chapter 3**.

Figure 9 Select the text you want to include.

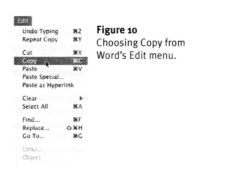

Figure 10 Choosing Copy from Word's Edit menu.

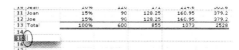

Figures 11 & 12 Position the insertion point in a cell (above) or text box (below).

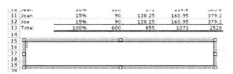

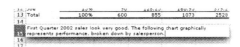

Figures 14 & 15 The text is pasted into the cell (above) or the text box (below).

Figure 13 Choosing Paste from Excel's Edit menu.

Figure 16 Start with an Excel list, like this one.

Figure 17 Choose Data Merge Manager from Word's Tools menu...

Figure 18 ...to open the Data Merge Manager.

Figure 19 Choose Open Data Source from the Get Data pop-up menu.

Figure 20 Use the Choose a File dialog to open the file you want to use as the data source.

To use an Excel list as a data source for a Word data merge

1. Follow the instructions in **Chapter 10** to create an Excel list and enter data into it (**Figure 16**).

2. Switch to Word and choose Tools > Data Merge Manager (**Figure 17**).

3. Use the Data Merge Manager (**Figure 18**) to create (or open) the main document.

4. Choose Open Data Source from the Get Data pop-up menu in the Data Source area of the Data Merge Manager (**Figure 19**).

5. Use the Choose a File dialog that appears (**Figure 20**) to locate, select, and open the Excel file containing the list.

6. Set options in the Open Worksheet dialog that appears (**Figure 21**) to specify which worksheet and cells contain the list you want to use for the merge.

7. Complete the main document with field names that appear in the Merge Field area of the Data Merge Manager (**Figure 22**) and perform the merge.

✔ Tip

- Because performing a data merge is primarily a function of Word rather than Excel, it is not covered in detail in this book.

Figure 21 Set options in the Open Worksheet dialog.

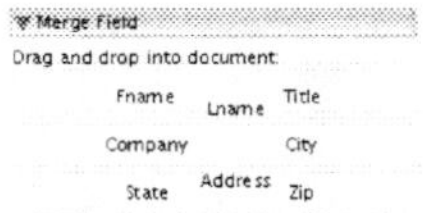

Figure 22 Field names from the Excel list appear in the Data Merge Manager.

Using Entourage with Excel

Entourage is the e-mail, newsgroup, and personal information management software component of Microsoft Office. *E-mail software* enables you to send and receive electronic mail messages (**Figure 23**). *Newsgroup software* enables you to participate in topical Internet message boards called *newsgroups*. *Personal information management software* enables you to store and organize address book (**Figure 24**) and calendar (**Figure 25**) data.

You can use Entourage with Excel to:

◆ E-mail an Excel document to a friend, family member, or co-worker.

◆ Flag a document for follow-up so Entourage reminds you about it.

✔ Tip

■ To learn more about using Entourage, consult the documentation that came with the program or its onscreen help feature.

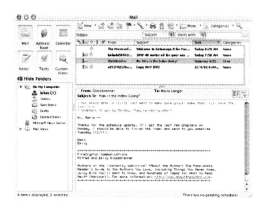

Figure 23 Entourage can handle e-mail, ...

Figure 24 ...address book information, ...

Figure 25 ...and calendar events.

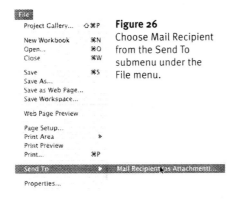

Figure 26
Choose Mail Recipient
from the Send To
submenu under the
File menu.

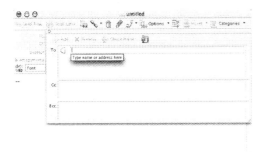

Figure 27 Entourage displays an untitled e-mail form.

Figure 28 Here's what a finished message might look like. Note that the name of the Excel document being sent appears in the Attachments area.

To send an Excel document via e-mail

1. Display the Excel document you want to send via e-mail.

2. Choose File > Send To > Mail Recipient (as Attachment) (**Figure 26**).

3. Excel launches Entourage and displays an empty e-mail window with the To field selected (**Figure 27**). Enter the e-mail address for the person you want to send the document to and press [Return].

4. In the Subject field, enter a subject for the message and press [Tab].

5. In the message body, enter a message to accompany the file. **Figure 28** shows an example.

6. To send the message immediately, click the Send Now button. Entourage connects to the Internet and sends the message.

   or

   To save the message in your outbox so it is sent the next time you send and receive messages, click Send Later.

7. Switch back to Excel to continue working with the document.

✔ Tips

- These instructions assume that Entourage is the default e-mail program as set in the Internet pane of System Preferences. If a different program, such as Eudora Pro, has been set as the default e-mail program, ignore steps 3 through 6 and send the message as you normally would with your e-mail program.

- Entourage (or your default e-mail program) must be properly configured to send and receive e-mail messages. Check the program's documentation or onscreen help if you need assistance with setup.

To flag a document for follow-up

1. Display the Excel document you want to flag for follow-up.

2. Click the Flag for Follow Up button  on the Standard toolbar.

3. In the Flag for Follow Up dialog that appears (**Figure 29**), set the date and time that you want to be reminded to work with the document. Then click OK.

   An entry is added to your Entourage Task list. When the date and time you specified approaches, a reminders window like the one in **Figure 30** appears. You can double-click the name of the document in the reminders window to open the document.

Figure 29 Use this dialog to enter a date and time to be reminded about a document.

Figure 30 Entourage reminds you with a dialog like this.

Figure 31 FileMaker Pro is an excellent program for storing, organizing, and reporting all kinds of data.

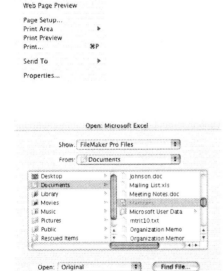

Figure 32 Choose Open from Excel's File menu.

Figure 33 Use the Open dialog to locate, select, and open the FileMaker Pro file.

Using FileMaker Pro with Excel

FileMaker Pro (**Figure 31**) is a database application from FileMaker, Inc. *Database software* enables you to store and organize information and create onscreen or printed reports. FileMaker Pro is easy to use and extremely flexible—it's no wonder that it's the top-selling database application for Macintosh users.

Excel can open a FileMaker Pro database file as an Excel list sheet. This enables you to perform complex calculations on or prepare charts from data stored in FileMaker Pro documents.

✔ Tip

- To learn more about using FileMaker Pro, pick up a copy of *FileMaker Pro 5: Visual QuickStart Guide*, a Peachpit Press book by Nolan Hester, or *FileMaker Pro 5 Companion*, a Morgan Kaufmann book by Maria Langer.

To open a FileMaker Pro database file as an Excel worksheet

1. In Excel, choose File > Open (**Figure 32**), or press ⌃ ⌘ O.

2. Use the Open dialog that appears (**Figure 33**) to locate, select, and open the FileMaker Pro file.

3. The first screen of the FileMaker Import Wizard appears (**Figure 34**). Use it to select the FileMaker Pro database fields you want to include in the Excel worksheet:

   ▲ To add a field to the Fields to import list, select it in the Available fields list and click the > button.

   ▲ To remove a field from the Fields to import list, select it and click the < button.

Continued on next page...

Continued on next page...

USING FILEMAKER PRO WITH EXCEL

Continued from previous page.

▲ To change the order of the fields in the Fields to import list, select one of the fields and click one of the triangle buttons to the right of the list.

4. When you are finished selecting fields, click Next.

5. In the next screen of the FileMaker Import Wizard (**Figure 35**), set criteria for selecting the records you want to import.

▲ To set the first criteria, choose options from the two pop-up menus in the Criteria 1 area to set the field and operator, then enter a value in the text box. Repeat this step to add additional criteria; be sure to select the And or Or radio button to specify how the criteria is to be used.

▲ To import all the records, leave the dialog as shown in **Figure 35**.

6. When you are finished setting criteria, click Finish. Excel imports the records and displays them in a new list sheet (**Figure 36**).

✔ Tip

■ I tell you more about Excel's list features in **Chapter 10**.

Figure 34 The first FileMaker Import Wizard dialog enables you to select the fields you want to import.

Figure 35 The second FileMaker Import Wizard dialog enables you to set criteria for importing records.

Figure 36 The FileMaker Pro data appears in a new list sheet.

ADVANCED TECHNIQUES

Figure 1 The reference to the selected range would be a lot easier to remember if it had a name like *FirstQtrSales* rather than just *A4:D7*.

=SUM('Qtr 1:Qtr 4'!E4)

Figure 2
3-D cell references make it possible to link information between worksheets or workbooks.

Figure 3 Excel's consolidation feature lets you combine information from multiple source areas into one destination area—with or without live links.

Advanced Techniques

Excel has many advanced features that you can use to tap into Excel's real power. In this chapter, I tell you about some of the advanced techniques I think you'll find most useful in your day-to-day work with Excel:

◆ **Names (Figure 1)** let you assign easy-to-remember names to cell references. You can then use the names in place of cell references in formulas.

◆ **3-D cell references (Figure 2)** let you write formulas with links to other worksheets and workbooks.

◆ **Consolidations (Figure 3)** let you summarize information from several source areas into one destination area.

◆ **Custom views** enable you to create predefined views of workbook contents that can include a variety of settings.

◆ **Macros** let you automate repetitive tasks.

✔ Tips

■ This chapter builds on information in previous chapters. It's a good idea to have a solid understanding of the information covered up to this point in this book before exploring the features in this chapter.

■ With Excel's built-in Visual Basic programming language, the macro feature also enables you to create highly customized workbook files, complete with special dialogs, menus, and commands. This, however, is far beyond the scope of this book.

Names

The trouble with using cell references in formulas is that they're difficult to remember. To make matters worse, cell references can change if cells above or to the left of them are inserted or deleted.

Excel's names feature eliminates both problems by letting you assign easy-to-remember names to individual cells or ranges of cells in your workbooks. The names, which you can use in formulas, don't change, no matter how much worksheet editing you do.

✔ Tips

- The Natural Language Formulas feature, which I discuss in **Chapter 2**, automatically recognizes cell column or row headings as cell names.

- Names can be up to 255 characters long and can include letters, numbers, periods, question marks, and underscore characters (_). The first character must be a letter. Names cannot contain spaces or "look" like cell references.

To define a name

1. Select the cell(s) you want to name (**Figure 1**).

2. Choose Insert > Name > Define (**Figure 4**).

3. In the Define Name dialog that appears, Excel may suggest a name in the Names in workbook text box. You can enter a name you prefer (**Figure 5**).

4. The cell reference in the Refers to text box should reflect the range you selected in step 1. To enter a different range, delete the range that appears in the text box and either type in a new range or reselect the cell(s) in the worksheet window.

5. Click OK.

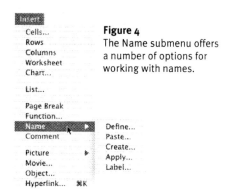

Figure 4
The Name submenu offers a number of options for working with names.

Figure 5 Use the Define Name dialog to set a name for one or more cells. As you can see, the name of the worksheet is part of the cell reference.

✔ Tip

- To define more than one name, follow the above steps for the first name but click the Add button in step 5. Then repeat steps 3 through 5 for each name you want to define. When you're finished, click OK.

Figure 6 To use the Create Names dialog, you must first select the cells you want to name, as well as adjoining cells with text you want to use as names.

Figure 7
In the Create Names dialog, tell Excel which cells contain the text for names.

Figure 8 Look in the Define Name dialog to see how many names were added.

To create names

1. Select the cells containing the ranges you want to name as well as text in adjoining cells that you want to use as names (**Figure 6**).

2. Choose Insert > Name > Create (**Figure 4**).

3. In the Create Names dialog (**Figure 7**), turn on the check box(es) for the cells that contain the text you want to use as names.

4. Click OK.

   Excel uses the text in the cells you indicated as names for the adjoining cells. You can see the results if you open the Define Name dialog (**Figure 8**).

✔ Tip

■ This is a quick way to create a lot of names all at once.

To delete a name

1. Choose Insert > Name > Define (**Figure 4**).

2. In the Define Name dialog (**Figure 8**), click to select the name in the scrolling list that you want to delete.

3. Click the Delete button. The name is removed from the list.

4. Repeat steps 2 and 3 to delete other names as desired.

5. Click OK to dismiss the Define Name dialog.

✔ Tip

■ Deleting a name does not delete the cells to which the name refers.

CREATING & DELETING NAMES

To enter a name in a formula

1. Position the cellpointer in the cell in which you want to write the formula.

2. Type in the formula, replacing any cell reference with the corresponding name (**Figure 9**).

3. Press [Return] or [Enter] or click the Enter button ✓ on the formula bar.

Excel performs the calculation just as if you'd typed in a cell reference.

✔ Tips

■ You can use the Paste Name command to enter a name for you. Follow the steps above, but when it's time to type in the name, choose Insert > Name > Paste (**Figure 4**). Use the Paste Name dialog that appears (**Figure 10**) to select and paste in the name you want. The Paste Name command even works when you use the Formula Palette to write formulas. I tell you about the Formula Palette in **Chapter 5**.

■ When you delete a name, Excel responds with a *#NAME?* error in each cell that contains a formula referring to that name (**Figure 11**). These formulas must be rewritten.

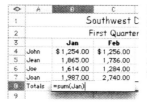

Figure 9
Once a range has been named, it can be used instead of a cell reference in a formula.

Figure 10 Use the Paste Name dialog to select and paste in a name.

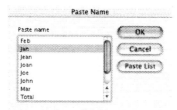

Figure 11
If you delete a name used in a formula, a *#NAME?* error results.

ENTERING NAMES IN FORMULAS

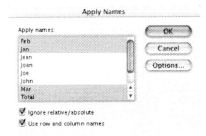

Figure 12 Select the names that you want to apply to formulas in your worksheet.

◇	A	B	C	D	E
1		Southwest Division			
2		First Quarter Sales			
3		Jan	Feb	Mar	Total
4	John	$ 1,254.00	$ 1,256.00	$ 2,435.00	$ 4,945.00
5	Jean	1,865.00	1,736.00	3,495.00	7,096.00
6	Joe	1,614.00	1,284.00	2,509.00	5,407.00
7	Joan	1,987.00	2,740.00	2,890.00	7,617.00
8	Totals	$ 6,720.00	$ 7,016.00	$ 11,329.00	$ 25,065.00

Figure 13
Excel applies the names you selected to formulas that reference their ranges.

Cell:	Before:	After:
B8	=SUM(B4:B7)	=SUM(Jan)
C8	=SUM(C4:C7)	=SUM(Feb)
D8	=SUM(D4:D7)	=SUM(Mar)
E8	=SUM(E4:E7)	=SUM(Total)

To apply names to existing formulas

1. Select the cells containing formulas for which you want to apply names. If you want to apply names throughout the worksheet, click any single cell.

2. Choose Insert > Name > Apply (**Figure 4**).

3. In the Apply Names dialog (**Figure 12**), select the names that you want to use in place of the cell reference. To select or deselect a name, click on it.

4. Click OK.

   Excel rewrites the formulas with the appropriate names from those you selected. **Figure 13** shows an example of formulas changed by selecting *Jan*, *Feb*, *Mar*, and *Total* in **Figure 12**.

✔ Tips

- If only one cell is selected, Excel applies names based on your selection(s) in the Apply Names dialog, not the selected cell.

- If you turn off the Ignore Relative/Absolute check box in the Apply Names dialog (**Figure 12**), Excel matches the type of reference. I tell you about relative and absolute references in **Chapter 3**.

APPLYING NAMES TO EXISTING FORMULAS

To select named cells

Choose the name of the cell(s) you want to select from the Name pop-up menu on the far-left end of the formula bar (**Figure 14**).

or

1. Click the Name box at the far left end of the formula bar to select it.

2. Type in the name of the cells you want to select (**Figure 15**).

3. Press $\boxed{\text{Return}}$ or $\boxed{\text{Enter}}$.

or

1. Choose Edit > Go To (**Figure 16**).

2. In the Go To dialog (**Figure 17**), click to select the name of the cell(s) you want to select in the Go to scrolling list.

3. Click OK.

✔ Tip

■ When named cells are selected, the name appears in the cell reference area at the far left end of the formula bar.

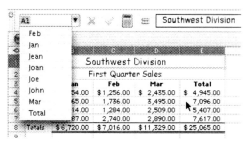

Figure 14 The Name pop-up menu on the left end of the formula bar lets you select named ranges quickly.

Figure 15 If you prefer, you can type in a name and press $\boxed{\text{Return}}$ to select it.

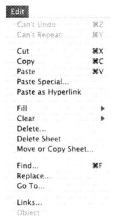

Figure 16
You can choose the Go To command under the Edit menu...

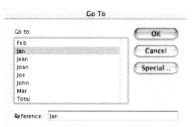

Figure 17 ...then select the name of the cell(s) you want to select from the Go to scrolling list.

=SUM(John,Joan,Joe,Jean)

Figure 18 This example uses the SUM function to add the contents of the cells named *John*, *Joan*, *Joe*, and *Jean* in the same workbook.

='Results for Year'!$B$9

Figure 19 This example refers to cell *B9* in a worksheet called *Results for Year* in the same workbook.

=SUM('Qtr 1:Qtr 4'!E9)

Figure 20 This example uses the SUM function to add the contents of cell *E9* in worksheets starting with *Qtr 1* and ending with *Qtr 4* in the same workbook.

=[Sales]'Results for Year'!$B$9

Figure 21 This example refers to cell *B9* in a worksheet called *Results for Year* in a workbook called *Sales*.

3-D References

3-D cell references let you write formulas that reference cells in other worksheets or workbooks. The links are live—when a cell's contents change, the results of formulas in cells that reference it change.

Excel offers several ways to write formulas with 3-D cell references:

- ◆ **Use cell names.** I tell you about cell names in the first part of this chapter. **Figure 18** shows an example.

- ◆ **Type them in.** When you type in a 3-D cell reference, you must include the name of the sheet (in single quotes, if the name contains a space), followed by an exclamation point (!) and cell reference. If the reference is for a cell in another workbook, you must also include the workbook name, in brackets. **Figures 19, 20**, and **21** show examples.

- ◆ **Click on them.** You'll get the same results as if you had typed the references, but Excel does all the typing for you.

- ◆ **Use the Paste Special command.** The Paste Link button in the Paste Special dialog lets you paste a link between cells in different sheets of a workbook or different workbooks.

✔ Tips

- ■ When you delete a cell, Excel displays a #REF! error in any cells that referred to it. The cells containing these errors must be revised to remove the error.

- ■ Do not make references to an unsaved file. If you do and you close the file with the reference before saving (and naming) the file it refers to, Excel won't be able to update the link.

To reference a named cell or range in another worksheet

1. Select the cell in which you want to enter the reference.

2. Type an equal sign (=).

3. If the sheet containing the cells you want to reference is in another workbook, type the name of the workbook (within single quotes, if the name contains a space) followed by an exclamation point (!).

4. Type the name of the cell(s) you want to reference (**Figures 22** and **23**).

5. Press [Return] or [Enter] or click the Enter button ✓ on the formula bar.

✔ Tip

- If the name you want to reference is in the same workbook, you can paste it in by choosing Insert > Name > Paste (**Figure 4**). I tell you how to use the Paste Name dialog earlier in this chapter.

To reference a cell or range in another worksheet by clicking

1. Select the cell in which you want to enter the reference.

2. Type an equal sign (=).

3. If the sheet containing the cells you want to reference is in another workbook, switch to that workbook.

4. Click on the sheet tab for the worksheet containing the cell you want to reference.

5. Select the cell(s) you want to reference (**Figure 24**).

6. Press [Return] or [Enter] or click the Enter button ✓ on the formula bar.

Figures 22 & 23 Two examples of 3-D references utilizing names. The first example refers to a name in the same workbook. The second example refers to a name in a different workbook.

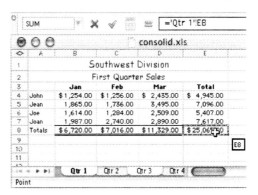

Figure 24 After typing an equal sign in the cell in which you want the reference to go, you can select the cell(s) you want to reference.

Figure 25 You can click the Paste Link button in the Paste Special dialog to paste a reference to cells you copied.

To reference a cell or range in another worksheet by typing

1. Select the cell in which you want to enter the reference.

2. Type an equal sign (=).

3. If the sheet containing the cells you want to reference is in another workbook, type the name of the workbook within brackets ([ ]).

4. Type the name of the sheet followed by an exclamation point (!).

5. Type the cell reference for the cell(s) you want to reference.

6. Press [Return] or [Enter] or click the Enter button ✓ on the formula bar.

✔ Tip

■ If the name of the sheet includes a space character, it must be enclosed within single quotes in the reference. See **Figures 19**, **20**, and **21** for examples.

To reference a cell with the Paste Special command

1. Select the cell you want to reference.

2. Choose Edit > Copy (**Figure 16**), press [⌃ ⌘ C], or click the Copy button on the Standard toolbar.

3. Switch to the worksheet in which you want to put the reference.

4. Select the cell in which you want the reference to go.

5. Choose Edit > Paste Special (**Figure 16**).

6. In the Paste Special dialog (**Figure 25**), click the Paste Link button.

✔ Tips

■ Do not press [Enter] after using the Paste Special command! Doing so pastes the contents of the Clipboard into the cell, overwriting the link.

■ Using the Paste Link button to paste a range of cells creates a special range called an *array*. Each cell in an array shares the same cell reference and cannot be changed unless all cells in the array are changed.

REFERENCING CELLS IN OTHER WORKSHEETS

To write a formula with 3-D references

1. Select the cell in which you want to enter the formula.

2. Type an equal sign (=).

3. Use any combination of the following techniques until the formula is complete.

   ▲ To enter a function, use the Formula Palette or type in the function. I tell you how to use the Formula Palette in **Chapter 5**.

   ▲ To enter an operator, type it in. I tell you about using operators in **Chapter 2**.

   ▲ To enter a cell reference, select the cell(s) you want to reference or type the reference in. If typing the reference, be sure to include single quotes, brackets, and exclamation points as discussed on the previous page.

4. Press **Return** or **Enter** or click the Enter button ✓ on the formula bar.

To write a formula that sums the same cell on multiple, adjacent sheets

1. Select the cell in which you want to enter the formula.

2. Type =SUM((**Figure 26**).

3. If the cells you want to add are in another workbook, switch to that workbook.

4. Click the sheet tab for the first worksheet containing the cell you want to sum.

5. Hold down **Shift** and click on the sheet tab for the last sheet containing the cell you want to sum. All tabs from the first to the last become selected (**Figure 27**). The formula in the formula bar should look something like the one in **Figure 28**.

Figure 26 Type the beginning of a formula with the SUM function...

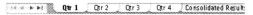

Figure 27 ...select all of the tabs for sheets that contain the cells you want to sum...

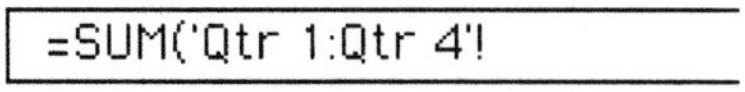

=SUM('Qtr 1:Qtr 4'!

Figure 28 ...so the sheet names are appended as a range in the formula bar.

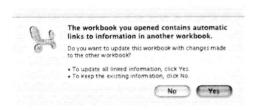

Figure 29 Then click on the cell you want to add...

```
=SUM('Qtr 1:Qtr 4'!E4
```

Figure 30 ...so that its reference is appended to the formula in the formula bar.

> **The workbook you opened contains automatic links to information in another workbook.**
>
> Do you want to update this workbook with changes made to the other workbook?
>
> • To update all linked information, click Yes.
> • To keep the existing information, click No.
>
> No   Yes

Figure 31 This dialog appears if you open a workbook that contains links to another workbook.

6. Click the cell you want to sum (**Figure 29**). The cell reference is added to the formula (**Figure 30**).

7. Type).

8. Press [Return] or [Enter] or click the Enter button ✓ on the formula bar.

✔ Tips

- Use this technique to link cells of identically arranged worksheets. This results in a "3-D worksheet" effect.

- Although you can use this technique to consolidate data, the Consolidate command, which I begin discussing on the next page, automates consolidations with or without links.

Opening Worksheets with Links

When you open a worksheet that has a link to another workbook file, a dialog like the one in **Figure 31** appears.

- If you click Yes, Excel checks the other file and updates linked information. If Excel can't find the other workbook, it displays a standard Open dialog so you can find it.

- If you click No, Excel does not check the data in the other file.

Consolidations

The Consolidate command lets you combine data from multiple sources. Excel lets you do this in two ways:

◆ **Consolidate based on the arrangement of data.** This is useful when data occupies the same number of cells in the same arrangement in multiple locations (**Figure 3**).

◆ **Consolidate based on identifying labels or categories.** This is useful when the arrangement of data varies from one source to the next.

✔ Tip

■ With either method, Excel can create links to the source information so the consolidation changes automatically when linked data changes.

To consolidate based on the arrangement of data

1. Select the cell(s) where you want the consolidated information to go (**Figure 32**).

2. Choose Data > Consolidate (**Figure 33**).

3. In the Consolidate dialog (**Figure 34**), choose a function from the Function pop-up menu (**Figure 35**).

4. Switch to the worksheet containing the first cell(s) to be included in the consolidation. The reference is entered into the Reference text box.

5. Select the cell(s) you want to include in the consolidation (**Figure 36**). The reference is entered into the Reference text box.

6. Click Add.

Figure 32
Select the cells in which you want the consolidated data to go.

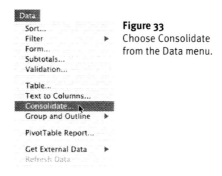

Figure 33
Choose Consolidate from the Data menu.

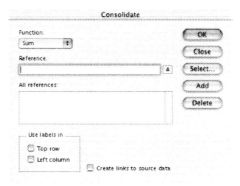

Figure 34 Use the Consolidate dialog to identify the cells you want to combine.

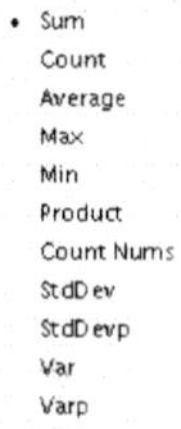

Figure 35
Choose a function for the consolidation from the Function pop-up menu.

CONSOLIDATING BASED ON ARRANGEMENT

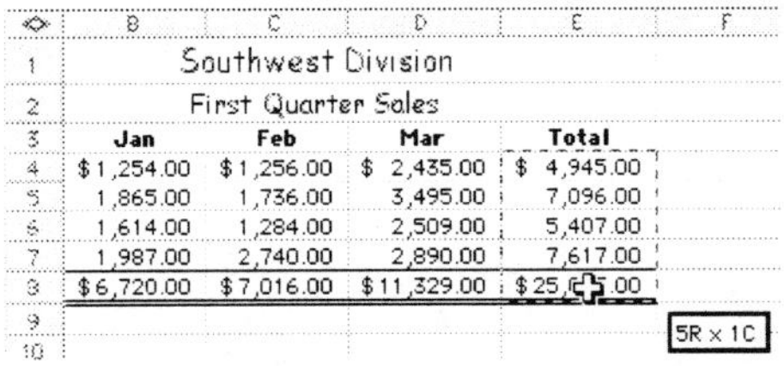

Figure 36 Enter references for cells in the Consolidate dialog by selecting them.

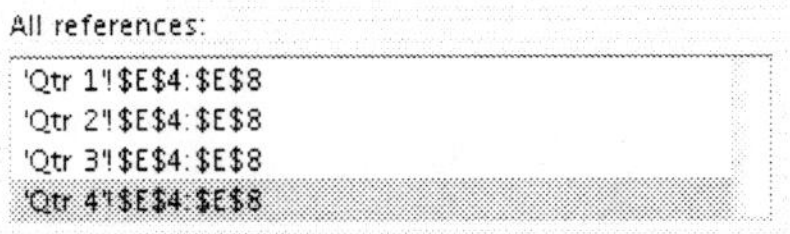

Figure 37 The cells you want to consolidate are listed in the All references scrolling list in the Consolidate dialog.

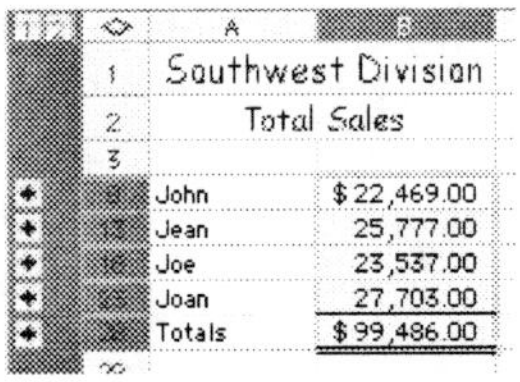

Figure 38 Excel combines the data in the cell(s) you originally selected.

7. Repeat steps 4, 5, and 6 for all of the cells that you want to include in the consolidation. When you're finished, the All references scrolling list in the Consolidate dialog might look something like **Figure 37**.

8. To create links between the source data and destination cell(s), turn on the Create links to source data check box.

9. Click OK.

   Excel consolidates the information in the originally selected cell(s) (**Figure 38**).

✔ Tips

■ For this technique to work, each source range must have the same number of cells with data arranged in the same way.

■ If the Consolidate dialog contains references when you open it, you can clear them by selecting each one and clicking the Delete button.

■ If you turn on the Create links to source data check box, Excel creates an outline with links to all source cells (**Figure 38**). You can expand or collapse the outline by clicking the outline buttons. I tell you more about outlines in **Chapter 10**.

CONSOLIDATING BASED ON ARRANGEMENT

To consolidate based on labels

1. Select the cell(s) in which you want the consolidated information to go. As shown in **Figure 39**, you can select just a single starting cell.

2. Choose Data > Consolidate (**Figure 33**).

3. In the Consolidate dialog (**Figure 34**), choose a function from the Function pop-up menu (**Figure 35**).

4. Switch to the worksheet containing the first cell(s) to be included in the consolidation. The reference is entered into the Reference text box.

5. Select the cell(s) you want to include in the consolidation, including any text that identifies data (**Figure 40**). The text must be in cells adjacent to the data. The reference is entered into the Reference text box.

6. Click Add.

7. Repeat steps 4, 5, and 6 for all cells you want to include in the consolidation. **Figures 41** and **42** show the other two ranges included for the example. When you're finished, the Consolidate dialog might look something like **Figure 43**.

8. Turn on the appropriate check box(es) in the Use labels in area to tell Excel where identifying labels for the data are.

9. Click OK.

   Excel consolidates the information in the originally selected cell(s) (**Figure 44**).

Figure 39
Select the destination cell(s).

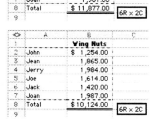

Figures 40, 41, & 42
Select the cell(s) you want to include in the consolidation.

Figure 43 The Consolidate dialog records all selections and enables you to specify where the data labels are.

Figure 44
The final consolidation accounts for all data.

Figure 45 Create a view you'd like to save.

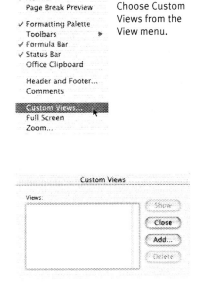

Figure 46
Choose Custom
Views from the
View menu.

Figure 47 The Custom Views dialog.

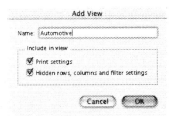

Figure 48 Use the Add View dialog to
name and set options for a view.

Custom Views

Excel's custom views feature lets you create
multiple *views* of a workbook file. A view
includes the window size and position, the
active cell, the zoom percentage, hidden
columns and rows, and print settings. Once
you set up a view, you can choose it from a
dialog to see it quickly.

✔ Tip

■ Including print settings in views makes it
possible to create and save multiple custom
reports for printing.

To add a custom view

1. Create the view you want to save. **Figure 45**
shows an example.

2. Choose View > Custom Views (**Figure 46**).

3. In the Custom Views dialog (**Figure 47**),
click the Add button.

4. In the Add View dialog (**Figure 48**), enter a
name for the view in the Name
text box.

5. Turn on the appropriate Include in view
check boxes:

▲ **Print settings** includes current Page
Setup and other printing options in
the view.

▲ **Hidden rows, columns and filter
settings** includes current settings for
hidden columns and rows, as well as
filter selections.

6. Click OK.

ADDING CUSTOM VIEWS

To switch to a view

1. Switch to the sheet containing the view you want to see.

2. Choose View > Custom Views (**Figure 46**).

3. In the Custom Views dialog (**Figure 49**), select the view you want to see from the Views scrolling list.

4. Click Show.

   Excel changes the window so it looks just like it did when you created the view.

To delete a view

1. Switch to the sheet containing the view you want to delete.

2. Choose View > Custom Views (**Figure 46**).

3. In the Custom Views dialog (**Figure 49**), select the view you want to delete from the Views scrolling list.

4. Click Delete.

5. In the confirmation dialog that appears (**Figure 50**), click Yes.

6. Follow steps 3 through 5 to delete other views if desired.

7. Click Close to dismiss the Custom Views dialog without changing the view.

✔ Tip

■ Deleting a view does not delete the information contained in the view. It simply removes the reference to the information from the Views scrolling list in the Custom Views dialog (**Figure 49**).

Figure 49 To see or delete a view, select the name of the view in the Custom Views dialog, then click Show or Delete.

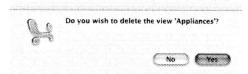

Figure 50 When you click the Delete button to delete a view, Excel asks you to confirm that you really do want to delete it.

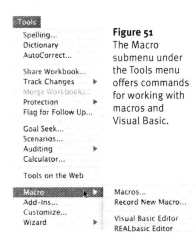

Figure 51
The Macro submenu under the Tools menu offers commands for working with macros and Visual Basic.

Figure 52 Enter a name and set options for a new macro in the Record Macro dialog.

Figure 53 When you're finished recording macro steps, click the Stop Recording button on the tiny Stop Recording toolbar.

Macros

A macro is a series of commands that Excel can perform automatically. You can create simple macros to automate repetitive tasks, like entering data or formatting cells.

Although macros are created with Excel's built-in Visual Basic programming language, you don't need to be a programmer to create them. Excel's Macro Recorder will record your keystrokes, menu choices, and dialog settings as you make them and will write the programming code for you. This makes macros useful for all Excel users, even raw beginners.

To record a macro with the Macro Recorder

1. Choose Tools > Macro > Record New Macro (**Figure 51**) to display the Record Macro dialog (**Figure 52**),

2. Enter a name for the macro in the Macro name text box.

3. If desired, enter a keystroke to use as a shortcut key in the Option+Cmd+ text box.

4. If desired, edit the description automatically entered in the Description text box.

5. Click OK.

6. Perform all the steps you want to include in your macro. Excel records them all—even the mistakes—so be careful!

7. When you're finished recording macro steps, click the Stop Recording button ▣ on the tiny Stop Recording toolbar (**Figure 53**).

To run a macro

Press the keystroke you specified as a shortcut key for the macro when you created it.

or

1. Choose Tools > Macro > Macros (**Figure 51**).

2. In the scrolling list of the Macro dialog (**Figure 54**), select the macro you want to run.

3. Click Run.

   Excel performs each macro step, just the way you recorded it.

✔ Tips

- Save your workbook *before* running a macro for the first time. You may be surprised by the results and need to revert the file to the way it was before you ran the macro. Excel's Undo command cannot undo the steps of a macro, so reverting to the last saved version of the file is the only way to reverse macro steps.

- Excel stores each macro as a *module* within the workbook. View and edit a macro by selecting it in the Macro dialog and clicking the Edit button. **Figure 55** shows an example. I don't recommend editing macro code unless you have at least a general understanding of Visual Basic!

- More advanced uses of macros include the creation of custom functions and applications that work within Excel.

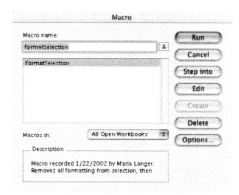

Figure 54 The Macro dialog enables you to run, edit, and delete macros.

Figure 55 Here's the code for a macro that removes cell formatting, then applies AutoFormatting.

WEB PAGES & HYPERLINKS

Web Pages

The World Wide Web has had a huge impact on publishing since 1995. Web pages, which can include text, graphics, and hyperlinks, can be published on the Internet or an intranet, making them available to audiences 24 hours a day, 7 days a week. They provide information quickly and inexpensively to anyone who needs it.

Microsoft Excel's Save as Web Page command enables you to save worksheets and charts as HTML documents, making it easy to publish Excel data on the Web.

✔ Tips

- This chapter explains how to create Web pages from Excel documents. Modifying the HTML underlying those pages is beyond the scope of this book.

- *HTML (or HyperText Markup Language)* is a system of codes for defining Web pages.

- To learn more about the Web publishing and HTML, check these Peachpit Press books:

  - ▲ *The Non-Designer's Web Book* by Robin Williams and John Tollett

  - ▲ *HTML 4 for the World Wide Web: Visual QuickStart Guide* by Elizabeth Castro

  - ▲ *Putting Your Small Business on the Web* by Maria Langer

- Web pages are normally viewed with *Web browser* software. Microsoft Internet Explorer and Netscape Navigator are two examples of Web browsers.

- To access the Internet, you need an Internet connection, either through an organizational network or dial-up connection. Setting up a connection is beyond the scope of this book; consult the documentation that came with your System or Internet access software for more information.

- To publish a Web page, you need access to a Web server. Contact your organization's Network Administrator or Internet Service Provider (ISP) for more information.

- A *hyperlink* (or *link*) is text or a graphic that, when clicked, displays other information from the Web.

- An *intranet* is like the Internet, but it exists only on the internal network of an organization and is usually closed to outsiders.

To preview a workbook as Web pages

1. Open the workbook that you want to save as Web pages (**Figure 1**).

2. Choose File > Web Page Preview (**Figure 2**). Excel launches your default Web browser and displays the current worksheet as a Web page (**Figure 3**).

3. To see other workbook sheets as Web pages, click the corresponding sheet tabs at the bottom of the Web page window.

4. When you are finished previewing the workbook as Web pages, close the Web browser window or quit the Web browser software.

✔ Tip

■ **Figure 3** shows what the Web page looks like with Microsoft Internet Explorer 5.1, which is the default Web browser on my system. If your system has a different default Web browser, the page may look different.

Figure 1 Here's a simple workbook ready to be converted into Web pages.

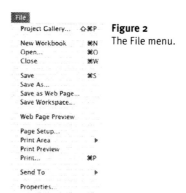

Figure 2
The File menu.

Figure 3 The workbook file in **Figure 1** previewed as Web pages. Note the sheet tabs at the bottom of the window; click them to view other sheets.

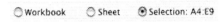

Figure 4 Use this Save dialog to save the workbook, current sheet, or current selection as Web pages.

Figure 5 If workbook cells are selected, the selection appears as an option in the Save dialog.

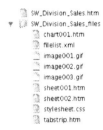

Figure 6
Excel creates all the HTML, image, and other supporting files necessary to view the workbook, sheet, or selection as Web pages. Here's what the files for the Web pages from **Figure 3** look like in the Finder.

To save a workbook as Web pages

1. Open the workbook that you want to save as a Web page (**Figure 1**).

2. Choose File > Save as Web Page (**Figure 2**).

3. A Save dialog like the one in **Figure 4** appears. Check to be sure that Web Page is selected from the Format pop-up menu.

4. Choose a disk location for the Web page and its supporting documents from the Where pop-up menu.

5. In the Save As text box, enter a name for the Web page. Make sure it follows the naming conventions of your Web server.

6. Select one of the radio buttons to specify what you want to save as a Web page:

   ▲ **Workbook** is the entire workbook.

   ▲ **Sheet** is the currently displayed workbook sheet.

   ▲ **Selection** is the currently selected cells. This option is only available if more than one cell is selected in the current worksheet; its wording will include the cell range (**Figure 5**).

7. Click Save.

   Excel creates the HTML, image (JPG and GIF), and other supporting files required to display the Excel document as Web pages. All supporting files are saved in a folder with the same name as the Web page file (**Figure 6**).

✔ Tips

- If you're not sure about the file naming conventions of your Web server, ask your System Administrator, Webmaster, or ISP.

- You can further customize the appearance of a Web page created by Excel by modifying its HTML document with your favorite Web authoring program or HTML editor.

SAVING WORKBOOKS AS WEB PAGES

265

To set Web page options

1. Follow steps 1 through 6 on the previous page to set basic options for saving the workbook as Web pages.

2. Click the Web Options button in the Save dialog (**Figure 4**). The Web Options dialog appears.

3. Click the General tab to display and set its options (**Figure 7**):

   ▲ **Web page title** is the title of the Web page. This is what appears in the title bar of the Web browser's document window when the page is open.

   ▲ **Web page keywords** are words and phrases a site visitor might enter to search for the Web page. Separate each word or phrase with a comma.

4. Click the Files tab to display and set its option (**Figure 8**). Turning on the Update links on save check box instructs Excel to automatically update links to the Web page's supporting files.

5. Click the Pictures tab to display and set its options (**Figure 9**):

   ▲ **Allow PNG as an output format** tells Excel that it can create PNG format graphics.

   ▲ **Screen size** is the size, in pixel dimensions, of the monitors used by most people who will view your Web pages. Choose an option from the pop-up menu (**Figure 10**).

   ▲ **Pixels per inch** is the resolution of the monitors used by most people who will view your Web pages. Choose an option from the pop-up menu (**Figure 11**).

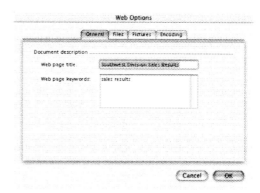

Figure 7 The General tab of the Web Options dialog.

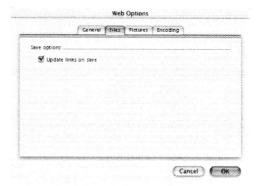

Figure 8 The Files tab of the Web Options dialog.

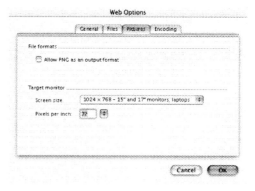

Figure 9 The Pictures tab of the Web Options dialog.

544 x 376 - Web TV
640 x 480 - 15" and smaller monitors
720 x 512 - 15" and smaller monitors
800 x 600 - 15" and smaller monitors
• 1024 x 768 - 15" and 17" monitors, laptops
1152 x 882 - 17" monitors
1152 x 900 - 17" monitors
1280 x 1024 - 17" and 19" monitors
1600 x 1200 - 19" and larger monitors
1800 x 1440 - 21" monitors
1920 x 1200 - 21" and larger monitors

Figure 10
Use this pop-up menu to choose a monitor screen size for most page visitors.

• 72
96
120

Figure 11 Use this pop-up menu to select the screen resolution of most page visitors.

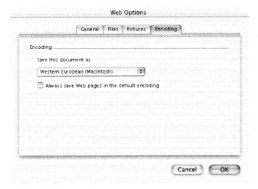

Figure 12 The Encoding tab of the Web Options dialog.

Arabic (ASMO 708)
Arabic (Macintosh)
Arabic (Windows)
Baltic (Windows)
Central European (Macintosh)
Central European (Windows)
Chinese Simplified (Macintosh)
Chinese Traditional (Macintosh)
Cyrillic (Macintosh)
Cyrillic (Windows)
Greek (Macintosh)
Greek (Windows)
Hebrew (Macintosh)
Hebrew (Windows)
Icelandic (Macintosh)
Japanese (EUC)
Japanese (JIS)
Japanese (JIS-Allow 1 byte Kana)
Japanese (Macintosh)
Japanese (Shift-JIS)
Korean (Macintosh)
OEM United States
Thai (Windows)
Turkish (Macintosh)
Turkish (Windows)
Unicode
Unicode (Big-Endian)
Unicode (UTF-8)
Western European (DOS)
• Western European (Macintosh)
Western European (Windows)

Figure 13
Use this pop-up menu to change the encoding option for publishing the Web pages on foreign systems.

6. Click the Encoding tab to display and set its options (**Figure 12**):

▲ **Save this document as** offers a pop-up menu of document encoding options (**Figure 13**). If necessary, choose an option from this menu.

▲ **Always save Web pages in the default encoding** tells Excel to always use the encoding chosen from the pop-up menu (**Figure 13**).

7. Click OK to return to the Save dialog.

8. Click Save to save the Web page(s) with the options you set.

✔ Tips

■ Keywords are used by search engines on the Web to help people find Web pages and sites.

■ PNG format images are not compatible with some older Web browsers.

■ To make your pages visible without requiring horizontal scrolling, in step 5 set the Screen size option to 800 x 600. This size is supported by the vast majority of Web site visitors.

■ Mac OS screen resolution is commonly 72 dpi; Windows screen resolution is commonly 96 dpi.

■ In step 6, if you don't know what encoding to select, leave it set as is. This is an advanced feature of Excel designed for publishing Web pages on foreign systems.

SETTING WEB PAGE OPTIONS

To automatically save a workbook as Web pages

1. Follow steps 1 through 7 on the previous two pages to set options for saving the workbook as Web pages.

2. Click the Automate button in the Save dialog (**Figure 4**).

3. In the Automate dialog (**Figure 14**), select a radio button for when you want the workbook automatically saved as a Web page:

   ▲ **Every time this workbook is saved** automatically saves the workbook as a Web page every time the workbook is saved.

   ▲ **According to schedule** saves the workbook according to a predefined schedule. If you select this option, click the Set Schedule button to display the Recurring Schedule dialog (**Figure 15**), use it to set up a schedule, and click OK. You can also turn on the **Warn me before saving as Web Page** check box to have Excel warn you before it saves the workbook as a Web page.

   ▲ **Never** disables the automation feature.

4. Click OK to return to the Save dialog.

5. Click Save to save the workbook as Web pages and save the automation options you set.

✔ Tip

■ This feature is especially useful if you can save your Web pages directly to a Web server. This way, the pages are automatically updated—with no additional work on your part—when changed or revised.

Figure 14 Use the Automate dialog to set up automatic Web page saving options.

Figure 15 The Recurring Schedule dialog lets you set up a schedule for automatically saving a workbook as Web pages.

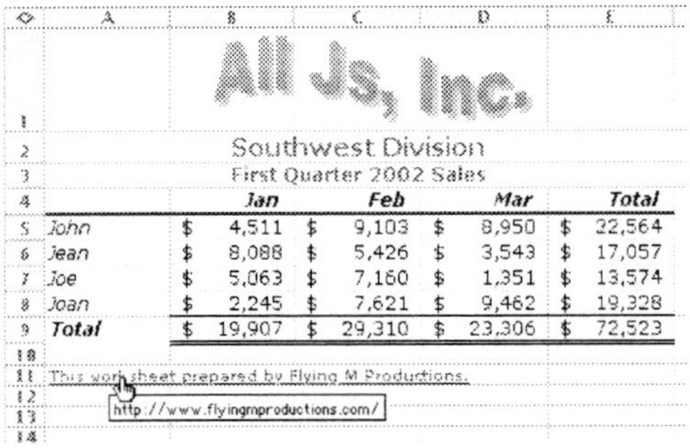

Figure 16 A hyperlink appears as blue, underlined text. When you point to it, the mouse pointer turns into a hand with a pointing finger and a ScreenTip appears.

Hyperlinks

A hyperlink is text or a graphic that, when clicked, displays other information. Excel enables you to create two kinds of hyperlinks:

◆ A link to a *URL* (*Uniform Resource Locator*), which is the Internet address of a document or individual. Excel makes it easy to create links to two types of URLs:

  ▲ **http://** links to a Web page on a Web server.

  ▲ **mailto:** links to an e-mail address.

◆ A link to another document on your hard disk or network.

By default, hyperlinks appear as colored, underlined text (**Figure 16**).

✔ Tip

■ Although you can create a link to any document on your hard disk or accessible over a local area network or the Internet, clicking the link will only open the document if you have a program capable of opening it—such as the program that created it.

To insert a hyperlink

1. Select the cell or object that you want to convert to a hyperlink.

2. Choose Insert > Hyperlink (**Figure 17**) or press ⌘ ⌘ K.

   The Insert Hyperlink dialog appears (**Figure 18**).

3. To link to a Web page, enter the complete URL of the page in the Link to text box (**Figure 19**).

   or

   To link to a document on your hard disk or another computer on your network, click the Select button in the Document tab and use the Choose a File dialog that appears (**Figure 20**) to locate, select, and open the document. Excel automatically fills in the Link to text box.

   or

   To link to an e-mail address, fill in the To and Subject fields in the E-mail Address tab. Excel automatically fills in the Link to text box (**Figure 21**).

4. Click OK to save your settings and dismiss the Insert Hyperlink dialog.

   The selected cell or object turns into a hyperlink.

✔ Tips

- You can also use the Favorites, History, Recent Documents, or Recent Addresses pop-up menu in the Insert Hyperlink dialog to link to a favorite or recently opened item.

Figure 17 Choose Hyperlink from the Insert menu.

Figure 18 Use the Insert Hyperlink dialog to enter hyperlink location information.

Figure 19 The Link to and Display text boxes determine how the link works and what appears in the cell.

Figure 20 You can use the Choose a File dialog to locate and select a file to link to on your hard disk or network.

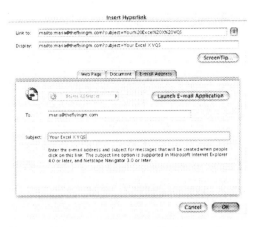

Figure 21 When you enter an e-mail address and subject in the To and Subject fields of the E-mail Address tab, Excel composes a complex URL in the Link to text box.

Figure 22 Use this dialog to set up a custom ScreenTip for a hyperlink.

■ The Display text box near the top of the Insert Hyperlink dialog (**Figure 18**) determines what text appears as the link in the worksheet cell. As shown in **Figures 19** and **21**, this does not have to be the same as what's in the Link to text box.

■ To specify what should appear in the yellow ScreenTip box when you point to the hyperlink, click the ScreenTip button in the Insert Hyperlink dialog (**Figure 18**). Then enter the text you want to appear in the Set Hyperlink ScreenTip dialog (**Figure 22**) and click OK. **Figure 16** shows an example of a ScreenTip. Keep in mind that this feature is not compatible with all Web browsers.

TIPS FOR INSERTING HYPERLINKS

To follow a hyperlink

1. Position the mouse pointer on the hyperlink. The mouse pointer turns into a pointing finger and a ScreenTip appears in a yellow box nearby (**Figure 16**).

2. Click once.

   If the hyperlink points to an Internet URL, Excel launches your default Web browser, connects to the Internet, and displays the URL.

   or

   If the hyperlink points to a file on your hard disk or another computer on the network, the file opens.

   or

   If the hyperlink points to an e-mail address, Excel launches your default e-mail application and prepares a preaddressed new message form.

To modify or remove a hyperlink

1. Select the cell or object containing the hyperlink. (You may have to use arrow keys to select the cell without clicking the link.)

2. Choose Insert > Hyperlink (**Figure 17**), or press ⌃ ⌘ K.

   or

   Click the Insert Hyperlink button on the Standard toolbar.

   The Edit Hyperlink dialog appears (**Figure 23**).

3. To change the link information, make changes as discussed on the previous two pages.

   or

   To remove the link, click the Remove Link button.

4. Click OK.

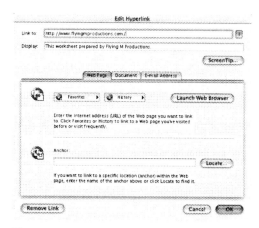

Figure 23 Use the Edit Hyperlink dialog to modify or remove a hyperlink.

SETTING EXCEL PREFERENCES

The Preferences Dialog

Microsoft Excel's Preferences dialog offers nine categories of options that you can set to customize the way Excel works for you:

◆ **View** preferences control Excel's on-screen appearance.

◆ **Save** preferences enable you to set Auto-Recover options.

◆ **Calculation** preferences control the way Excel calculates formulas.

◆ **Edit** preferences control editing.

◆ **General** preferences control general Excel operations.

◆ **Transition** preferences control options for Excel users who also work with other spreadsheet programs.

◆ **Custom Lists** preferences enable you to create or modify series lists.

◆ **Chart** preferences control the active chart and chart tips.

◆ **Color** preferences control standard, chart fill, and chart line colors.

✔ Tips

■ Excel's default preference settings are discussed and illustrated throughout this book.

■ Some of the preference settings affect only the active sheet or workbook file while others affect all Excel operations. If you want a setting to affect a specific sheet or file, be sure to open and activate it before opening the Preferences dialog.

To set preferences

1. Choose Excel > Preferences (**Figure 1**) to display the Preferences dialog (**Figure 3**).

2. On the left side of the window, click the name of the category of options you want to set. The dialog changes to display that preferences pane.

3. Set options as desired.

4. Repeat steps 2 and 3 for other categories of options that you want to set.

5. Click OK to save your settings.

✔ Tip

■ I illustrate and discuss all Preferences dialog options throughout this chapter.

To restore preferences to the default settings

1. If Excel is running, choose Excel > Quit Excel or press ⌃⌘Q to quit it.

2. In the Finder, open the folder at this path: ~/Library/Preferences/Microsoft/ (where ~/ represents your home folder).

3. Locate the file named *Excel Settings (10)* (**Figure 2**) and drag it to the Trash.

4. Choose Finder > Empty Trash.

5. Launch Excel.

✔ Tips

■ When the Excel Settings (10) file is deleted, Excel automatically creates a new file with the same name, using default preference settings.

■ As you may have guessed, Excel creates an Excel Settings (10) file for each user on your computer.

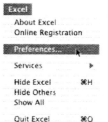

Figure 1
To open the Preferences dialog, choose Preferences from the Excel menu.

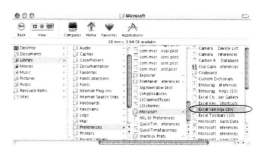

Figure 2 Excel preferences are stored in the Excel Settings (10) file.

Figure 3 The default options in the View pane of the Preferences dialog. Some of the Window options are not available when a chart sheet is active.

View Preferences

The View pane of the Preferences dialog (**Figure 3**) offers options in four categories: Show, Comments, Objects, and Window options.

✔ Tip

■ The available options in the View pane vary depending on the type of sheet that is active when you open the Preferences dialog. When a chart sheet is active, many of the Window options are gray.

Show

Show options determine what Excel elements appear on screen:

◆ **Formula bar** displays the formula bar above the document window.

◆ **Status bar** displays the status bar at the bottom of the screen.

Comments

The Comments area enables you to select one of three radio buttons for displaying comments:

◆ **None** does not display comments or comment indicators.

◆ **Comment indicator only** displays a small red triangle in the upper-right corner of a cell containing a comment. When you point to the cell, the comment appears in a yellow box.

◆ **Comment & indicator** displays cell comments in yellow boxes as well as a small red triangle in the upper-right corner of each cell containing a comment.

Objects

The Objects area enables you to select one of three radio buttons for displaying graphic objects, buttons, text boxes, drawn objects, and pictures:

◆ **Show all** displays all objects.

◆ **Show placeholders** displays gray rectangles as placeholders for pictures and charts. This can speed up scrolling through a window with many graphic objects.

◆ **Hide all** does not display any objects. Excel will not print objects with this option selected.

Window options

Window options determine how various Excel elements are displayed in the active window.

◆ **Page breaks** displays horizontal and vertical page breaks.

◆ **Formulas** displays formulas instead of formula results (**Figure 4**). You may find this feature useful to document your worksheets.

◆ **Gridlines** displays the boundaries of cells as gray lines.

◆ **Color** offers a pop-up menu (**Figure 5**) for selecting a gridline color. Automatic (the default option) displays gridlines in gray.

◆ **Row & column headers** displays the numeric row headings and alphabetical column headings.

◆ **Outline symbols** displays outline symbols when the worksheet includes an outline.

◆ **Zero values** displays a 0 (zero) in cells that contain zero values. Turning off this check box instructs Excel to leave a cell blank if it contains a zero value.

◆ **Horizontal scroll bar** displays a scroll bar along the bottom of the window.

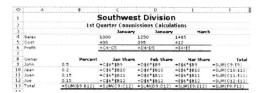

Figure 4 If desired, you can display formulas rather than their results.

Figure 5
Use the Color pop-up menu to select a color for the gridlines that appear in a worksheet window.

◆ **Vertical scroll bar** displays a scroll bar along the right side of the window.

◆ **Sheet tabs** displays tabs at the bottom of the window for each sheet in the workbook file.

Figure 6 The default settings in the Save pane of the Preferences dialog.

Save Preferences

The Save pane of the Preferences dialog (**Figure 6**) enables you to configure Excel's AutoRecover feature. This feature can automatically recover files you are working on if Excel unexpectedly quits due to a power outage or system problem. It does this by saving a special version of the file in the background while you work. The process is transparent to you and does not affect normal Excel operations.

✔ Tip

■ The AutoRecover feature is enabled by default.

To configure AutoRecover

1. In the Save pane of the Preferences dialog (**Figure 6**), make sure the Save AutoRecover info check box is turned on.

2. Enter the number of minutes Excel should wait between AutoRecover info saves in the text box. The higher the number you enter, the fewer automatic saves are completed.

✔ Tip

■ If you use Excel on a laptop computer that frequently runs on battery power, configure the AutoRecover feature so it saves less frequently. This can help conserve battery power.

To disable AutoRecover

In the Save pane of the Preferences dialog (**Figure 6**), turn off the Save AutoRecover info check box.

SAVE PREFERENCES

Calculation Preferences

Calculation preferences (**Figure 7**) control the way formulas are calculated (or recalculated) in a worksheet. There are several groups of options: Calculation, Iteration, Calc buttons, and Workbook options.

Calculation

The Calculation area enables you to select one of three radio buttons for specifying how formulas should be calculated:

◆ **Automatic** tells Excel to recalculate all dependent formulas whenever you change a value, formula, or name.

◆ **Automatic except tables** is the same as Automatic, but does not recalculate data tables. With this option selected, you must click the Calc Now button or press ⌃ ⌘ = to recalculate data tables.

◆ **Manual** recalculates formulas only when you click the Calc Now button or press ⌃ ⌘ =. With this option selected, you can turn on the **Recalculate before save** check box to ensure that the worksheet is recalculated each time you save it.

Iteration

The Iteration check box enables you to set limits for the number of times Excel tries to resolve circular references or complete goal-seeking calculations. To use this advanced option, turn on the check box, then enter values in the two text boxes below it:

◆ **Maximum iterations** is the maximum number of times Excel should try to resolve circular references or solve goal-seeking problems.

◆ **Maximum change** is the maximum amount of result change below which iteration stops.

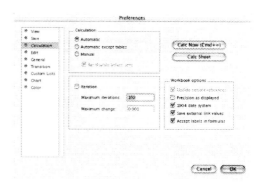

Figure 7 The default settings for the Calculation pane of the Preferences dialog.

Calc buttons

The Calculation Preferences dialog offers two buttons for calculating formulas:

◆ **Calc Now (Cmd+=)** recalculates all open worksheets and updates all open chart sheets. You can also access this option by pressing ⌘ ⌘ =.

◆ **Calc Sheet** recalculates the active worksheet and updates linked charts or updates the active chart sheet.

Workbook options

Workbook options control calculation in the active workbook file.

◆ **Update remote references** calculates formulas with references to documents created with other applications.

◆ **Precision as displayed** permanently changes values stored in cells from 15-digit precision to the precision of the applied formatting. This may result in rounding.

◆ **1904 date system** changes the starting date from which all dates are calculated to January 2, 1904. This is the date system used on Macintosh computers. Wintel computers begin dates at January 1, 1900. Turning off this option enhances compatibility with Wintel system spreadsheet programs.

◆ **Save external link values** saves copies of values from linked documents within the workbook file. If many values are linked, storing them can increase the file size; turning off this option can reduce the file size.

◆ **Accept labels in formulas** enables the Natural Language Formulas feature, which allows you to use column and row headings to identify ranges of cells.

CALCULATION PREFERENCES

Edit Preferences

Edit preferences (**Figure 8**) control the way certain editing tasks work:

◆ **Edit directly in cell** enables you to edit a cell's value or formula by double-clicking the cell. With this option turned off, you must edit a cell's contents in the formula bar.

◆ **Allow cell drag and drop** enables you to copy or move cells by dragging them to a new location. With this option turned on, you can also turn on the **Alert before overwriting cells** check box to have Excel warn you if a drag-and-drop operation will overwrite the contents of destination cells.

◆ **Move selection after Return** tells Excel to move the cellpointer when you press Return. With this option turned on, you can use the **Direction** pop-up menu (**Figure 9**) to choose a direction: Down, Right, Up, or Left.

◆ **Fixed decimal** instructs Excel to automatically place a decimal point when you enter a value. Turn on the check box and enter a value in the **Places** text box. A positive value moves the decimal to the left; a negative value moves the decimal to the right.

◆ **Cut, copy, and sort objects with cells** keeps objects (such as graphics) with cells that you cut, copy, filter, or sort.

◆ **Ask to update automatic links** prompts you to update links when you open a workbook containing links to other files.

◆ **Provide feedback with animation** displays worksheet movement when you insert or delete cells. Turning on this option may slow Excel's performance on some systems.

◆ **Enable AutoComplete for cell values** turns on the AutoComplete feature for entering values in cells based on entries in the same column.

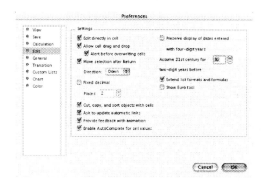

Figure 8 The default options in the Edit pane of the Preferences dialog.

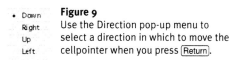

Figure 9
Use the Direction pop-up menu to select a direction in which to move the cellpointer when you press Return.

Figure 10 Excel's Formatting toolbar, with the Euro Style button displayed. This toolbar does not appear by default. To display it, choose Formatting from the Toolbars submenu under the View menu.

◆ **Preserve display of dates entered with four-digit years** changes the default date format from two-digit years to four-digit years. For example, Excel would display a date as *6/30/2001* instead of *6/30/01*.

◆ **Assume 21st century for two-digit years before** enables you to enter a two digit year number that Excel should use as a breaking point for twenty-first century dates. For example, with 30 set as the value in this text box, Excel assumes that if you enter *1/15/25*, you mean *1/15/2025* rather than *1/15/1925*. On the other hand, *1/15/40* would be interpreted as *1/15/1940* rather than *1/15/2040*.

◆ **Extend list formats and formulas** tells Excel that it should copy the formats and formulas in list cells to new rows added at the bottom of the list.

◆ **Show Euro tool** displays the Euro Style button € on the Formatting toolbar (**Figure 10**) and turns on the Euro Currency Tool add-in for converting Euro values.

General Preferences

General preferences (**Figure 11**) control basic Excel operations. There is one main category—Settings—and a number of other options.

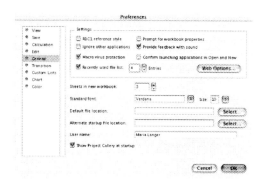

Settings

The Settings options offer check boxes to set a variety of options:

◆ **R1C1 reference style** changes the style of cell references so both rows and columns have numbers.

◆ **Ignore other applications** prevents the exchange of data with other applications that use Dynamic Data Exchange (DDE).

◆ **Macro virus protection** displays a warning like the one in **Figure 12** when you open an Excel workbook file that contains macros or customized toolbars, menus, or shortcut keys. (These features could contain Excel macro viruses.) When this dialog appears, you have three options:

▲ **Enable Macros** opens the file so the macros will function as intended. If the file contains a macro virus, your Excel files may become infected. Use this option only if you are certain that the file does not contain any viruses.

▲ **Do Not Open** does not open the file. Your Excel files cannot become infected if the file contains a macro virus.

▲ **Disable Macros** opens the file so the macros cannot operate as intended. Your Excel files cannot become infected if the file contains a macro virus.

◆ **Recently used file list** enables you to specify the number of recently opened files that should appear near the bottom of the File menu. Turn on the check box and enter a value in the **Entries** text box. This feature is handy for quickly reopening recently accessed files.

Figure 11 The default options in the General pane of the Preferences dialog.

Figure 12 Excel displays a warning dialog like this when you open a workbook file that contains macros or other Visual Basic modules.

Figure 13 You can use the Summary pane of the Properties dialog to enter information about the file the first time you save it. You can also open this dialog by choosing Properties from the File menu.

◆ **Prompt for workbook properties** displays the Properties dialog (**Figure 13**) the first time you save a file. You can use this dialog to enter summary information about a file.

◆ **Provide feedback with sound** plays sounds at certain events, such as opening, saving, and printing files and displaying error messages. If this option is turned on in one Microsoft Office application, it is automatically turned on in all Office applications.

◆ **Confirm launching apps in Open and New** tells Excel to display a confirmation dialog any time you use the Open or New command to open or create a document with another application.

◆ **Web Options** displays the Web Options dialog, which you can use to edit default settings for saving workbooks as Web pages. (I discuss these options in **Chapter 14**.)

Other options

The bottom half of the dialog lets you set a variety of other workbook options:

◆ **Sheets in new workbook** enables you to specify the number of worksheets that should be included in each new workbook you create. Enter a value in the text box.

◆ **Standard font** enables you to select the default font for worksheets and charts.

◆ **Default file location** allows you to specify the default location in which new workbook files should be saved. Click the Select button and use the dialog that appears to locate and select a location on your hard disk or a network.

◆ **Alternate startup file location** lets you specify a secondary startup folder in which Excel should look for files when it launches.

◆ **User name** is the name that appears when Excel displays a user name.

◆ **Show Project Gallery at startup** displays the Project Gallery when you start Excel.

Transition Preferences

Transition preferences (**Figure 14**) offer options to help you transition between Excel and other spreadsheet software packages, such as Lotus 1-2-3.

◆ **Default save as type** enables you to specify the default file format for every Excel file you save. Choose an option from the pop-up menu (**Figure 15**). The option you select will automatically appear in the Save As dialog. You can override this choice if desired when you save a file. This option is useful if you often share the Excel files you create with people who use a different version of Excel or some other spreadsheet or database application.

◆ **Transition formula evaluation** instructs Excel to evaluate Lotus 1-2-3 formulas without changing them. This option may be extremely helpful if you often open files created with Lotus 1-2-3.

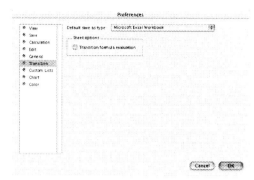

Figure 14 The default settings in the Transition pane of the Preferences dialog.

- Microsoft Excel Workbook
  Web Page
  Template
  Formatted Text (Space delimited)
  Text (Tab delimited)
  Microsoft Excel 5.0/95 Workbook
  Microsoft Excel 97-2002, X & 5.0/95 Workbook
  CSV (Comma delimited)
  Microsoft Excel 4.0 Worksheet
  Microsoft Excel 3.0 Worksheet
  Microsoft Excel 2.2 Worksheet
  Microsoft Excel 4.0 Workbook
  WK4 (1-2-3)
  WK3,FM3 (1-2-3)
  WK3 (1-2-3)
  WK1,FMT (1-2-3)
  WK1,ALL (1-2-3)
  WK1 (1-2-3)
  WKS (1-2-3)
  DBF 4 (dBASE IV)
  DBF 3 (dBASE III)
  DBF 2 (dBASE II)
  Unicode Text
  Text (Windows)
  Text (OS/2 or MS-DOS)
  CSV (Windows)
  CSV (OS/2 or MS-DOS)
  DIF (Data Interchange Format)
  SYLK (Symbolic Link)
  Microsoft Excel Add-In

Figure 15 Use the Default save as type pop-up menu to select a default file format in which to save files.

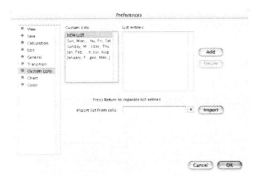

Figure 16 The default settings in the Custom Lists pane of the Preferences dialog.

Figure 17
Enter the values you want to include in the list, one per line.

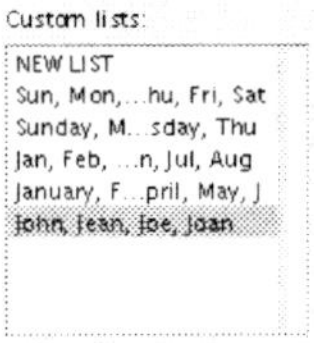

Custom lists:
Figure 18
The list appears in the Custom lists scrolling list.

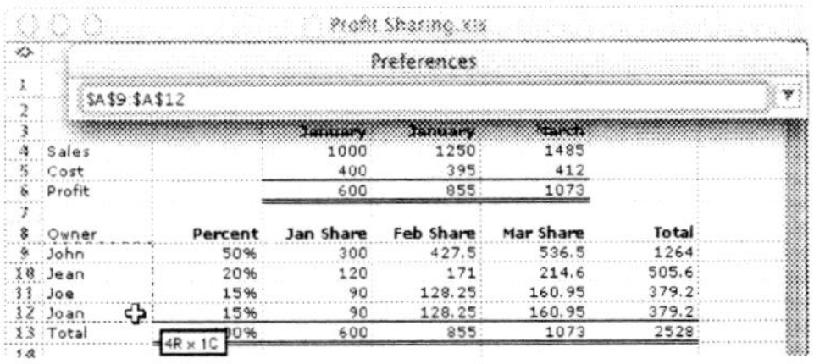

Figure 19 Select the cells containing the values you want to appear in the custom list.

Custom Lists Preferences

The Custom Lists preferences (**Figure 16**) enable you to create, modify, and delete custom lists. Once created, you can use the AutoFill feature I discuss in **Chapter 3** to enter list contents into cells.

✔ Tip

- You cannot modify or delete the predefined lists in the Custom lists scrolling list (**Figure 16**).

To create a custom list

1. In the Custom Lists pane of the Preferences dialog, select NEW LIST in the Custom lists scrolling list (**Figure 16**).

2. Enter the list contents in the List entries area (**Figure 17**). Be sure to press Return after each item.

3. Click Add.

   The list appears in the Custom lists scrolling list (**Figure 18**).

To import cell contents as a custom list

1. In the Custom Lists pane of the Preferences dialog, select NEW LIST in the Custom lists scrolling list (**Figure 16**).

2. Click in the Import list from cells text box.

3. In the worksheet window, drag to select the cells containing the values you want to use as a custom list. The Preferences dialog collapses while you make your selection, as shown in **Figure 19**.

4. Click Import.

   The list appears in the Custom lists scrolling list (**Figure 18**).

CUSTOM LISTS PREFERENCES

To modify a custom list

1. In the Custom Lists pane of the Preferences dialog, select the list you want to modify in the Custom lists scrolling list.

2. Edit the list contents as desired in the List entries area.

3. Click Add.

The custom list changes.

To delete a custom list

1. In the Custom Lists pane of the Preferences dialog, select the list you want to delete in the Custom lists scrolling list.

2. Click Delete.

3. A confirmation dialog like the one in **Figure 20** appears. Click OK.

The list disappears from the Custom list scrolling list.

✔ Tip

■ Deleting a custom list does not delete any data from your workbook files. It simply removes the list from the Custom Lists pane of the Preferences dialog so you can no longer use it with the AutoFill feature.

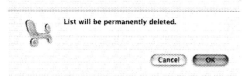

Figure 20 Excel displays this dialog when you delete a custom list.

Figure 21 The default settings in the Chart pane of the Preferences dialog.

Chart Preferences

Chart preferences (**Figure 21**) let you set options for the active chart and chart tips.

Active chart

Active chart options affect the active chart only. Be sure to activate the chart for which you want to set these options before opening the Preferences dialog.

◆ **Empty cells plotted as** enables you to select one of two or three options to specify how Excel should plot empty cells on the chart:

▲ **Not plotted (leave gaps)** tells Excel not to plot the cell values at all. This leaves gaps in the chart.

▲ **Zero** tells Excel to plot empty cells as zeros, thus including a zero data point for each empty cell.

▲ **Interpolated** tells Excel to interpolate data points for blank cells and fill in the chart gaps with connecting lines. This option is not available for all chart types.

◆ **Plot visible cells only** tells Excel to plot only the cells that are displayed on the worksheet. If one or more cells are in hidden columns or rows, they are not plotted.

◆ **Chart sizes with window frame** resizes the chart in a chart sheet window so it fills the window, no matter how the window is sized. This option is not available for charts embedded in worksheets.

Chart tips

Chart tips options enable you to specify what displays in chart tips.

◆ **Show names** displays the names of data points.

◆ **Show values** displays the values of data points.

Color Preferences

The Color pane of the Preferences dialog (**Figure 22**) enables you to set the color palettes used within the Excel workbook file.

- **Standard colors** are the colors that appear in color pop-up menus throughout Excel.

- **Chart fills** are the first eight colors Excel uses as chart fills.

- **Chart lines** are the first eight colors Excel uses as chart lines.

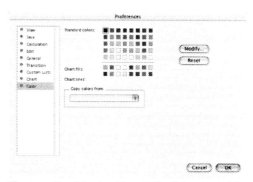

Figure 22 The default settings in the Color pane of the Preferences dialog.

To modify the color palette

1. Click the color that you want to change to select it.

2. Click the Modify button.

3. Use the Color Picker dialog (**Figure 23** or **24**) to select a color.

4. Click OK. The selected color changes.

5. Repeat steps 1 through 4 for each color you want to change.

To copy colors from another workbook file

1. Before opening the Preferences dialog, open the workbook file from which you want to copy colors.

2. Open the Color pane of the Preferences dialog.

3. From the Copy colors from pop-up menu (**Figure 25**), choose the workbook file from which you want to copy colors.

   The palette changes to reflect the colors from the other workbook file.

To reset the color palette

Click the Reset button. The colors change back to the default colors.

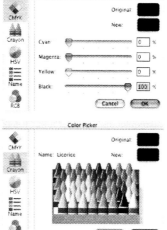

Figures 23 & 24 Use the Color Picker dialog to select a different color. Here are two versions of the Color Picker; click an icon on the left side of the window to switch from one picker to another.

Figure 25 You can copy the color palette from another open workbook file by choosing it from the Copy colors from pop-up menu.

MENUS &
SHORTCUT KEYS

Menus & Shortcut Keys

This appendix illustrates all of Excel's standard menus for worksheets and charts and provides a list of shortcut keys you can use to access menu commands.

To use a shortcut key, hold down the modifier key (usually ⌘ ⌘) and press the keyboard key corresponding to the command. For example, to use the Save command's shortcut key, hold down ⌘ ⌘ and press ⑤. I tell you more about menus and shortcut keys in **Chapter 1**.

Excel menu

| ⌘ ⌘ Ⓗ | Hide Excel |
| ⌘ ⌘ ⓠ | Quit Excel |

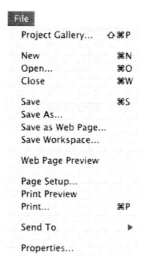

File menu (worksheets)

Shift ⌃ ⌘ P	Project Gallery
⌃ ⌘ N	New Workbook
⌃ ⌘ O	Open
⌃ ⌘ W	Close
⌃ ⌘ S	Save
⌃ ⌘ P	Print

File menu (charts)

Shift ⌃ ⌘ P	Project Gallery
⌃ ⌘ N	New
⌃ ⌘ O	Open
⌃ ⌘ W	Close
⌃ ⌘ S	Save
⌃ ⌘ P	Print

FILE MENU

Edit

Undo Paste	⌘Z
Can't Repeat	⌘Y
Cut	⌘X
Copy	⌘C
Paste	⌘V
Paste Special...	
Paste as Hyperlink	
Fill	▶
Clear	▶
Delete...	
Delete Sheet	
Move or Copy Sheet...	
Find...	⌘F
Replace...	
Go To...	
Links...	
Object	

Edit menu (worksheets)

⌃ ⌘ Z	Undo
⌃ ⌘ Y	Repeat/Redo
⌃ ⌘ X	Cut
⌃ ⌘ C	Copy
⌃ ⌘ V	Paste
Control D	Fill Down
Control R	Fill Right
Control B	Clear Contents
Control K	Delete
⌃ ⌘ F	Find
⌃ ⌘ H	Replace

Edit

Can't Undo	⌘Z
Redo Paste	⌘Y
Cut	⌘X
Copy	⌘C
Paste	⌘V
Paste Special...	
Clear	▶
Delete Sheet	
Move or Copy Sheet...	
Links...	

Edit menu (charts)

⌃ ⌘ Z	Undo
⌃ ⌘ Y	Repeat/Redo
⌃ ⌘ X	Cut
⌃ ⌘ C	Copy
⌃ ⌘ V	Paste

EDIT MENU

View menu (worksheets)

(no shortcut keys)

View menu (charts)

(no shortcut keys)

Insert menu (charts)

(no shortcut keys)

Insert menu (worksheets)

Control I	Cells
⌃ ⌘ K	Hyperlink

Cells...　　　　　　⌘1
Row　　　　　　　▶
Column　　　　　　▶
Sheet　　　　　　　▶

AutoFormat...
Conditional Formatting...
Style...

Format menu (worksheets)

⌘1　　　　Cells

Selected Chart Area...　⌘1

Sheet　　　　　　▶

Format menu (charts)

⌘1　　　Selection

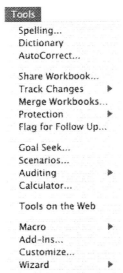

Spelling...
Dictionary
AutoCorrect...

Share Workbook...
Track Changes　　▶
Merge Workbooks...
Protection　　　　▶
Flag for Follow Up...

Goal Seek...
Scenarios...
Auditing　　　　▶
Calculator...

Tools on the Web

Macro　　　　　▶
Add-Ins...
Customize...
Wizard　　　　　▶

Tools menu (worksheets)

(no shortcut keys)

Spelling...
AutoCorrect...

Share Workbook...
Track Changes　　▶
Merge Workbooks...
Protection　　　　▶

Tools on the Web

Macro　　　　　▶
Add-Ins...
Customize...

Tools menu (charts)

(no shortcut keys)

Data

Sort...
Filter   ▶
Form...
Subtotals...
Validation...

Table...
Text to Columns...
Consolidate...
Group and Outline   ▶

PivotTable Report...

Get External Data   ▶
Refresh Data

Data menu (worksheets)

(no shortcut keys)

Chart

Chart Type...
Source Data...
Chart Options...
Location...

Add Data...
Add Trendline...
3-D View...

Chart menu (charts)

(no shortcut keys)

Window

Zoom Window
Minimize Window   ⌘M

Bring All to Front

New Window
Arrange...
Hide
Unhide...

Split
Freeze Panes

1 Members.xls
✓ 2 SW Division Sales.xls

Window menu (worksheets)

   Minimize Window

Window

New Window
Arrange...
Hide
Unhide...

1 Members.xls
✓ 2 SW Division Sales.xls

Window menu (charts)

(no shortcut keys)

Help

Search Excel Help
Excel Help Contents
Additional Help Resources

Use the Office Assistant

Downloads and Updates
Visit the Mactopia Web Site
Send Feedback on Excel

Help menu

(no shortcut keys)

MENUS & SHORTCUT KEYS

Menus & Shortcut Keys

This appendix illustrates all of Excel's standard menus for worksheets and charts and provides a list of shortcut keys you can use to access menu commands.

To use a shortcut key, hold down the modifier key (usually ⌘) and press the keyboard key corresponding to the command. For example, to use the Save command's shortcut key, hold down ⌘ and press S. I tell you more about menus and shortcut keys in **Chapter 1**.

Excel	
About Excel	
Online Registration	
Preferences...	
Services	▶
Hide Excel	⌘H
Hide Others	
Show All	
Quit Excel	⌘Q

Excel menu

⌘H	Hide Excel
⌘Q	Quit Excel

File

Project Gallery...	⇧⌘P
New Workbook	⌘N
Open...	⌘O
Close	⌘W
Save	⌘S
Save As...	
Save as Web Page...	
Save Workspace...	
Web Page Preview	
Page Setup...	
Print Area	▶
Print Preview	
Print...	⌘P
Send To	▶
Properties...	

File

Project Gallery...	⇧⌘P
New	⌘N
Open...	⌘O
Close	⌘W
Save	⌘S
Save As...	
Save as Web Page...	
Save Workspace...	
Web Page Preview	
Page Setup...	
Print Preview	
Print...	⌘P
Send To	▶
Properties...	

File menu (worksheets)

Shift ⌃ ⌘ P	Project Gallery
⌃ ⌘ N	New Workbook
⌃ ⌘ O	Open
⌃ ⌘ W	Close
⌃ ⌘ S	Save
⌃ ⌘ P	Print

File menu (charts)

Shift ⌃ ⌘ P	Project Gallery
⌃ ⌘ N	New
⌃ ⌘ O	Open
⌃ ⌘ W	Close
⌃ ⌘ S	Save
⌃ ⌘ P	Print

FILE MENU

Edit

Undo Paste	⌘Z
Can't Repeat	⌘Y
Cut	⌘X
Copy	⌘C
Paste	⌘V
Paste Special...	
Paste as Hyperlink	
Fill	▶
Clear	▶
Delete...	
Delete Sheet	
Move or Copy Sheet...	
Find...	⌘F
Replace...	
Go To...	
Links...	
Object	

Edit

Can't Undo	⌘Z
Redo Paste	⌘Y
Cut	⌘X
Copy	⌘C
Paste	⌘V
Paste Special...	
Clear	▶
Delete Sheet	
Move or Copy Sheet...	
Links...	

Edit menu (worksheets)

⌘ ⌘ Z	Undo
⌘ ⌘ Y	Repeat/Redo
⌘ ⌘ X	Cut
⌘ ⌘ C	Copy
⌘ ⌘ V	Paste
Control D	Fill Down
Control R	Fill Right
Control B	Clear Contents
Control K	Delete
⌘ ⌘ F	Find
⌘ ⌘ H	Replace

Edit menu (charts)

⌘ ⌘ Z	Undo
⌘ ⌘ Y	Repeat/Redo
⌘ ⌘ X	Cut
⌘ ⌘ C	Copy
⌘ ⌘ V	Paste

EDIT MENU

View menu (worksheets)

(no shortcut keys)

View menu (charts)

(no shortcut keys)

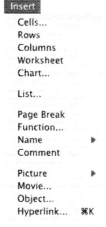

Insert menu (worksheets)

| Control I | Cells |
| ⌘K | Hyperlink |

Insert menu (charts)

(no shortcut keys)

Cells... ⌘1
Row ▶
Column ▶
Sheet ▶

AutoFormat...
Conditional Formatting...
Style...

Format menu (worksheets)

 Cells

Format

Selected Chart Area... ⌘1

Sheet ▶

Format menu (charts)

⌃⌘1 Selection

Spelling...
Dictionary
AutoCorrect...

Share Workbook...
Track Changes ▶
Merge Workbooks...
Protection ▶
Flag for Follow Up...

Goal Seek...
Scenarios...
Auditing ▶
Calculator...

Tools on the Web

Macro ▶
Add-Ins...
Customize...
Wizard ▶

Tools menu (worksheets)

(no shortcut keys)

Spelling...
AutoCorrect...

Share Workbook...
Track Changes ▶
Merge Workbooks...
Protection ▶

Tools on the Web

Macro ▶
Add-Ins...
Customize...

Tools menu (charts)

(no shortcut keys)

Data

Sort...
Filter   ▶
Form...
Subtotals...
Validation...

Table...
Text to Columns...
Consolidate...
Group and Outline   ▶

PivotTable Report...

Get External Data   ▶
Refresh Data

Data menu (worksheets)

(no shortcut keys)

Chart

Chart Type...
Source Data...
Chart Options...
Location...

Add Data...
Add Trendline...
3-D View...

Chart menu (charts)

(no shortcut keys)

Window

Zoom Window
Minimize Window   ⌘M

Bring All to Front

New Window
Arrange...
Hide
Unhide...

Split
Freeze Panes

1 Members.xls
✓ 2 SW Division Sales.xls

Window menu (worksheets)

 Minimize Window

Window

New Window
Arrange...
Hide
Unhide...

1 Members.xls
✓ 2 SW Division Sales.xls

Window menu (charts)

(no shortcut keys)

Help

Search Excel Help
Excel Help Contents
Additional Help Resources

Use the Office Assistant

Downloads and Updates
Visit the Mactopia Web Site
Send Feedback on Excel

Help menu

(no shortcut keys)

FUNCTION REFERENCE

Functions

Functions are predefined formulas for making specific kinds of calculations. Functions make it quicker and easier to write formulas. I tell you about functions in **Chapter 5**. In this appendix, I provide a complete list of every function installed as part of a standard installation of Excel X, along with its arguments and a brief description of what it does.

Financial Functions

DB(cost,salvage,life,period,month)	Returns the depreciation of an asset for a specified period using the fixed-declining balance method.
DDB(cost,salvage,life,period,factor)	Returns the depreciation of an asset for a specified period using the double-declining balance method or some other method you specify.
FV(rate,nper,pmt,pv,type)	Returns the future value of an investment.
IPMT(rate,per,nper,pv,fv,type)	Returns the interest payment for an investment for a given period.
IRR(values,guess)	Returns the internal rate of return for a series of cash flows.
ISPMT(rate,per,nper,pv)	Returns the straight-loan payment interest.
MIRR(values,finance_rate,reinvest_rate)	Returns the internal rate of return where positive and negative cash flows are financed at different rates.
NPER(rate,pmt,pv,fv,type)	Returns the number of periods for an investment.
NPV(rate,value1,value2,...)	Returns the net present value of an investment based on a series of periodic cash flows and a discount rate.
PMT(rate,nper,pv,fv,type)	Returns the period payment for an annuity.
PPMT(rate,per,nper,pv,fv,type)	Returns the payment on the principal for an investment for a given period.
PV(rate,nper,pmt,fv,type)	Returns the present value of an investment.

RATE(nper,pmt,pv,fv,type,guess)   Returns the interest rate per period of an annuity.

SLN(cost,salvage,life)   Returns the straight-line depreciation of an asset for one period.

SYD(cost,salvage,life,per)   Returns the sum-of-years'-digits depreciation of an asset for a specified period.

VDB(cost,salvage,life,start_period,end_period,factor,...)

Returns the depreciation of an asset for a specified or partial period using a declining balance method.

Date & Time Functions

DATE(year,month,day)   Returns the serial number of a particular date.

DATEVALUE(date_text)   Converts a date in the form of text to a serial number.

DAY(serial_number)   Converts a serial number to a day of the month.

DAYS360(start_date,end_date,method)   Calculates the number of days between two dates based on a 360-day year.

HOUR(serial_number)   Converts a serial number to an hour.

MINUTE(serial_number)   Converts a serial number to a minute.

MONTH(serial_number)   Converts a serial number to a month.

NOW()   Returns the serial number of the current date and time.

SECOND(serial_number)   Converts a serial number to a second.

TIME(hour,minute,second)   Returns the serial number of a particular time.

TIMEVALUE(time_text)   Converts a time in the form of text to a serial number.

TODAY()   Returns the serial number of today's date.

WEEKDAY(serial_number,return_type)   Converts a serial number to a day of the week.

YEAR(serial_number)   Converts a serial number to a year.

Math & Trig Functions

ABS(number)   Returns the absolute value of a number.

ACOS(number)   Returns the arccosine of a number.

ACOSH(number)   Returns the inverse hyperbolic cosine of a number.

ASIN(number)   Returns the arcsine of a number.

ASINH(number)   Returns the inverse hyperbolic sine of a number.

ATAN(number)   Returns the arctangent of a number.

ATAN2(x_num,y_num)   Returns the arctangent from x- and y-coordinates.

ATANH(number)   Returns the inverse hyperbolic tangent of a number.

CEILING(number,significance)	Rounds a number to the nearest whole number or to the nearest multiple of significance.
COMBIN(number,number_chosen)	Returns the number of combinations for a given number of objects.
COS(number)	Returns the cosine of a number.
COSH(number)	Returns the hyperbolic cosine of a number.
DEGREES(angle)	Converts radians to degrees.
EVEN(number)	Rounds a number up to the nearest even whole number.
EXP(number)	Returns e raised to the power of a given number.
FACT(number)	Returns the factorial of a number.
FLOOR(number, significance)	Rounds a number down, toward 0.
INT(number)	Rounds a number down to the nearest whole number.
LN(number)	Returns the natural logarithm of a number.
LOG(number,base)	Returns the logarithm of a number to a specified base.
LOG10(number)	Returns the base-10 logarithm of a number.
MDETERM(array)	Returns the matrix determinant of an array.
MINVERSE(array)	Returns the matrix inverse of an array.
MMULT(array1,array2)	Returns the matrix product of two arrays.
MOD(number,divisor)	Returns the remainder from division.
ODD(number)	Rounds a number up to the nearest odd whole number.
PI( )	Returns the value of pi.
POWER(number,power)	Returns the result of a number raised to a power.
PRODUCT(number 1,number2,...)	Multiplies its arguments.
RADIANS(angle)	Converts degrees to radians.
RAND( )	Returns a random number between 0 and 1.
ROMAN(number,form)	Converts an Arabic numeral to a Roman numeral, as text.
ROUND(number,num_digits)	Rounds a number to a specified number of digits.
ROUNDDOWN(number,num_digits)	Rounds a number down, toward 0.
ROUNDUP(number,num_digits)	Rounds a number up, away from 0.
SIGN(number)	Returns the sign of a number.
SIN(number)	Returns the sine of a number.
SINH(number)	Returns the hyperbolic sine of a number.
SQRT(number)	Returns a positive square root.

MATH & TRIG FUNCTIONS

SUBTOTAL(function_num,ref1,...)	Returns a subtotal in a list or database.
SUM(number1,number2,...)	Adds its arguments.
SUMIF(range,criteria, sum_range)	Adds the cells specified by a given criteria.
SUMPRODUCT(array1,array2,array3,...)	Returns the sum of the products of corresponding array components.
SUMSQ(number1,number2,...)	Returns the sum of the squares of its arguments.
SUMX2MY2(array_x,array_y)	Returns the sum of the difference of squares of corresponding values in two arrays.
SUMX2PY2(array_x,array_y)	Returns the sum of the sum of squares of corresponding values in two arrays.
SUMXMY2(array_x,array_y)	Returns the sum of squares of differences of corresponding values in two arrays.
TAN(number)	Returns the tangent of a number.
TANH(number)	Returns the hyperbolic tangent of a number.
TRUNC(number,num_digits)	Truncates a number to a whole number.

Statistical Functions

AVEDEV(number1,number2,...)	Returns the average of the absolute deviations of data points from their mean.
AVERAGE(number1,number2,...)	Returns the average of its arguments.
AVERAGEA(value1,value2,...)	Returns the average of its arguments, including text and logical values.
BETADIST(x,alpha,beta,A,B)	Returns the cumulative beta probability density function.
BETAINV(probability,alpha,beta,A,B)	Returns the inverse of the cumulative beta probability density function.
BINOMDIST(number_s,trials,probability_s,cumulative)	
	Returns the individual term binomial distribution probability.
CHIDIST(x,degrees_freedom)	Returns the one-tailed probability of the chi-squared distribution.
CHIINV(probability,degrees_freedom)	Returns the inverse of the one-tailed probability of the chi-squared distribution.
CHITEST(actual_range,expected_range)	Returns the test for independence.
CONFIDENCE(alpha,standard_dev,size)	Returns the confidence interval for a population mean.
CORREL(array1,array2)	Returns the correlation coefficient between two data sets.

COUNT(value1,value2,...)	Counts how many numbers are in the list of arguments.
COUNTA(value2,value2,...)	Counts how many values are in the list of arguments.
COUNTBLANK(range)	Counts the number of blank cells within a range.
COUNTIF(range,criteria)	Counts the number of nonblank cells within a range which meet the given criteria.
COVAR(array1,array2)	Returns covariance, the average of the products of paired deviations.
CRITBINOM(trials,probability_s,alpha)	Returns the smallest value for which the cumulative binomial distribution is greater than or equal to a criterian value.
DEVSQ(number1,number2,...)	Returns the sum of squares of deviations.
EXPONDIST(x,lambda,cumulative)	Returns the exponential distribution.
FDIST(x,degrees_freedom1,degrees_freedom2)	
	Returns the F probability distribution.
FINV(probability,degrees_freedom1,degrees_freedom2)	
	Returns the inverse of the F probability distribution.
FISHER(x)	Returns the Fisher transformation.
FISHERINV(y)	Returns the inverse of the Fisher transformation.
FORECAST(x,known_y's,known_x's)	Returns a value along a linear trend.
FREQUENCY(data_array,bins_array)	Returns a frequency distribution as a vertical array.
FTEST(array1,array2)	Returns the result of an F-test.
GAMMADIST(x,alpha,beta,cumulative)	Returns the gamma distribution.
GAMMAINV(probability,alpha,beta)	Returns the inverse of the gamma cumulative distribution.
GAMMALN(x)	Returns the natural logarithm of the gamma function.
GEOMEAN(number1,number2,...)	Returns the geometric mean.
GROWTH(knowy_y's,known_x's,new_x's,const)	
	Returns values along an exponential trend.
HARMEAN(number1,number2,...)	Returns the harmonic mean.
HYPGEOMDIST(sample_s,number_sample,population_s,...)	
	Returns the hypergeometric distribution.
INTERCEPT(known_y's,known_x's)	Returns the intercept of the linear regression line.
KURT(number1,number2,...)	Returns the kurtosis of a data set.
LARGE(array,k)	Returns the k-th largest value in a data set.
LINEST(known_y's,known_x's,const,stats)	Returns the parameters of a linear trend.
LOGEST(known_y's,known_x's,const,stats)	Returns the parameters of an exponential trend.

LOGINV(probability,mean,standard_dev)	Returns the inverse of the lognormal distribution.
LOGNORMDIST(x,mean,standard_dev)	Returns the cumulative lognormal distribution.
MAX(number1,number2,...)	Returns the maximum value in a list of arguments.
MAXA(value1,value2,...)	Returns the maximum value in a list of arguments, including text and logical values.
MEDIAN(number1,number2,...)	Returns the median of the given numbers.
MIN(number1,number2,...)	Returns the minimum value in a list of arguments.
MINA(value1,value2,...)	Returns the minimum value in a list of arguments, including text and logical values.
MODE(number1,number2,...)	Returns the most common value in a data set.
NEGBINOMDIST(number_f,number_s,probability_s)	
	Returns the negative binomial distribution.
NORMDIST(x,mean,standard_dev,cumulative)	
	Returns the normal cumulative distribution.
NORMINV(probability,mean,standard_dev)	Returns the inverse of the normal cumulative distribution.
NORMSDIST(z)	Returns the standard normal cumulative distribution.
NORMSINV(probability)	Returns the inverse of the standard normal cumulative distribution.
PEARSON(array1,array2)	Returns the Pearson product moment correlation coefficient.
PERCENTILE(array,k)	Returns the k-th percentile of values in a range.
PERCENTRANK(array,x,significance)	Returns the percentage rank of a value in a data set.
PERMUT(number,number_chosen)	Returns the number of permutations for a given number of objects.
POISSON(x,mean,cumulative)	Returns the Poisson distribution.
PROB(x_range,prob_range,lower_limit,upper_limit)	
	Returns the probability that values in a range are between two limits.
QUARTILE(array,quart)	Returns the quartile of a data set.
RANK(number,ref,order)	Returns the rank of a number in a list of numbers.
RSQ(known_y's,known_x's)	Returns the square of the Pearson product moment correlation coefficient. (If you know what that means, I hope you're making a lot of money.)
SKEW(number1,number2,...)	Returns the skewness of a distribution.
SLOPE(known_y's,known_x's)	Returns the slope of the linear regression line.
SMALL(array,k)	Returns the k-th smallest value in a data set.

STANDARDIZE(x,mean,standard_dev)	Returns a normalized value.
STDEV(number1,number2,...)	Estimates standard deviation based on a sample.
STDEVA(value1,value2,...)	Estimates standard deviation based on a sample, including text and logical values.
STDEVP(number1,number2,...)	Calculates standard deviation based on the entire population.
STDEVPA(value1,value2,...)	Calculates standard deviation based on the entire population, including text and logical values.
STEYX(known_y's,known_x's)	Returns the standard error of the predicted y-value for each x in the regression.
TDIST(x,degrees_freedom,tails)	Returns the Student's t-distribution.
TINV(probability,degrees_freedom)	Returns the inverse of the Student's t-distribution.
TREND(known_y's,known_x's,new_x's,const)	Returns values along a linear trend.
TRIMMEAN(array,percent)	Returns the mean of the interior of a data set.
TTEST(array1,array2,tails,type)	Returns the probability associated with a Student's t-test.
VAR(number1,number2,...)	Estimates variance based on a sample.
VARA(value1,value2,...)	Estimates variance based on a sample, including text and logical values.
VARP(number1,number2,...)	Calculates variance based on the entire population.
VARPA(value1,value2,...)	Calculates variance based on the entire population, including text and logical values.
WEIBULL(x,alpha,beta,cumulative)	Returns the Weibull distribution.
ZTEST(array,x,sigma)	Returns the two-tailed P-value of a z-test. Really.

STATISTICAL FUNCTIONS

Lookup & Reference Functions

ADDRESS(row_num,column_num,abs_num,a1,sheet_text)	Returns a reference as text to a single cell in a worksheet.
AREAS(reference)	Returns the number of areas in a reference.
CHOOSE(index_num,value1,value2,...)	Chooses a value from a list of values.
COLUMN(reference)	Returns the column number of a reference.
COLUMNS(array)	Returns the number of columns in a reference.
HLOOKUP(lookup_value,table_array,row_index_num,...)	Looks in the top row of a table and returns the value of the indicated cell.

HYPERLINK(link_location,friendly_name)	Creates a shortcut that opens a document stored on a network computer or the Internet.
INDEX(...)	Uses an index to choose a value from a reference or array.
INDIRECT(ref_text,a1)	Returns a reference indicated by a text value.
LOOKUP(...)	Looks up values in a vector or array.
MATCH(lookup_value,lookup_array,match_type)	Looks up values in a reference or array.
OFFSET(reference,rows,cols,height,width)	Returns a reference offset from a given reference.
ROW(reference)	Returns the row number of a reference.
ROWS(array)	Returns the number of rows in a reference.
TRANSPOSE(array)	Returns the transpose of an array.
VLOOKUP(lookup_value,table_array,col_index_num,...)	Looks in the first column of a table and moves across the row to return the value of a cell.

Database Functions

DAVERAGE(database,field,criteria)	Returns the average of selected database entries.
DCOUNT(database,field,criteria)	Counts the cells containing numbers from a specified database and criteria.
DCOUNTA(database,field,criteria)	Counts nonblank cells from a specified database and criteria.
DGET(database,field,criteria)	Extracts from a database a single record that matches the specified criteria.
DMAX(database,field,criteria)	Returns the maximum value from selected database entries.
DMIN(database,field,criteria)	Returns the minimum value from selected database entries.
DPRODUCT(database,field,criteria)	Multiplies the values in a particular field of records that match the criteria in a database.
DSTDEV(database,field,criteria)	Estimates the standard deviation based on a sample of selected database entries.
DSTDEVP(database,field,criteria)	Calculates the standard deviation based on the entire population of selected database entries.
DSUM(database,field,criteria)	Adds the numbers in the field column of records in the database that match the criteria.
DVAR(database,field,criteria)	Estimates the variance based on a sample from selected database entries.

DVARP(database,field,criteria)	Calculates variance based on the entire population of selected database entries.
GETPIVOTDATA(pivot_table,name)	Returns data stored in a pivot table.

Text Functions

CHAR(number)	Returns the character specified by the code number.
CLEAN(text)	Removes all nonprintable characters from text.
CODE(text)	Returns a numeric code for the first character in a text string.
CONCATENATE(text1,text2,...)	Joins several text items into one text item.
DOLLAR(number,decimals)	Converts a number to text, using currency format.
EXACT(text1,text2)	Checks to see if two text values are identical.
FIND(find_text,within_text,start_num)	Finds one text value within another. This function is case-sensitive.
FIXED(number,decimals,no_commas)	Formats a number as text with a fixed number of decimals.
LEFT(text,num_chars)	Returns the leftmost characters from a text value.
LEN(text)	Returns the number of characters in a text string.
LOWER(text)	Converts text to lowercase.
MID(text,start_num,num_chars)	Returns a specific number of characters from a text string.
PROPER(text)	Capitalizes the first letter in each word of a text value.
REPLACE(old_text,start_num,num_chars,new_text)	Replaces characters within text.
REPT(text,number_times)	Repeats text a given number of times.
RIGHT(text,num_chars)	Returns the rightmost characters from a text value.
SEARCH(find_text,within_text,start_num)	Finds one text value within another. This function is not case-sensitive.
SUBSTITUTE(text,old_text,new_text,instance_num)	Substitutes new text for old text in a text string.
T(value)	Converts its arguments to text.
TEXT(value,format_text)	Formats a number and converts it to text.
TRIM(text)	Removes spaces from text.
UPPER(text)	Converts text to uppercase.
VALUE(text)	Converts a text argument to a number.

Logical Functions

AND(logical1,logical2,...)	Returns TRUE if all of its arguments are TRUE.
FALSE()	Returns the logical value FALSE.
IF(logical_test,value_if_true,value_if_false)	
	Specifies a logical test to perform and the value to return based on a TRUE or FALSE result.
NOT(logical)	Reverses the logic of its argument.
OR(logical1,logical2,...)	Returns TRUE if any argument is TRUE.
TRUE()	Returns the logical value TRUE.

Information Functions

CELL(info_type,reference)	Returns information about the formatting, location, or contents of a cell.
ERROR.TYPE(error_val)	Returns a number corresponding to an error value.
INFO(type_text)	Returns information about the current operating environment.
ISBLANK(value)	Returns TRUE if the value is blank.
ISERR(value)	Returns TRUE if the value is any error value except #N/A.
ISERROR(value)	Returns TRUE if the value is any error value.
ISLOGICAL(value)	Returns TRUE if the value is a logical value.
ISNA(value)	Returns TRUE if the value is the #N/A error value.
ISNONTEXT(value)	Returns TRUE if the value is not text.
ISNUMBER(value)	Returns TRUE if the value is a number.
ISREF(value)	Returns TRUE if the value is a reference.
ISTECT(value)	Returns TRUE if the value is text.
N(value)	Returns a value converted to a number.
NA()	Returns the error value #N/A.
TYPE(value)	Returns a number indicating the data type of a value.

INDEX

INDEX

INDEX

INDEX

INDEX

WWW.PEACHPIT.COM

Quality How-to Computer Books

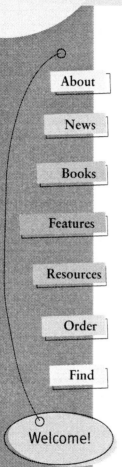

- About
- News
- Books
- Features
- Resources
- Order
- Find

Welcome!

Visit Peachpit Press on the Web at www.peachpit.com

- Check out new feature articles each Monday: excerpts, interviews, tips, and plenty of how-tos

- Find any Peachpit book by title, series, author, or topic on the Books page

- See what our authors are up to on the News page: signings, chats, appearances, and more

- Meet the Peachpit staff and authors in the About section: bios, profiles, and candid shots

- Use Resources to reach our academic, sales, customer service, and tech support areas and find out how to become a Peachpit author

Peachpit.com is also the place to:

- Chat with our authors online
- Take advantage of special Web-only offers
- Get the latest info on new books